CW00968116

LAMBETH Praise

Compiled by Geoff Weaver
Director of Music for the 1998 Lambeth Conference
Canterbury, England

ΕΛΕΥΘΕΡΩΣΕΙ ΥΜΑΣ Η ΑΛΗΘΕΙΑ

Published for
the Anglican Consultative Council
by
Morehouse Publishing
Harrisburg, Pennsylvania, USA

Morehouse Publishing
P.O. Box 1321
Harrisburg, PA 17105

Morehouse Publishing is a division of The Morehouse Group.

The publisher wishes to express gratitude to the copyright owners who have granted permission to include their copyright material in this book. Full details are indicated on the respective pages. Every effort has been made to trace the owners of existing copyright material, and apology is made for any copyright inadvertently not cited.

Grateful acknowledgement is made to those who assisted Geoff Weaver with the selection of songs: James Rosenthal, Anne-Christine Ballard, John Bell, Fred Kaan, Alan Luff, Michael Sadgrove, and Robert Willis.

Special thanks are extended to Morehouse Publishing's Laura Hudson, Project Coordinator, Trisha Mason, Page Designer, and Corey Kent, Cover Designer, for their remarkable work in preparing this songbook, and to June Williams for her invaluable assistance to Geoff Weaver in processing material.

Printed in the United States of America

ISBN 0-8192-1777-8

CONTENTS

FOREWORD

The haunting chants of Asia, the lilting tunes of the Americas, the vibrant melodies of Africa, the majestic anthems of Europe, are some of the rich variety of music and melody that forms the Anglican Communion.

The rich heritage we enjoy harks back to the earlier Hebrew and Christian expression of faith. The Reformation gave us a vast array of carefully thought-through hymnody. Various movements since then have added to the great library of the Christian music tradition. These movements, be they catholic, evangelical, charismatic, traditional, contemporary, prophetic, or the rediscovery of simple chants, move beyond the boundaries of geography and culture, piety and context to bind Christians together.

This compilation takes the context and the participants of the Lambeth Conference seriously. Mr. Geoff Weaver has given us a resource which reflects the vast variety. I hope that this book will be used across the Provinces. With our hearts bound in common partnership, let us be united in the Spirit of song as well.

George Leonard Carey
Archbishop of Canterbury

PREFACE

Communities have always sung together—to express their joys and sorrows, their hopes, fears and convictions.

Christian communities in particular have always expressed their faith in song—and often it has been communal singing that has given them the strength and the courage to persevere.

I hope that, as we sing songs from other parts of the World Church, we shall discover that, in a mysterious way, we can enter into their experience, and discover the truth of Paul's words that "when one part of the body rejoices, the other parts rejoice—and when one part suffers, the other parts suffer too".

For Lambeth 1998, we can guarantee many opportunities to "sing a new song—and an old song—unto the Lord". I hope you will come in good voice!

Geoff Weaver
Director of Music
Lambeth 1998

INTRODUCTION

Music, hymns, songs, chants, lift us into another dimension. The inner person begins to rise above the mundane to respond. It is this very special character that makes words and music, style and rhythm the ground for dissension and conflict. Our unique temperaments and backgrounds cause different tastes and different 'risings'.

This book, carefully woven together, seeks to enhance our common worship. It cannot claim to link the various divides. No one bridge can span the whole river. Some people's favourites would have been left out, while a song one may consider 'unworthy' is included.

I do trust that there is sufficient material here to warm the heart, stir the intellect and lift our voices.

Mr. Geoff Weaver, the Director of Music for the Lambeth Conference, has spent many hours prayerfully gathering the material, responding to specific requests. We owe a debt of gratitude to him for it is not often that we have, as one of our song leaders, the Editor of the Hymn Book itself.

Rejoice!—may our prayers and supplications be made before God with songs and praises, in the echoes of sound and in the still silences.

Roger Herft
Chaplain to Lambeth 1998

Classical Hymnody

1 A TOUCHING PLACE

Words & arrangement by John L. Bell & Graham Maule © 1986, 1989 WGRG, Iona Community, 840 Govan Road, Glasgow G51 3UU Scotland; melody "Dream Angus" Scots traditional.

DREAM ANGUS
1.Christ's is the world in which we move, Christ's are the
folk we're sum-moned to love, Christ's is the voice which
calls us to care, and Christ is the one who meets us here.
Refrain
To the lost Christ shows his face; to the un - loved he
Em7 Bm7
gives his em - brace; to those who cry in pain or dis -
Cmaj7 G Em Bm7 E7
grace, Christ makes with his friends a touch - ing place.
Am D Am G D

2. Feel for the people we most avoid,
strange or bereaved or never employed;
feel for the women, and feel for the men
who fear that their living is all in vain.

3. Feel for the parents who've lost their child,
feel for the women whom men have defiled,
feel for the baby for whom there's no breast,
and feel for the weary who find no rest.

4. Feel for the lives by life confused,
riddled with doubt, in loving abused;
feel for the lonely heart, conscious of sin,
which longs to be pure but fears to begin.

2 ALL CREATURES OF OUR GOD AND KING

Lasst uns erfreuen 88 44 88 with alleluias

Melody from *Geistliche Kirchengesäng*, Cologne, 1623
arr. R. VAUGHAN WILLIAMS (1872–1958)

Unison
Harmony
Unison
Harmony
O___ praise him, O___ praise him, al - le -
Unison
- lu - ia, al - le - lu - ia, al - le - lu - - ia!

ALL creatures of our God and King,
lift up your voice and with us sing,
alleluia, alleluia!
Thou burning sun with golden beam,
thou silver moon with softer gleam:

O praise him, O praise him,
alleluia, alleluia, alleluia!

2 Thou rushing wind that art so strong,
ye clouds that sail in heaven along,
O praise him, alleluia!
Thou rising morn, in praise rejoice;
ye lights of evening, find a voice:

3 Thou flowing water, pure and clear,
make music for thy Lord to hear,
alleluia, alleluia!
Thou fire, so masterful and bright,
that givest us both warmth and light:

4 Dear mother earth, who day by day
unfoldest blessings on our way,
O praise him, alleluia!
The flowers and fruits that in thee grow,
let them his glory also show:

5 All ye that are of tender heart,
forgiving others, take your part,
O sing ye, alleluia!
Ye who long pain and sorrow bear,
praise God, and on him cast your care:

6 And thou, most kind and gentle death,
waiting to hush our latest breath,
O praise him, alleluia!
Thou leadest home the child of God,
and Christ our Lord the way has trod:

7 Let all things their creator bless,
and worship him in humbleness;
O praise him, alleluia!
Praise, praise the Father, praise the Son,
and praise the Spirit, Three in One:

W. H. DRAPER (1855–1933)
based on ST FRANCIS OF ASSISI (1182–1226)

Music used by permission of Oxford University Press

3 ALL MY HOPE ON GOD IS FOUNDED

Meine Hoffnung 87 87 337

Later form of a melody by JOACHIM NEANDER (1650–80)

SECOND TUNE

Michael 87 87 337

HERBERT HOWELLS (1892–1983)

Unison

ALL my hope on God is founded;
he doth still my trust renew.
Me through change and chance he guideth,
only good and only true.
God unknown,
he alone
calls my heart to be his own.

2 Human pride and earthly glory,
sword and crown betray our trust;
what with care and toil is builded,
tower and temple, fall to dust.
But God's power
hour by hour
is my temple and my tower.

3 God's great goodness aye endureth,
deep his wisdom, passing thought;
splendour, light and life attend him,
beauty springeth out of naught.
Evermore
from his store
new-born worlds rise and adore.

4 Daily doth the almighty giver
bounteous gifts on us bestow;
his desire our soul delighteth
pleasure leads us where we go.
Love doth stand
at his hand;
joy doth wait on his command.

5 Still from earth to God eternal
sacrifice of praise be done,
high above all praises praising
for the gift of Christ his Son.
Christ doth call
one and all;
ye who follow shall not fall.

ROBERT BRIDGES (1844–1930)
based on JOACHIM NEANDER (1650–80)

4 ALL PEOPLE THAT ON EARTH DO DWELL

Old 100th L.M. Melody in Genevan Psalter, 1551

All people that on earth do dwell,
 sing to the Lord with cheerful voice;
him serve with fear, his praise forth tell,
 come ye before him, and rejoice.

2

The Lord, ye know, is God indeed;
 without our aid he did us make;
we are his folk, he doth us feed,
 and for his sheep he doth us take.

3

O enter then his gates with praise,
 approach with joy his courts unto;
praise, laud, and bless his name always,
 for it is seemly so to do.

4

For why? the Lord our God is good;
 his mercy is for ever sure;
his truth at all times firmly stood,
 and shall from age to age endure.

5

To Father, Son, and Holy Ghost,
 the God whom heaven and earth adore,
from men and from the angel-host
 be praise and glory evermore.

W. KETHE (d. 1594)
in *Anglo-Genevan Psalter* (1560)

5 ALLELUIA, SING TO JESUS

Reproduced by permission of Hymns Ancient & Modern Ltd.

Hyfrydol 8 7.8 7. D

Melody by
R. H. Prichard (1811–87)

Music used by permission of Oxford University Press

Classical

Alleluia, sing to Jesus!
his the sceptre, his the throne;
Alleluia, his the triumph,
his the victory alone:
hark, the songs of peaceful Sion
thunder like a mighty flood;
Jesus out of every nation
hath redeemed us by his blood.

2

Alleluia, not as orphans‿
are we left in sorrow now;
Alleluia, he is near us,
faith believes, nor questions how:
though the cloud from sight received him,
when the forty days were o'er,
shall our hearts forget his promise,
'I am with you evermore'?

3

Alleluia, bread of angels,
thou on earth our food, our stay;
Alleluia, here the sinful‿
flee to thee from day to day:
Intercessor, Friend of sinners,
earth's Redeemer, plead for me,
where the songs of all the sinless
sweep across the crystal sea.

4

Alleluia, King eternal,
thee the Lord of lords we own;
Alleluia, born of Mary,
earth thy footstool, heaven thy throne:
thou within the veil hast entered,
robed in flesh, our great High Priest;
thou on earth both Priest and Victim
in the eucharistic feast.

W. Chatterton Dix (1837–98)

Alelwia, mawl i'r Iesu

Ar orseddfainc nef y nef;
Alelwia, buddugoliaeth
Byth sy'n eiddo iddo ef;
Clywch ganiadau hyfryd Sion
Yn taranu megis lli:
Allan o'r holl wledydd, Iesu
Trwy ei Waed a'n prynodd ni.

Alelwia, ni'n gadawyd
Yn amddifaid ar y llawr;
Alelwia, ffydd a'i cenfydd
Yn y canol yma'n awr;
Er i'r cwmwl ar Olewydd
Guddio'i annwyl wedd a'i bryd,
Byth y cofiwn "Wele'r ydwyf
Gyda chwi hyd ddiwedd byd."

Alelwia, Bara'r Engyl,
Ymborth nefol yma sydd;
Alelwia, ffy y truan
Atat ti o ddydd i ddydd;
Eiriol drosof, O fy Mhrynwr,
Cyfaill pechaduriaid, clyw,
Lle y daw dros for o risial
Ber alawon meibion Duw.

Alelwia, Ior tragwyddol,
Nefoedd yw d'orseddfainc di;
Alelwia, Fab y Forwyn.
Mainc dy draed yw'n daear ni;
Fry ein Harchoffeiriad ydwyt,
Brawd i ni yng ngwlad yr hedd;
Yma'n Aberth ac Offeiriad
Yn y sanctaidd Ddiolch-wledd.

W.C. Dix—Welsh translation

6 AMAZING GRACE

AMAZING GRACE CM
1. A - maz - ing grace! How sweet the sound that
Capo 1 E A E
saved a wretch like me. I
B7
once was lost, but now I'm found; was
E A E
blind, but now I see.
B7 E

2. 'Twas grace that taught my heart to fear,
and grace my fears relieved.
How precious did that grace appear
the hour I first believed.

3. Through many dangers, toils and snares
I have already come.
'Tis grace hath brought me safe thus far,
and grace will lead me home.

4. The Lord has promised good to me,
his word my hope secures;
he will my shield and portion be
as long as life endures.

5. When we've been there a thousand years,
bright shining as the sun,
we've no less days to sing God's praise
than when we first begun.

Text: vs.1-4: John Newton (1725 - 1807) alt, v.5: John Rees (1828 - 1900)
Music: American folk melody arr. Richard Lloyd (*b.* 1933)

7 AND CAN IT BE

Music used by permission of Oxford University Press

SAGINA 88 88 88 extended

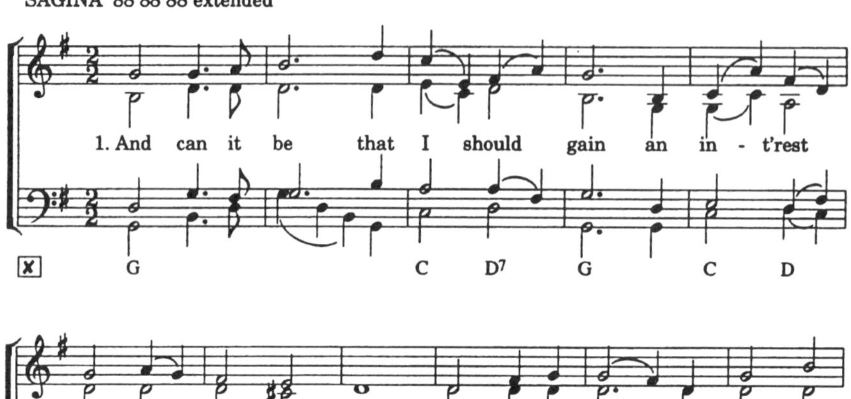
1. And can it be that I should gain an in - t'rest
G C D7 G C D

in the Sa - viour's blood? Died he for me, who caused his
G D A7 D G D G

pain? For me, who him to death pur - sued? A - maz - ing
D C G D7 G D

love! How can it be that thou, my God, shouldst
G D C A D7 G C

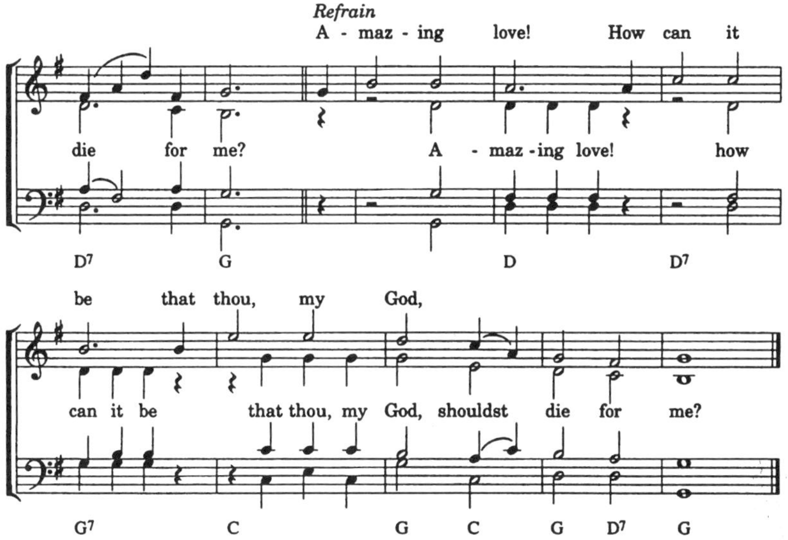
Refrain
A - maz - ing love! How can it
die for me? A - maz -ing love! how
D7 G D D7
be that thou, my God,
can it be that thou, my God, shouldst die for me?
G7 C G C G D7 G

2. 'Tis myst'ry all! th'Immortal dies:
who can explore his strange design?
In vain the first-born seraph tries
to sound the depths of love divine!
'Tis mercy all! Let earth adore,
let angel minds inquire no more.

3. He left his Father's throne above
so free, so infinite his grace;
emptied himself of all but love,
and bled for Adam's helpless race;
'tis mercy all, immense and free;
for, O my God, it found out me.

4. Long my imprisoned spirit lay
fast bound in sin and nature's night;
thine eye diffused a quick'ning ray,
I woke, the dungeon flamed with light;
my chains fell off, my heart was free;
I rose, went forth, and followed thee.

5. No condemnation now I dread;
Jesus, and all in him, is mine!
Alive in him, my living Head,
and clothed in righteousness divine,
bold I approach the eternal throne,
and claim the crown, through Christ my own.

Text: Charles Wesley (1707 - 1788)
Music: Thomas Campbell (1825 - 1876)

8 ANGEL VOICES EVER SINGING

Angel voices 85 85 843 E. G. MONK (1819–1900)

ANGEL voices ever singing
  round thy throne of light,
angel harps for ever ringing
  rest not day nor night;
thousands only live to bless thee,
  and confess thee,
    Lord of might.

2 Lord, we know that thou rejoicest
  o'er each work of thine;
thou didst ears and hands and voices
  for thy praise design;
craftsman's art and music's measure
  for thy pleasure
    all combine.

3 In thy house, great God, we offer
  of thine own to thee,
and for thine acceptance proffer,
  all unworthily,
hearts and minds and hands and voices,
  in our choicest
    psalmody.

4 Honour, glory, might and merit
  thine shall ever be,
Father, Son, and Holy Spirit,
  blessèd Trinity;
of the best that thou hast given
  earth and heaven
    render thee.

FRANCIS POTT (1832–1909)

9 AT EVENING WHEN THE SUN WAS SET

Angelus LM

Founded on a melody in *Heilige Seelen-Lust*, 1657

At evening, when the sun was set,
  the sick, O Lord, around you lay;
O in what various pains they met!
  O with what joy they went away!

2 O Saviour Christ, our ills dispel:
  for some are sick, and some are sad,
and some have never loved you well,
  and some have lost the love they had;

3 and some are pressed with worldly care,
  and some are tried with fear and doubt,
and some such grievous passions tear,
  that only you can cast them out;

4 and none, O Lord, have perfect rest,
  for none are wholly free from sin;
and those who long to serve you best
  are conscious most of wrong within.

5 O Christ our Saviour, Son of Man;
  you have been troubled, tempted, tried;
your kind but searching glance can scan
  the very wounds that shame would hide.

6 Your touch has still its ancient power;
  no word from you can fruitless fall;
hear in this solemn evening hour,
  and in your mercy heal us all.

HENRY TWELLS (1823–1900)*

10 AT THE NAME OF JESUS

Evelyns 65 65 D — W. H. MONK (1823–89)

At the Name of Jesus
   every knee shall bow,
every tongue confess him
   King of glory now.
'Tis the Father's pleasure
   we should call him Lord,
who from the beginning
   was the mighty Word.

2 Humbled for a season,
   to receive a Name
from the lips of sinners
   unto whom he came,
he became a witness,
   faithful to the last,
and returned victorious
   when from death he passed.

3 In your hearts enthrone him;
   there let him make new
all that is not holy,
   all that is not true.
He is God the Saviour,
   he is Christ the Lord,
ever to be worshipped,
   trusted and adored.

4 When this same Lord Jesus
   shall appear again
in his Father's glory,
   there with him to reign,
then may we adore him,
   all before him bow,
as our hearts confess him
   King of glory now.

CAROLINE M. NOEL (1817–77)*

11 BE THOU MY VISION

Music used by permission of Oxford University Press

Slane 10 10 10 10 (Dactylic)

Irish traditional melody
harm. ERIK ROUTLEY (1917–82)

BE thou my vision, O Lord of my heart,
naught be all else to me, save that thou art—
thou my best thought in the day and the night,
waking and sleeping, thy presence my light.

2 Be thou my wisdom, be thou my true word,
thou ever with me and I with thee, Lord;
thou my great Father, thy child let me be,
thou in me dwelling, and I one with thee.

3 Be thou my breastplate, my sword for the fight;
be thou my dignity, thou my delight,
thou my soul's shelter, and thou my strong tower;
raise thou me heav'nward, great Power of my power.

4 Riches I heed not, nor earth's empty praise,
thou mine inheritance, now and always;
thou and thou only, the first in my heart,
High King of heaven, my treasure thou art.

5 High King of heaven, thou heaven's bright sun,
grant me its joys after vict'ry is won;
heart of my own heart, whatever befall,
still be my vision, O Ruler of all.

Ancient Irish poem
tr. MARY E. BYRNE (1880–1931)
and ELEANOR H. HULL (1860–1935)

12 BEFORE THE ENDING OF THE DAY

Te Lucis L.M. **Mode viii**

A - men.

Before the ending of the day,
Creator of the world, we pray,
that with thy wonted favour thou‿
wouldst be our guard and keeper now.

2

From all ill dreams defend our eyes,
from nightly fears and fantasies;
tread under foot our ghostly foe,
that no pollution we may know.

3

O Father, that we ask be done,
through Jesus Christ thine only Son,
who, with the Holy Ghost and thee,
doth live and reign eternally. Amen.

Latin, tr. J. M. Neale (1818–66)

13 BREAD OF HEAVEN, ON THEE WE FEED

Bread of Heaven 7 7·7 7·7 7·

W. D. Maclagan (1826–1910)

1

Bread of heaven, on thee we feed,
for thy flesh is meat indeed;
ever may our souls be fed
with this true and living bread;
day by day with strength supplied
through the life of him who died.

2

Vine of heaven, thy blood supplies‿
this blest cup of sacrifice;
Lord, thy wounds our healing give,
to thy Cross we look and live:
Jesus, may we ever be‿
grafted, rooted, built in thee.

J. Conder (1789–1855)

14 BREATHE ON ME, BREATH OF GOD

FIRST TUNE

Veni Spiritus SM JOHN STAINER (1840–1901)

Second Tune

Carlisle S.M. C. Lockhart (1745–1815)

Breathe on me, breath of God,
fill me with life anew,
that I may love what thou dost love,
and do what thou wouldst do.

2 Breathe on me, breath of God,
until my heart is pure,
until with thee I will one will
to do and to endure.

3 Breathe on me, breath of God,
till I am wholly thine,
until this earthly part of me
glows with thy fire divine.

4 Breathe on me, breath of God;
so shall I never die,
but live with thee the perfect life
of thine eternity.

EDWIN HATCH (1835–89)

15 CHRIST BE BESIDE ME

Unison

Bunessan 55 54 D
Words © 1969, 1985 James Quinn

Scots Gaelic traditional melody
arr. Donald Davison

1 Christ be beside me,
Christ be before me,
Christ be behind me,
Kind of my heart.
Christ be within me,
Christ be below me,
Christ be above me,
never to part.

2 Christ on my right hand,
Christ on my left hand,
Christ all around me,
shield in the strife.
Christ in my sleeping,
Christ in my sitting,
Christ in my rising,
light of my life.

3 Christ be in all hearts
thinking about me,
Christ be on all tongues
telling of me.
Christ be the vision
in eyes that see me,
in ears that hear me,
Christ ever be.

James Quinn (b. 1919)
adapted from 'St Patrick's Breastplate

16 CHRIST IS MADE THE SURE FOUNDATION

1 Christ is made the sure foundation,
Christ the head and corner-stone,
chosen of the Lord, and precious,
binding all the Church in one,
holy Sion's help for ever,
and her confidence alone.

2 All that dedicated city,
dearly loved of God on high,
in exultant jubilation
pours perpetual melody,
God the One in Three adoring
in glad hymns eternally.

3 To this temple, where we call thee,
come, O Lord of Hosts, to-day;
with thy wonted loving-kindness
hear thy servants as they pray,
and thy fullest benediction
shed within its walls alway.

4 Here vouchsafe to all thy servants
what they ask of thee to gain,
what they gain from thee for ever
with the blessèd to retain,
and hereafter in thy glory
evermore with thee to reign.

This Doxology may be sung at the end of any part, or of the whole hymn

5 Laud and honour to the Father,
laud and honour to the Son,
laud and honour to the Spirit,
ever Three, and ever One,
consubstantial, co-eternal,
while unending ages run.

Latin, 7th–8th cent.
tr. J. M. NEALE* (1818–66)

17 CHRIST IS THE KING, O FRIENDS REJOICE

Vulpius 888 with alleluias

Melody by MELCHIOR VULPIUS (c.1570–1615)
harm. ERIK ROUTLEY (1917–82)

CHRIST is the King! O friends rejoice;
brothers and sisters, with one voice
tell all the earth he is your choice:

Alleluia! Alleluia! Alleluia!

2 O magnify the Lord, and raise
anthems of joy and holy praise
for Christ's brave saints of ancient days:

3 Christ through all ages is the same:
place the same hope in his great name,
with the same faith his word proclaim:

4 Let Love's unconquerable might
your scattered companies unite
in service to the Lord of light:

5 So shall God's will on earth be done,
new lamps be lit, new tasks begun,
and the whole Church at last be one:

G. K. A. BELL (1883–1958)*

18 CHRIST IS THE WORLD'S TRUE LIGHT

Rinkart 67 67 66 66 J. S. BACH (1685–1750)

Small notes for organ only

Words and music used by permission of Oxford University

CHRIST is the world's true light,
  its captain of salvation,
the daystar clear and bright
  and joy of every nation;
new life, new hope awakes,
  where'er we own his sway:
freedom her bondage breaks,
  and night is turned to day.

2 In Christ all races meet,
  their ancient feuds forgetting,
the whole round world complete,
  from sunrise to its setting:
when Christ is throned as Lord,
  all shall forsake their fear,
to ploughshare beat the sword,
  to pruning-hook the spear.

3 One Lord, in one great name
  unite us all who own thee;
cast out our pride and shame
  that hinder to enthrone thee;
the world has waited long,
  has travailed long in pain;
to heal its ancient wrong,
  come, Prince of Peace, and reign.

G. W. BRIGGS (1875–1959)

19 CHRIST WHOSE GLORY FILLS THE SKIES

Ratisbon 7 7.7 7.7 7. Melody from Werner's *Choralbuch* (Leipzig, 1815)

Christ, whose glory fills the skies,
  Christ, the true, the only light,
Sun of Righteousness, arise,
  triumph o'er the shades of night;
Dayspring from on high, be near;
Daystar, in my heart appear.

2

Dark and cheerless is the morn
  unaccompanied by thee;
joyless is the day's return,
  till thy mercy's beams I see,
till they inward light impart,
glad my eyes, and warm my heart.

3

Visit then this soul of mine,
  pierce the gloom of sin and grief;
fill me, radiancy divine,
  scatter all my unbelief;
more and more thyself display,
shining to the perfect day.

CHARLES WESLEY (1707–88)

20 COME DOWN, O LOVE DIVINE

Music used by permission of Oxford University Press

Down Ampney 66 11 D R. VAUGHAN WILLIAMS (1872–1958)

COME down, O Love Divine,
seek thou this soul of mine,
and visit it with thine own ardour glowing;
O Comforter, draw near,
within my heart appear,
and kindle it, thy holy flame bestowing.

2 O let it freely burn,
till earthly passions turn
to dust and ashes in its heat consuming;
and let thy glorious light
shine ever on my sight,
and clothe me round, the while my path illuming.

3 Let holy charity
mine outward vesture be,
and lowliness become mine inner clothing;
true lowliness of heart,
which takes the humbler part,
and o'er its own shortcomings weeps with loathing.

4 And so the yearning strong
with which the soul will long,
shall far outpass the power of human telling;
for none can guess its grace,
till he become the place
wherein the Holy Spirit makes his dwelling.

BIANCO DA SIENA (d. 1434)
tr. R. F. LITTLEDALE (1833–90)

21 COME HOLY GHOST, OUR SOULS INSPIRE

Veni Creator Spiritus LM with doxology Mechlin melody

Unison
DOXOLOGY
Praise__ to thy__ e -
- ter - nal me-rit, Fa - ther, Son,_ and Ho - ly Spi-rit.

COME, Holy Ghost, our souls inspire,
and lighten with celestial fire;
thou the anointing Spirit art,
who dost thy sevenfold gifts impart.

2 Thy blessèd unction from above
is comfort, life, and fire of love;
enable with perpetual light
the dullness of our blinded sight.

3 Anoint and cheer our soilèd face
with the abundance of thy grace:
keep far our foes, give peace at home:
where thou art guide no ill can come.

4 Teach us to know the Father, Son,
and thee, of both, to be but One;
that through the ages all along
this may be our endless song:

Praise to thy eternal merit,
Father, Son, and Holy Spirit.

Latin, 9th cent.
tr. JOHN COSIN (1594–1672)

This alternative version of verse 1 may be used if preferred:

Come, Holy Spirit, souls inspire
and lighten with celestial fire;
thou the anointing Spirit art,
who dost thy sevenfold gifts impart.

22 COME LET US JOIN OUR CHEERFUL SONGS

Nativity CM H. LAHEE (1826–1912)

COME, let us join our cheerful songs
  with angels round the throne;
ten thousand thousand are their tongues,
  but all their joys are one.

2 Worthy the Lamb that died, they cry,
  to be exalted thus:
worthy the Lamb, our lips reply,
  for he was slain for us.

3 Jesus is worthy to receive
  honour and power divine;
and blessings more than we can give
  be, Lord, for ever thine.

4 Let all the hosts of heaven combine
  with air and earth and sea,
to lift in glorious songs divine
  their endless praise to thee.

5 Let all creation join in one,
  to bless the sacred name
of him that sits upon the throne,
  and to adore the Lamb.

ISAAC WATTS (1674–1748)*

23 COME RISEN LORD, AND DEIGN TO BE OUR GUEST

Blackbird Leys 10 10.10 10. Peter Cutts (b. 1937)

The breaking of bread

Come, risen Lord, and deign to be our guest;
nay, let us be thy guests; the feast is thine;
thyself at thine own board make manifest,
in thine own sacrament of bread and wine.

2

We meet, as in that upper room they met;
thou at the table, blessing, yet dost stand:
'This is my body': so thou givest yet:
faith still receives the cup as from thy hand.

3

One body we, one body who partake,
one church united in communion blest;
one name we bear, one bread of life we break,
with all thy saints on earth and saints at rest.

4

One with each other, Lord, for one in thee,
who art one Saviour and one living Head;
then open thou our eyes, that we may see;
be known to us in breaking of the bread.

G. W. Briggs (1875–1959)

24 CROWN HIM WITH MANY CROWNS

Reproduced by permission of Hymns Ancient & Modern Ltd.

Diademata D.S.M.
G. J. Elvey (1816–93)

Crown him with many crowns,
the Lamb upon his throne;
hark, how the heavenly anthem drowns‿
all music but its own:
awake, my soul, and sing
of him who died for thee,
and hail him as thy matchless King
through all eternity.

2

Crown him the Virgin's Son,
the God incarnate born,
whose arm those crimson trophies won
which now his brow adorn:
Fruit of the mystic Rose,
as of that Rose the Stem;
the Root whence mercy ever flows,
the Babe of Bethlehem.

3

Crown him the Lord of love;
behold his hands and side,
those wounds yet visible above
in beauty glorified:
no angel in the sky
can fully bear that sight,
but downward bends his burning eye
at mysteries so bright.

4

Crown him the Lord of peace,
whose power a sceptre sways
from pole to pole, that wars may cease,
and all be prayer and praise:
his reign shall know no end,
and round his piercèd feet
fair flowers of paradise extend‿
their fragrance ever sweet.

5

Crown him the Lord of years,
the Potentate of time,
Creator of the rolling spheres,
ineffably sublime:
all hail, Redeemer, hail!
for thou hast died for me;
thy praise shall never, never fail
throughout eternity.

The expression 'mystic Rose' in verse 2, line 5, is a medieval title for the Blessed Virgin, and is combined here with a reference to Isaiah 11.1

MATTHEW BRIDGES* (1800–94)
Revelation 19. 12

25 DEAR LORD AND FATHER OF MANKIND

Repton 8 6. 8 8 6.

C. H. H. Parry (1848–1918)
arr. Michael Fleming

For manuals only

Dear Lord and Father of mankind,
forgive our foolish ways;
re-clothe us in our rightful mind,
in purer lives thy service find,
in deeper reverence praise.

2

In simple trust like theirs who heard,
beside the Syrian sea,
the gracious calling of the Lord,
let us, like them, without a word
rise up and follow thee.

*3

O Sabbath rest by Galilee!
O calm of hills above,
where Jesus knelt to share with thee
the silence of eternity,
interpreted by love!

4

Drop thy still dews of quietness,
till all our strivings cease;
take from our souls the strain and stress,
and let our ordered lives confess
the beauty of thy peace.

5

Breathe through the heats of our desire
thy coolness and thy balm;
let sense be dumb, let flesh retire;
speak through the earthquake, wind, and fire,
O still small voice of calm.

J. G. WHITTIER (1807–92)

The last line of each verse is repeated

26 FATHER HEAR THE PRAYER WE OFFER

Sussex 87 87 (Trochaic)

English traditional melody
adpt. and arr. R. VAUGHAN WILLIAMS (1872–1958)

Music used by permission of Oxford University Press.

FATHER, hear the prayer we offer;
not for ease that prayer shall be,
but for strength that we may ever
live our lives courageously.

2 Not for ever in green pastures
do we ask our way to be;
but the steep and rugged pathway
may we tread rejoicingly.

3 Not for ever by still waters
would we idly rest and stay;
but would smite the living fountains
from the rocks along our way.

4 Be our strength in hours of weakness,
in our wanderings be our guide;
through endeavour, failure, danger,
Father, be thou at our side.

LOVE MARIA WILLIS (1824–1908) and others

27 FILL THOU MY LIFE

Billing CM

R. R. TERRY (1865–1938)

Fill thou my life, O Lord my God,
in every part with praise,
that my whole being may proclaim
thy being and thy ways.

2 Not for the lip of praise alone
nor ev'n the praising heart
I ask, but for a life made up
of praise in every part:

3 praise in the common things of life,
its goings out and in;
praise in each duty and each deed,
however small and mean.

4 Fill every part of me with praise;
let all my being speak
of thee and of thy love, O Lord,
poor though I be and weak.

5 So shalt thou, glorious Lord, from me
receive the glory due;
and so shall I begin on earth
the song for ever new.

6 So shall no part of day or night
from sacredness be free;
but all my life, in every step,
be fellowship with thee.

H. BONAR (1808–89)

28 FOR ALL THE SAINTS

Verses 4, 5, 6 in Harmony
(small notes v. 6)

For all the saints who from their labours rest,
who thee by faith before the world confessed,
thy name, O Jesu, be for ever blest.
Alleluia.

2

Thou wast their rock, their fortress, and their might;
thou, Lord, their Captain in the well-fought fight;
thou, in the darkness, still their one true Light.
Alleluia.

3

O may thy soldiers, faithful, true, and bold,
fight as the saints who nobly fought of old,
and win, with them, the victor's crown of gold.
Alleluia.

4

O blest communion, fellowship divine!
we feebly struggle, they in glory shine;
yet all are one in thee, for all are thine.
Alleluia.

5

And when the strife is fierce, the warfare long,
steals on the ear the distant triumph-song,
and hearts are brave again and arms are strong.
Alleluia.

6

The golden evening brightens in the west;
soon, soon to faithful warriors comes their rest:
sweet is the calm of Paradise the blest.
Alleluia.

7

But lo, there breaks a yet more glorious day;
the saints triumphant rise in bright array:
the King of Glory passes on his way.
Alleluia.

8

From earth's wide bounds, from ocean's farthest coast,
through gates of pearl streams in the countless host,
singing to Father, Son, and Holy Ghost
Alleluia.

W. Walsham How (1823–97)

29 FOR THE BEAUTY

Dix 77.77.77.

Adapted from C. Kocher (1786–1872)
by W. H. Monk (1823–89)

DESCANT

If preferred, the harmonies for lines 1 and 2 may be repeated for lines 3 and 4. The descant may be sung by sopranos for verses 3 and 5, the main melody being sung in unison. In this case, the above harmonies should be played as printed.

FOR the beauty of the earth,
for the beauty of the skies,
for the love which from our birth
over and around us lies:

Gracious God, to thee we raise
this our sacrifice of praise.

2 For the beauty of each hour
of the day and of the night,
hill and vale, and tree and flower,
sun and moon, and stars of light:

3 For the joy of ear and eye,
for the heart and mind's delight,
for the mystic harmony
linking sense to sound and sight:

4 For the joy of human love,
brother, sister, parent, child,
friends on earth, and friends above;
for all gentle thoughts and mild:

5 For each perfect gift of thine
to our race so freely given,
graces human and divine,
flowers of earth and buds of heaven:

6 For thy people, evermore
lifting holy hands above,
offering up on every shore
their pure sacrifice of love:

F. S. PIERPOINT (1835–1917)

30 FORTH IN THY NAME O LORD I GO

Melody and bass by
Orlando Gibbons (1583–1625)

1

Forth in thy name, O Lord, I go,
  my daily labour to pursue;
thee, only thee, resolved to know,
  in all I think or speak or do.

2

The task thy wisdom hath assigned
  O let me cheerfully fulfil;
in all my works thy presence find,
  and prove thy good and perfect will.

3

Thee may I set at my right hand,
  whose eyes my inmost substance see
and labour on at thy command,
  and offer all my works to thee.

4

Give me to bear thy easy yoke,
  and every moment watch and pray,
and still to things eternal look,
  and hasten to thy glorious day;

5

for thee delightfully employ
  whate'er thy bounteous grace hath given,
and run my course with even joy,
  and closely walk with thee to heaven.

CHARLES WESLEY* (1707–88)

31 GLORIOUS THINGS OF THEE ARE SPOKEN

Abbot's Leigh 87 87 D CYRIL V. TAYLOR (1907–91)

Music used by permission of Oxford University Press

GLORIOUS things of thee are spoken,
  Zion, city of our God;
he whose word cannot be broken
  formed thee for his own abode.
On the Rock of Ages founded,
  what can shake thy sure repose?
With salvation's walls surrounded,
  thou may'st smile at all thy foes.

2 See! The streams of living waters,
  springing from eternal love,
well supply thy sons and daughters,
  and all fear of want remove;
who can faint, while such a river
  ever flows, their thirst to assuage—
grace, which, like the Lord, the giver,
  never fails from age to age.

3 Saviour, if of Zion's city
  I, through grace, a member am,
let the world deride or pity,
  I will glory in thy name.
Fading is the worldling's pleasure,
  all his boasted pomp and show;
solid joys and lasting treasure
  none but Zion's children know.

JOHN NEWTON (1725–1807)

32 GLORY TO THEE MY GOD, THIS NIGHT

Tallis's Canon L.M.

Thomas Tallis (*c.* 1505–85)
as shortened by T. Ravenscroft (1621)

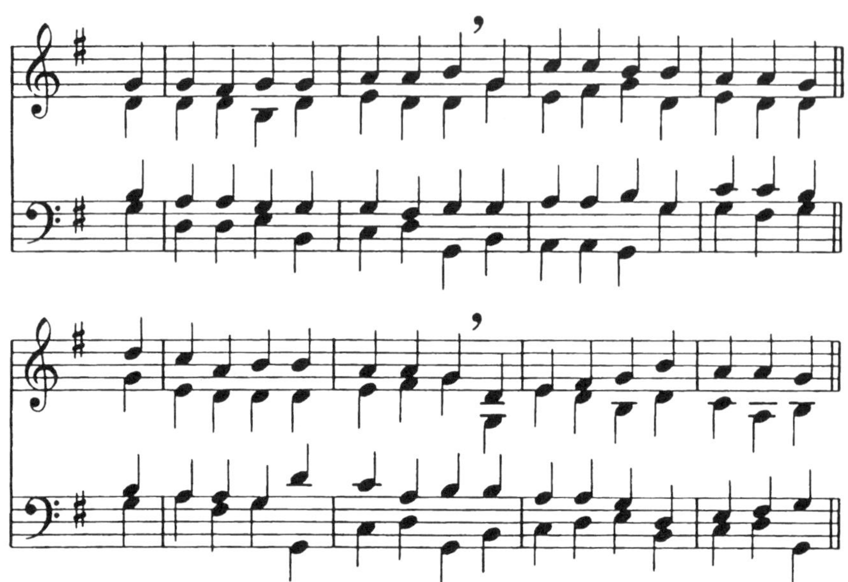

Glory to thee, my God, this night
for all the blessings of the light;
keep me, O keep me, King of kings,
beneath thy own almighty wings.

2

Forgive me, Lord, for thy dear Son,
the ill that I this day have done,
that with the world, myself, and thee,
I, ere I sleep, at peace may be.

3

Teach me to live, that I may dread‿
the grave as little as my bed;
teach me to die, that so I may‿
rise glorious at the aweful day.

4

O may my soul on thee repose,
and may sweet sleep mine eyelids close,
sleep that may me more vigorous make
to serve my God when I awake.

5

When in the night I sleepless lie,
my soul with heavenly thoughts supply;
let no ill dreams disturb my rest,
no powers of darkness me molest.

6

Praise God, from whom all blessings flow,
praise him, all creatures here below,
praise him above, angelic host,
praise Father, Son, and Holy Ghost.

THOMAS KEN (1637–1711)

33 GOD IS LOVE, LET HEAVEN ADORE HIM

Blaenwern 87 87 D W. P. ROWLANDS (1860–1937)

GOD is love: let heaven adore him;
God is love: let earth rejoice;
let creation sing before him,
and exalt him with one voice.
He who laid the earth's foundation,
he who spread the heavens above,
he who breathes through all creation,
he is love, eternal love.

2 God is love, and is enfolding
all the world in one embrace;
his unfailing grasp is holding
every child of every race;
and when human hearts are breaking
under sorrow's iron rod,
that same sorrow, that same aching
wrings with pain the heart of God.

3 God is love: and though with blindness
sin afflicts and clouds the will,
God's eternal loving-kindness
holds us fast and guides us still.
Sin and death and hell shall never
o'er us final triumph gain;
God is love, so Love for ever
o'er the universe must reign.

TIMOTHY REES (1874–1939)*

34 GOD OF GRACE AND GOD OF GLORY

Rhuddlan 87 87 87 Welsh traditional melody

God of grace and God of glory,
on thy people pour thy power;
crown thine ancient Church's story;
bring her bud to glorious flower.
Grant us wisdom,
grant us courage,
for the facing of this hour.

2 Lo! the hosts of evil round us
scorn thy Christ, assail his ways!
From the fears that long have bound us,
free our hearts to faith and praise.
Grant us wisdom,
grant us courage,
for the living of these days.

3 Cure thy children's warring madness;
bend our pride to thy control;
shame our wanton, selfish gladness,
rich in things and poor in soul.
Grant us wisdom,
grant us courage,
lest we miss thy kingdom's goal.

4 Save us from weak resignation
to the evils we deplore;
let the gift of thy salvation
be our glory evermore.
Grant us wisdom,
grant us courage,
serving thee whom we adore.

H. E. FOSDICK (1878–1969)

35 GOD OF MERCY, GOD OF GRACE

Heathlands 77 77 77 HENRY SMART (1813–79)

GOD of mercy, God of grace,
show the brightness of your face;
shine upon us, Saviour, shine,
fill your Church with light divine;
and your saving health extend
unto earth's remotest end.

2 Let the peoples praise you, Lord!
Be by all that live adored;
let the nations shout and sing
glory to their Saviour King;
at your feet their tribute pay
and your holy will obey.

3 Let the peoples praise you, Lord!
Earth shall all her fruits afford;
God to us his blessing give,
we to God devoted live:
all below, and all above,
one in joy and light and love.

H. F. LYTE (1793–1847)
based on Psalm 67

36 GREAT IS THY FAITHFULNESS

Faithfulness 11 10 11 10 (Dactylic) with refrain W. M. RUNYAN (1870–1957)

REFRAIN
Great is thy faith-ful-ness, great is thy faith-ful-ness, morn-ing by

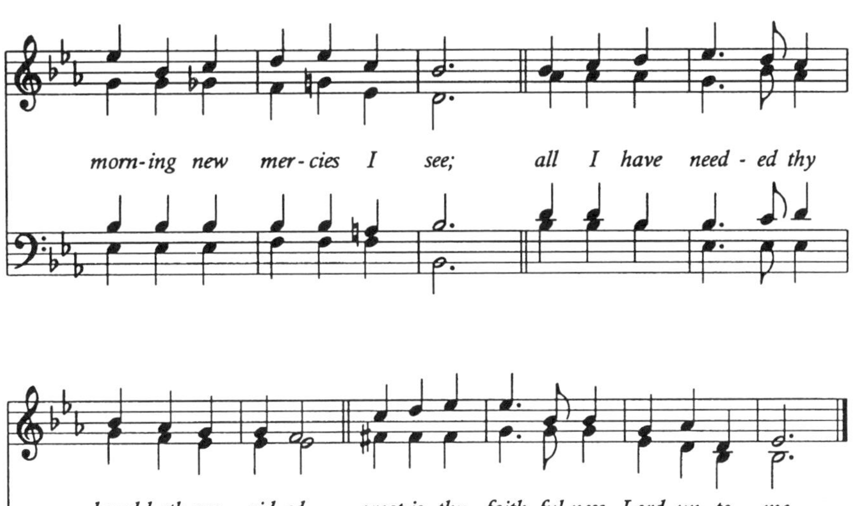
morn-ing new mer-cies I see; all I have need-ed thy
hand hath pro - vid-ed, great is thy faith-ful-ness, Lord, un-to me.

GREAT is thy faithfulness, O God my Father,
there is no shadow of turning with thee;
thou changest not, thy compassions, they fail not;
as thou hast been thou for ever wilt be.

Great is thy faithfulness, great is thy faithfulness,
morning by morning new mercies I see;
all I have needed thy hand hath provided,
great is thy faithfulness, Lord, unto me.

2 Summer and winter, and springtime and harvest,
sun, moon and stars in their courses above,
join with all nature in manifold witness
to thy great faithfulness, mercy and love.

3 Pardon for sin and a peace that endureth,
thine own dear presence to cheer and to guide;
strength for today and bright hope for tomorrow,
blessings all mine, with ten thousand beside!

T. O. CHISHOLM (1866–1960)

37 GUIDE ME, O THOU GREAT JEHOVAH

Cwm Rhondda 87 87 47 extended JOHN HUGHES (Pontypridd) (1873–1932)

ARGLWYDD, arwain drwy'r anialwch
fi, bererin gwael ei wedd;
nad oes ynof nerth na bywyd,
fel yn gorwedd yn y bedd;
Hollalluog
ydyw'r un a'm cwyd i'r lan.

2 Agor y ffynhonnau melys
sydd yn tarddu o'r Graig i maes;
'r hyd yr anial mawr canlyned
afon iachawdwriaeth gras:
rho im' hynny—
dim i mi ond dy fwynhau.

3 Pan fwy'n myned trwy'r Iorddonen,
angau creulon yn ei rym,
aethost trywddi gynt dy hunan,
pam yr ofnaf bellach ddim?
Buddogoliaeth!
Gwna im' weiddi yn y llif. (Welsh)

WILLIAM WILLIAMS, Pantycelyn (1717–91)

GUIDE me, O thou great Jehovah,
pilgrim through this barren land;
I am weak, but thou art mighty,
hold me with thy powerful hand:
bread of heaven,
feed me now and evermore.

2 Open thou the crystal fountain
whence the healing stream doth flow;
let the fiery, cloudy pillar
lead me all my journey through:
strong deliverer,
be thou still my strength and shield.

3 When I tread the verge of Jordan,
bid my anxious fears subside;
death of death, and hell's destruction,
land me safe on Canaan's side:
songs of praises,
I will ever give to thee.

v. 1 tr. PETER WILLIAMS (1722–96)
vv. 2–3 tr. WILLIAM WILLIAMS
(or JOHN WILLIAMS, 1754–1828)

1 Niongoze, Bwana
Mungu,
Ni msafiri chini;
Ni mnyonge, nguvu sina:
Nishike mkononi;
U Mkate wa mbinguni,
Nilishe siku zote.

2 Kijito cha maji mema
Kitokacho mwambani,
Nguzo yako, moto, wingu,
Yaongoza nyikani;
Niokoe Mwenye nguvu;
Nguvu zangu na ngao.

3 Nikikaribia kufa,
Sichi neno lolote,
Wewe kifo umeshinda
Zinawe nguvu zote,
Tutaimba sifa zako,
Kwako juu milele.

(Swahili)

38 HAIL, TO THE LORD'S ANOINTED

Crüger 76 76 D

adpt. W. H. MONK (1823–89)
from a chorale by JOHANN CRÜGER (1598–1662)

HAIL to the Lord's Anointed,
  great David's greater Son!
Hail, in the time appointed,
  his reign on earth begun!
He comes to break oppression,
  to set the captive free,
to take away transgression,
  and rule in equity.

2 He comes with succour speedy
  to those who suffer wrong;
to help the poor and needy,
  and bid the weak be strong;
to give them songs for sighing,
  their darkness turn to light,
whose souls, condemned and dying,
  were precious in his sight.

3 He shall come down like showers
  upon the fruitful earth;
and love, joy, hope, like flowers,
  spring in his path to birth:
before him on the mountains,
  shall peace the herald go,
and righteousness in fountains
  from hill to valley flow.

4 Kings shall fall down before him,
  and gold and incense bring;
and nations shall adore him,
  his praise all people sing;
for he shall have dominion
  o'er river, sea, and shore,
far as the eagle's pinion
  or dove's light wing can soar.

5 O'er every foe victorious,
  he on his throne shall rest;
from age to age more glorious,
  all-blessing and all-blest:
the tide of time shall never
  his covenant remove;
his name shall stand for ever;
  that name to us is Love.

Psalm 72
para. JAMES MONTGOMERY (1771–1854)

39 HILLS OF THE NORTH REJOICE

Words used by permission of Oxford University Press

LITTLE CORNARD 66 66 88 — Martin Shaw 1875–1958

Unison
*
* vv. 4, 5

HILLS of the North, rejoice,
  Echoing songs arise,
Hail with united voice
  Him who made earth and skies:
He comes in righteousness and love,
He brings salvation from above.

2 Isles of the Southern seas,
  Sing to the listening earth,
Carry on every breeze
  Hope of a world's new birth:
In Christ shall all be made anew,
His word is sure, his promise true.

3 Lands of the East, arise,
  He is your brightest morn,
Greet him with joyous eyes,
  Praise shall his path adorn:
The God whom you have longed to know
In Christ draws near, and calls you now.

4 Shores of the utmost West,
  Lands of the setting sun,
Welcome the heavenly guest
  In whom the dawn has come:
He brings a never-ending light
Who triumphed o'er our darkest night.

5 Shout, as you journey on,
  Songs be in every mouth,
Lo, from the North they come,
  From East and West and South:
In Jesus all shall find their rest,
In him the sons of earth be blest.

Based on
C. E. Oakley 1832–65

40 HOLY, HOLY, HOLY

Nicaea 11 12 12 10 J. B. DYKES (1823–76)

HOLY, holy, holy! Lord God Almighty,
early in the morning our song shall rise to thee;
Holy, holy, holy! merciful and mighty,
God in three Persons, blessed Trinity!

2 Holy, holy, holy! All the saints adore thee,
casting down their golden crowns around the glassy sea,
cherubim and seraphim falling down before thee,
who wast and art and evermore shalt be.

3 Holy, holy, holy! Though the darkness hide thee,
though the sinful human eye thy glory may not see,
only thou art holy, there is none beside thee,
perfect in power, in love, and purity.

4 Holy, holy, holy! Lord God Almighty,
all thy works shall praise thy name, in earth, and sky, and sea;
Holy, holy, holy! merciful and mighty,
God in three Persons, blessed Trinity!

REGINALD HEBER (1783–1826)*

41 HOW SHALL I SING THAT MAJESTY

Coe Fen DCM KEN NAYLOR (1931–91)

Unison

How shall I sing that majesty
which angels do admire?
Let dust in dust and silence lie;
sing, sing, ye heavenly choir.
Thousands of thousands stand around
thy throne, O God most high;
ten thousand times ten thousand sound
thy praise; but who am I?

2 Thy brightness unto them appears,
while I thy footsteps trace;
a sound of God comes to my ears;
but they behold thy face:
I shall, I fear, be dark and cold,
with all my fire and light;
yet when thou dost accept their gold,
Lord, treasure up my mite.

3 Enlighten with faith's light my heart,
inflame it with love's fire,
then shall I sing and take my part
with that celestial choir.
They sing, because thou art their Sun;
Lord, send a beam on me;
for where heaven is but once begun,
there alleluias be.

4 How great a being, Lord, is thine,
which doth all beings keep!
Thy knowledge is the only line
to sound so vast a deep:
thou art a sea without a shore,
a sun without a sphere;
thy time is now and evermore,
thy place is everywhere.

JOHN MASON (1646–94)*

42 HOW SWEET THE NAME OF JESUS

St. Peter C.M. A. R. Reinagle (1799–1877)

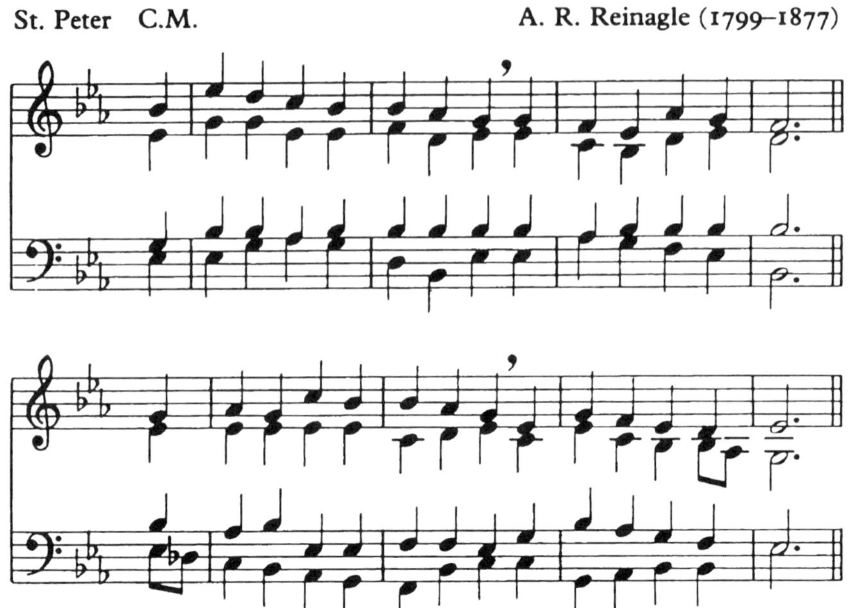

Classical

How sweet the name of Jesus sounds
in a believer's ear!
It soothes his sorrows, heals his wounds,
and drives away his fear.

2

It makes the wounded spirit whole,
and calms the troubled breast;
'tis manna to the hungry soul,
and to the weary rest.

3

Dear name! the rock on which I build,
my shield and hiding-place,
my never-failing treasury filled‿
with boundless stores of grace.

4

Jesus! my Shepherd, Brother, Friend,
my Prophet, Priest, and King,
my Lord, my Life, my Way, my End,
accept the praise I bring.

5

Weak is the effort of my heart,
and cold my warmest thought;
but when I see thee as thou art,
I'll praise thee as I ought.

6

Till then I would thy love proclaim
with every fleeting breath;
and may the music of thy name
refresh my soul in death.

JOHN NEWTON* (1725–1807)

43 I CANNOT TELL

Irish traditional melody
arr. compilers

Londonderry Air 11 10 11 10 11 10 11 12

Unison
Harmony (optional)

Classical

*v. 4, optional

I cannot tell why he, whom angels worship,
should set his love upon the human race,
or why, as Shepherd, he should seek the wanderers,
to bring them back within the fold of grace.
But this I know, that he was born of Mary,
when Bethlehem's manger was his only home,
and that he lived at Nazareth and laboured,
and so the Saviour, Saviour of the world, is come.

2 I cannot tell how silently he suffered,
as with his peace he graced this place of tears,
or how his heart upon the cross was broken,
the crown of pain to three and thirty years.
But this I know, he heals the broken-hearted,
and stays our sin, and calms our lurking fear,
and lifts the burden from the heavy-laden,
for yet the Saviour, Saviour of the world, is here.

3 I cannot tell how he will win the nations,
how he will claim his earthly heritage,
how satisfy the needs and aspirations
of East and West, of sinner and of sage.
But this I know, all flesh shall see his glory,
and he shall reap the harvest he has sown,
and some glad day his sun shall shine in splendour
when he the Saviour, Saviour of the world, is known.

4 I cannot tell how all the lands shall worship
when, at his bidding, every storm is stilled,
or who can say how great the jubilation
when all the hearts on earth with love are filled.
But this I know, the skies will thrill with rapture,
and myriad, myriad human voices sing,
and earth to heaven, and heaven to earth, will answer:
At last the Saviour, Saviour of the world, is King!

W. Y. FULLERTON (1857–1932)*

44 IMMORTAL, INVISIBLE

St. Denio 11 11.11 11. Welsh Hymn Melody (1839)

IMMORTAL, invisible, God only wise,
in light inaccessible hid from our eyes,
most blessed, most glorious, the Ancient of Days,
almighty, victorious, thy great name we praise.

2 Unresting, unhasting, and silent as light,
nor wanting, nor wasting, thou rulest in might;
thy justice like mountains, high soaring above
thy clouds which are fountains of goodness and love.

3 To all life thou givest, to both great and small;
in all life thou livest, the true life of all;
we blossom and flourish as leaves on the tree,
and wither and perish—but naught changeth thee.

4 Great Father of glory: O help us to see
'tis only the splendour of light hideth thee.
And so let thy glory, Almighty, impart,
through Christ in the story, thy Christ to the heart.

W. CHALMERS SMITH (1824–1908)*

45 JESUS, LOVER OF MY SOUL

Aberystwyth 77 77 D JOSEPH PARRY (1841–1903)

JESUS, lover of my soul,
   let me to thy bosom fly,
while the nearer waters roll,
   while the tempest still is high.
Hide me, O my Saviour, hide,
   till the storm of life is past;
safe into the haven guide,
   O receive my soul at last!

2 Other refuge have I none,
   hangs my helpless soul on thee;
leave, ah leave me not alone,
   still support and comfort me.
All my trust on thee is stayed,
   all my help from thee I bring;
cover my defenceless head
   with the shadow of thy wing.

3 Thou, O Christ, art all I want;
   more than all in thee I find;
raise the fallen, cheer the faint,
   heal the sick, and lead the blind.
Just and holy is thy name,
   I am all unrighteousness;
false and full of sin I am,
   thou art full of truth and grace.

4 Plenteous grace with thee is found,
   grace to cover all my sin;
let the healing streams abound,
   make and keep me pure within.
Thou of life the fountain art,
   freely let me take of thee;
spring thou up within my heart,
   rise to all eternity.

CHARLES WESLEY (1707–88)

46 JESU, SON OF MARY

First Tune

SWAHILI 65 65 D

J. A. P. Schulz 1747–1800 in *Lieder im Volkston* Berlin 1785

Slow

At Holy Communion.

JESU, Son of Mary,
  Fount of life alone,
Here we hail thee present
  On thine altar-throne.
Humbly we adore thee,
  Lord of endless might,
In the mystic symbols
  Veiled from earthly sight.

2 Think, O Lord, in mercy
  On the souls of those
Who, in faith gone from us,
  Now in death repose.
Here 'mid stress and conflict
  Toils can never cease;
There, the warfare ended,
  Bid them rest in peace.

Second Tune

CORPUS DOMINI 65 65 D G. E. W. Malet 1839–1918

3 Often were they wounded
In the deadly strife;
Heal them, Good Physician,
With the balm of life.
Every taint of evil,
Frailty and decay,
Good and gracious Saviour,
Cleanse and purge away.

4 Rest eternal grant them,
After weary fight;
Shed on them the radiance
Of thy heavenly light.
Lead them onward, upward,
To the holy place,
Where thy saints made perfect
Gaze upon thy face.

Swahili, *Tr* EDMUND PALMER 1856–1931

47 JESUS IS LORD, CREATION'S VOICE PROCLAIMS IT

Jesus is Lord 11 12 11 12 with refrain DAVID MANSELL (1936–)

Unison
A
Adim
Bm
E6
E7
A
D
A
E7
A
Adim
Bm
E6
E7
A
D
E6
E7
A

REFRAIN
E7 A E7 A E7 A
Je - sus is Lord, Je - sus is Lord!
A D E6 E7 A
Praise him with Al - le - lu - ias, for Je - sus is Lord!

JESUS is Lord! Creation's voice proclaims it,
for by his power
each tree and flower
was planned and made.
Jesus is Lord! The universe declares it—
sun, moon and stars in heaven cry: 'Jesus is Lord!'

Jesus is Lord, Jesus is Lord!
Praise him with Alleluias,
for Jesus is Lord!

2 Jesus is Lord! Yet from his throne eternal
in flesh he came
to die in pain
on Calvary's tree.
Jesus is Lord! From him all life proceeding,
he gave his life a ransom thus setting us free.

3 Jesus is Lord! O'er sin the mighty conqueror,
from death he rose
and all his foes
shall own his name.
Jesus is Lord! God sends his Holy Spirit
showing by works of power that Jesus is Lord.

DAVID MANSELL (1936–)*

48 JESUS LIVES

Music used by permission of Oxford University Press.

First Tune

Mowsley 78 78 4 CYRIL V. TAYLOR (1907–91)

Second Tune

St Albinus 78 78 4 H. J. GAUNTLETT (1805–76)

JESUS lives! Thy terrors now
can, O death, no more appal us;
Jesus lives! By this we know
thou, O grave, canst not enthral us:
Alleluia!

2 Jesus lives! For us he died;
hence may we, to Jesus living,
pure in heart and act abide,
praise to him and glory giving:
Alleluia!

3 Jesus lives! Our hearts know well
naught from us his love shall sever;
life, nor death, nor powers of hell
part us now from Christ for ever:
Alleluia!

4 Jesus lives! Henceforth is death
entrance-gate of life immortal;
this shall calm our trembling breath,
when we pass its gloomy portal:
Alleluia!

5 Jesus lives! To him the throne
over all the world is given;
may we go where he is gone,
live and reign with him in heaven:
Alleluia!

C. F. GELLERT (1715–69)
tr. FRANCES E. COX (1812–97)

49 JESU, THE VERY THOUGHT OF THEE

Metzler's Redhead C.M. R. Redhead (1820–1901)

Jesu, the very thought of thee
with sweetness fills the breast;
but sweeter far thy face to see,
and in thy presence rest.

2

No voice can sing, no heart can frame,
nor can the memory find,
a sweeter sound than Jesu's name,
the Saviour of mankind.

3

O hope of every contrite heart,
O joy of all the meek,
to those who ask how kind thou art,
how good to those who seek!

4

But what to those who find? Ah, this
   nor tongue nor pen can show;
the love of Jesus, what it is
   none but his loved ones know.

5

Jesu, our only joy be thou,
   as thou our prize wilt be;
in thee be all our glory now,
   and through eternity.

50 JUST AS I AM

FIRST TUNE

Saffron Walden 8 8 8.6. A. H. Brown (1830–1926)

Org.

SECOND TUNE

Misericordia 8 8 8.6. Henry Smart (1813–79)

1

Just as I am, without one plea
but that thy blood was shed for me,
and that thou bidst me come to thee,
O Lamb of God, I come.

2

Just as I am, though tossed about
with many a conflict, many a doubt,
fightings and fears within, without,
O Lamb of God, I come.

3

Just as I am, poor, wretched, blind;
sight, riches, healing of the mind,
yea, all I need, in thee to find,
O Lamb of God, I come.

4

Just as I am, thou wilt receive,
wilt welcome, pardon, cleanse, relieve:
because thy promise I believe,
O Lamb of God, I come.

5

Just as I am (thy love unknown
has broken every barrier down),
now to be thine, yea, thine alone,
O Lamb of God, I come.

6

Just as I am, of that free love‿
the breadth, length, depth, and height
here for a season, then above,
O Lamb of God, I come.

Charlotte Elliott (1789–1871)

51 LEAD US, HEAVENLY FATHER

Mannheim 87 87 87

Melody adapted from a chorale by
FRIEDRICH FILITZ (1804–76)

LEAD us, heavenly Father, lead us
   o'er the world's tempestuous sea;
guard us, guide us, keep us, feed us,
   for we have no help but thee;
yet possessing every blessing
   if our God our Father be.

2 Saviour, breathe forgiveness o'er us;
   all our weakness thou dost know,
thou didst tread this earth before us,
   thou didst feel its keenest woe;
lone and dreary, faint and weary,
   through the desert thou didst go.

3 Spirit of our God, descending,
   fill our hearts with heavenly joy,
love with every passion blending,
   pleasure that can never cloy:
thus provided, pardoned, guided,
   nothing can our peace destroy.

JAMES EDMESTON (1791–1867)

In verse 2 line 5 the word 'dreary' has its older meaning, 'sad', rather than the modern 'dismal' or 'gloomy'.

52 LET ALL MORTAL FLESH

Reproduced by permission of Hymns Ancient & Modern Ltd.

Picardy 8 7.8 7.8 7.
(French Carol)

French Carol Melody

Unison

Let all mortal flesh keep silence
  and with fear and trembling stand;
ponder nothing earthly-minded,
  for with blessing in his hand
Christ our God to earth descendeth,
  our full homage to demand.

2

King of kings, yet born of Mary,
  as of old on earth he stood,
Lord of lords, in human vesture –
  in the body and the blood –
he will give to all the faithful
  his own self for heavenly food.

3

Rank on rank the host of heaven
  spreads its vanguard on the way,
as the Light of light descendeth
  from the realms of endless day,
that the powers of hell may vanish
  as the darkness clears away.

4

At his feet the six-winged seraph;
  cherubim with sleepless eye
veil their faces to the Presence,
  as with ceaseless voice they cry,
Alleluia, Alleluia,
  Alleluia, Lord most high.

Liturgy of St. James
tr. G. MOULTRIE (1829–85)

53 LET ALL THE WORLD

Music published by permission of the Executors of the late Dr. Basil Harwood

Luckington 10 4.6 6.6 6.10 4. Basil Harwood (1859–1949)

Antiphon

Let all the world in every corner sing,
        my God and King.
    The heavens are not too high,
    his praise may thither fly:
    the earth is not too low,
    his praises there may grow.
Let all the world in every corner sing,
        my God and King.

2

Let all the world in every corner sing,
        my God and King.
    The Church with psalms must shout,
    no door can keep them out;
    but above all the heart
    must bear the longest part.
Let all the world in every corner sing,
        my God and King.

George Herbert (1593–1632)

54 LIGHT'S ABODE, CELESTIAL SALEM

Regent Square 8 7.8 7.8 7. Henry Smart (1813–79)

*

Light's abode, celestial Salem,
  vision whence true peace doth spring,
brighter than the heart can fancy,
  mansion of the highest King;
O how glorious are the praises
  which of thee the prophets sing!

2

There for ever and for ever
  alleluia is outpoured;
for unending, for unbroken
  is the feast-day of the Lord;
all is pure and all is holy
  that within thy walls is stored.

3

There no cloud or passing vapour
  dims the brightness of the air;
endless noon-day, glorious noon-day,
  from the Sun of suns is there;
there no night brings rest from labour,
  for unknown are toil and care.

*4

O how glorious and resplendent,
  fragile body, shalt thou be,
when endued with so much beauty,
  full of health and strong and free,
full of vigour, full of pleasure
  that shall last eternally.

*5

Now with gladness, now with courage,
  bear the burden on thee laid,
that hereafter these thy labours
  may with endless gifts be paid;
and in everlasting glory
  thou with brightness be arrayed.

6

Laud and honour to the Father,
  laud and honour to the Son,
laud and honour to the Spirit,
  ever Three and ever One,
consubstantial, co-eternal,
  while unending ages run.

Ascribed to THOMAS À KEMPIS (c. 1380–1471)
tr. J. M. NEALE* (1818–66)

55 LORD CHRIST, WHO ON THY HEART DIDST BEAR

Gonfalon Royal L.M. P. C. Buck (1871–1947)

Unison
A - - - men.

Music used by permission of Oxford University Press

1
Lord Christ, who on thy heart didst bear
The burden of our shame and sin,
And now on high dost stoop to share
The fight without, the fear within.

2
Thy patience cannot know defeat,
Thy pity will not be denied,
Thy loving-kindness still is great,
Thy tender mercies still abide.

3
So in our present need we pray
To thee, our living, healing Lord,
That we thy people, day by day,
May follow thee and keep thy word;

4
That we may care, as thou hast cared,
For sick and lame, for deaf and blind,
And freely share, as thou hast shared,
In all the sorrows of mankind;

5
That ours may be the holy task
To help and bless, to heal and save;
This is the privilege we ask,
And this the happiness we crave.

6
So in thy mercy make us wise,
And lead us in the ways of love,
Until, at last, our wondering eyes
Look on thy glorious face above.

Arnold Thomas

56 LORD ENTHRONED IN HEAVENLY SPLENDOUR

FIRST TUNE

St. Helen 8 7.8 7.8 7. G. C. Martin (1844–1916)

Unison
Harmony
Organ

Lord, enthroned in heavenly splendour,
first-begotten from the dead,
thou alone, our strong defender,
liftest up thy people's head.
Alleluia,
Jesu, true and living bread.

2

Here our humblest homage pay we,
here in loving reverence bow;
here for faith's discernment pray we,
lest we fail to know thee now.
Alleluia,
thou art here, we ask not how.

SECOND TUNE

Rhuddlan 8 7.8 7.8 7. Welsh Traditional Melody

3

Though the lowliest form doth veil thee
as of old in Bethlehem,
here as there thine angels hail thee,
Branch and Flower of Jesse's Stem.
Alleluia,
we in worship join with them.

4

Paschal Lamb, thine offering, finished
once for all when thou wast slain,
in its fulness undiminished
shall for evermore remain,
Alleluia,
cleansing souls from every stain.

5

Life-imparting heavenly Manna,
stricken Rock with streaming side,
heaven and earth with loud hosanna
worship thee, the Lamb who died,
Alleluia,
risen, ascended, glorified.

G. H. Bourne (1840–1925)

57 LORD OF ALL HOPEFULNESS

Words and music used by permission of Oxford University Press

Slane 10 11 11 12

Irish traditional melody
harm. ERIK ROUTLEY (1917–82)

LORD of all hopefulness, Lord of all joy,
whose trust, ever child-like, no cares could destroy,
be there at our waking, and give us, we pray,
your bliss in our hearts, Lord, at the break of the day.

2 Lord of all eagerness, Lord of all faith,
whose strong hands were skilled at the plane and the lathe,
be there at our labours, and give us, we pray,
your strength in our hearts, Lord, at the noon of the day.

3 Lord of all kindliness, Lord of all grace,
your hands swift to welcome, your arms to embrace,
be there at our homing, and give us, we pray,
your love in our hearts, Lord, at the eve of the day.

4 Lord of all gentleness, Lord of all calm,
whose voice is contentment, whose presence is balm,
be there at our sleeping, and give us, we pray,
your peace in our hearts, Lord, at the end of the day.

'JAN STRUTHER' (1901–53)

58 LOVE DIVINE ALL LOVES EXCELLING

First Tune

Hyfrydol 87 87 D

Melody by R. H. PRICHARD (1811–87)
harm. R. VAUGHAN WILLIAMS (1872–1958)

Second Tune

Love Divine 87 87 (Trochaic) John Stainer (1840–1901)

Music used by permission of Oxford University Press.

Love divine, all loves excelling,
joy of heaven, to earth come down,
fix in us thy humble dwelling,
all thy faithful mercies crown.
Jesus, thou art all compassion,
pure, unbounded love thou art;
visit us with thy salvation,
enter every trembling heart.

2 Come, almighty to deliver,
let us all thy life receive;
suddenly return, and never,
never more thy temples leave.
Thee we would be always blessing,
serve thee as thy hosts above,
pray, and praise thee without ceasing,
glory in thy perfect love.

3 Finish then thy new creation,
pure and spotless let us be;
let us see thy great salvation,
perfectly restored in thee;
changed from glory into glory,
till in heaven we take our place,
till we cast our crowns before thee,
lost in wonder, love and praise.

59 LOVE'S REDEEMING WORK IS DONE

Savannah 7 7.7 7. John Wesley's *Foundery Collection*, 1742

Love's redeeming work is done;
fought the fight, the battle won:
lo, our Sun's eclipse is o'er,
lo, he sets in blood no more.

2

Vain the stone, the watch, the seal;
Christ has burst the gates of hell;
death in vain forbids his rise;
Christ has opened Paradise.

3

Lives again our glorious King;
where, O death, is now thy sting?
Dying once, he all doth save;
where thy victory, O grave?

4

Soar we now where Christ has led,
following our exalted Head;
made like him, like him we rise;
ours the cross, the grave, the skies.

5

Hail the Lord of earth and heaven!
praise to thee by both be given:
thee we greet triumphant now;
hail, the Resurrection thou!

CHARLES WESLEY (1707–88)

60 MY SONG IS LOVE UNKNOWN

Love Unknown 6 6.6 6.4 4.4 4. John Ireland (1879–1962)

Classical

1

My song is love unknown,
my Saviour's love to me,
love to the loveless shown,
that they might lovely be.
O who am I,
that for my sake
my Lord should take‿
frail flesh, and die?

2

He came from his blest throne,
salvation to bestow;
but men made strange, and none‿
the longed-for Christ would know.
But O, my Friend,
my Friend indeed,
who at my need‿
his life did spend!

3

Sometimes they strew his way,
and his sweet praises sing;
resounding all the day
hosannas to their King.
Then 'Crucify!'‿
is all their breath,
and for his death‿
they thirst and cry.

*4

Why, what hath my Lord done?
What makes this rage and spite?
He made the lame to run,
he gave the blind their sight.
Sweet injuries!
yet they at these‿
themselves displease,
and 'gainst him rise.

5

They rise, and needs will have‿
my dear Lord made away;
a murderer they save,
the Prince of Life they slay.
Yet cheerful he‿
to suffering goes,
that he his foes‿
from thence might free.

*6

In life, no house, no home
my Lord on earth might have;
in death, no friendly tomb
but what a stranger gave.
What may I say?
Heaven was his home;
but mine the tomb‿
wherein he lay.

7

Here might I stay and sing:
no story so divine;
never was love, dear King,
never was grief like thine!
This is my Friend,
in whose sweet praise
I all my days‿
could gladly spend.

SAMUEL CROSSMAN (1624–83)

61 NEW EVERY MORNING

Melcombe L.M. S. Webbe the elder (1740–1816)

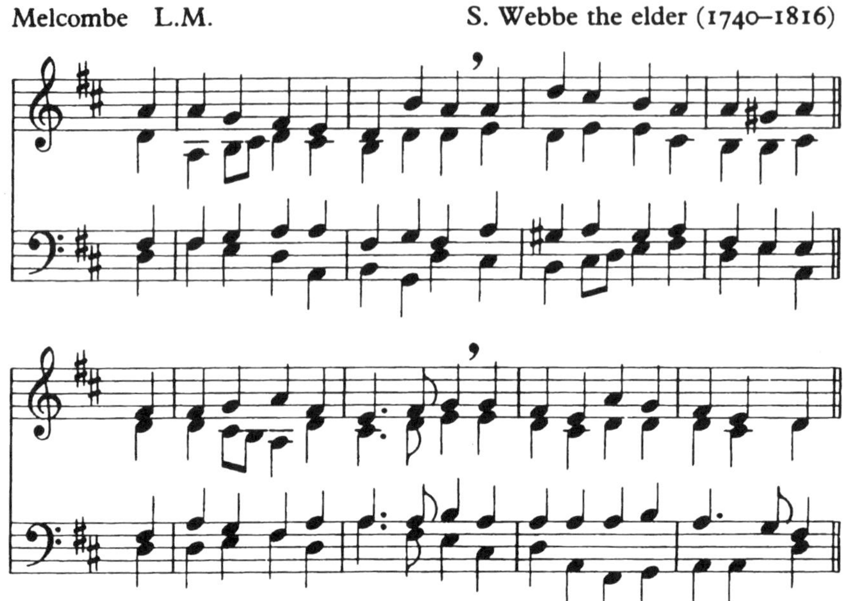

Classical

New every morning is the love
our wakening and uprising prove;
through sleep and darkness safely brought,
restored to life and power and thought.

2

New mercies, each returning day,
hover around us while we pray;
new perils past, new sins forgiven,
new thoughts of God, new hopes of heaven.

3

If on our daily course our mind‿
be set to hallow all we find,
new treasures still, of countless price,
God will provide for sacrifice.

4

The trivial round, the common task,
will furnish all we need to ask,
room to deny ourselves, a road‿
to bring us daily nearer God.

5

Only, O Lord, in thy dear love
fit us for perfect rest above;
and help us, this and every day,
to live more nearly as we pray.

JOHN KEBLE* (1792–1866)

62 NOW THANK WE ALL OUR GOD

Nun danket 67 67 66 66

Later form of a melody in
JOHANN CRÜGER'S *Praxis Pietatis Melica*, 1647
Harmony adpt. from MENDELSSOHN'S *Lobgesang*, 1840

Now thank we all our God,
  with hearts and hands and voices,
who wondrous things has done,
  in whom his world rejoices;
who from our mothers' arms
  has blessed us on our way
with countless gifts of love,
  and still is ours today.

2 O may this bounteous God
  through all our life be near us,
with ever joyful hearts
  and blessed peace to cheer us;
and keep us in his grace,
  and guide us when perplexed,
and free us from all ills
  in this world and the next.

3 All praise and thanks to God
  the Father now be given,
the Son, and him who reigns
  with them in highest heaven,
the one eternal God,
  whom heaven and earth adore;
for thus it was, is now,
  and shall be evermore.

MARTIN RINKART (1586–1649)
tr. CATHERINE WINKWORTH (1827–78)

63 O BREATH OF LIFE

Spiritus Vitae 98 98 MARY J. HAMMOND (1878–1964)

O BREATH of life, come sweeping through us,
revive your Church with life and power;
O Breath of life, come, cleanse, renew us,
and fit your Church to meet this hour.

2 O Wind of God, come, bend us, break us,
till humbly we confess our need;
then in your tenderness remake us,
revive, restore; for this we plead.

3 O Breath of love, come, breathe within us
renewing thought and will and heart;
come, love of Christ, afresh to win us,
revive your Church in every part.

BESSIE PORTER HEAD (1850–1936)

64 O FOR A CLOSER WALK

Caithness CM

Melody from *Scottish Psalter,* 1635

O FOR a closer walk with God,
a calm and heavenly frame;
a light to shine upon the road
that leads me to the Lamb.

2 Where is the blessedness I knew
when first I saw the Lord?
Where is the soul-refreshing view
of Jesus and his word?

3 What peaceful hours I once enjoyed,
how sweet their memory still!
But they have left an aching void
the world can never fill.

4 Return, O holy dove, return,
sweet messenger of rest:
I hate the sins that made thee mourn
and drove thee from my breast.

5 The dearest idol I have known,
whate'er that idol be,
help me to tear it from thy throne
and worship only thee.

6 So shall my walk be close with God,
calm and serene my frame;
so purer light shall mark the road
that leads me to the Lamb.

WILLIAM COWPER (1731–1800)

65 O FOR A THOUSAND TONGUES

LYNGHAM

Words: C. Wesley
Spanish: Esteban Sywulka B.
German: E. Gensichen
Music: T. Jarman

G
C
G/D
D7
G
D7/A
G
D/F♯
A7/E
D
G
Em
D/A
A
D
G
D7/A
G
D/F♯
A7/E

D
G
C
G
D
D7
G
C
G/B
D7/A
G
Dsus
D
D7
G

O FOR a thousand tongues to sing
  my great Redeemer's praise,
the glories of my God and King,
  the triumphs of his grace.

2 Jesus, the name that charms our
      fears,
  that bids our sorrows cease;
'tis music in the sinner's ears,
  'tis life and health and peace.

3 He breaks the power of cancelled sin,
  he sets the prisoner free;
his blood can make the foulest clean,
  his blood availed for me.

4 He speaks, and listening to his voice
  new life the dead receive;
the mournful, broken hearts rejoice,
  the humble poor believe.

5 Hear him, ye deaf; his praise, ye
      dumb,
  your loosened tongues employ;
ye blind, behold your Saviour come;
  and leap, ye lame, for joy!

6 My gracious Master and my God,
  assist me to proclaim,
to spread through all the earth abroad
  the honours of thy name.

CHARLES WESLEY (1707–88)

66 O JESUS I HAVE PROMISED

Music used by permission of Oxford University Press

Wolvercote 7 6.7 6. D. W. H. Ferguson (1874–1950)

Unison

O Jesus, I have promised
  to serve thee to the end;
be thou for ever near me,
  my Master and my Friend:
I shall not fear the battle
  if thou art by my side,
nor wander from the pathway
  if thou wilt be my guide.

*2

O let me feel thee near me:
  the world is ever near;
I see the sights that dazzle,
  the tempting sounds I hear;
my foes are ever near me,
  around me and within;
but, Jesus, draw thou nearer,
  and shield my soul from sin.

3

O let me hear thee speaking
  in accents clear and still,
above the storms of passion,
  the murmurs of self-will;
O speak to reassure me,
  to hasten or control;
O speak, and make me listen,
  thou guardian of my soul.

4

O Jesus, thou hast promised
  to all who follow thee,
that where thou art in glory
  there shall thy servant be;
and, Jesus, I have promised
  to serve thee to the end:
O give me grace to follow,
  my Master and my Friend.

5

O let me see thy foot-marks,
  and in them plant mine own;
my hope to follow duly
  is in thy strength alone:
O guide me, call me, draw me,
  uphold me to the end;
and then in heaven receive me,
  my Saviour and my Friend.

J. E. BODE (1816–74)

67 O PRAISE YE THE LORD

FIRST TUNE

Laudate Dominum (Parry) — C. Hubert H. Parry (1848–1918)

10 10.11 11.

1

O praise ye the Lord! praise him in the height;
rejoice in his word, ye angels of light;
ye heavens adore him by whom ye were made,
and worship before him, in brightness arrayed.

2

O praise ye the Lord! praise him upon earth,
in tuneful accord, sing praise for new birth;
praise him who hath brought you his grace from above,
praise him who hath taught you to sing of his love.

3

O praise ye the Lord, all things that give sound;
each jubilant chord re-echo around;
loud organs, his glory forth tell in deep tone,
and, sweet harp, the story of what he hath done.

4

O praise ye the Lord! thanksgiving and song
to him be outpoured all ages along:
for love in creation, for heaven restored,
for grace of salvation, O praise ye the Lord!

H.W. Baker

67 contd.

Optional setting for verse 4
All voices
f
4 O praise ye the Lord! thanks - giv - ing and
Organ
f
song to him be out - poured all
a - ges a - long: for love in cre -
mf

Praise and Thanksgiving
cresc.
-a - tion, for hea - ven re - stored, for
ff
grace of sal - va - tion, O praise ye the Lord!
ff
Congregation
A - men, A - men.
Choir and Organ
(Small notes Organ only)

68 O THOU, WHO AT THY EUCHARIST

Song 1 10 10.10 10.10 10.

Melody and bass by
Orlando Gibbons (1583–1625)

Music used by permission of Oxford University Press

O thou, who at thy Eucharist didst pray
  that all thy Church might be for ever one,
grant us at every Eucharist to say
  with longing heart and soul, 'Thy will be done:'
O may we all one bread, one body be,
through this blest sacrament of unity.

2

For all thy Church, O Lord, we intercede;
  make thou our sad divisions soon to cease;
draw us the nearer each to each, we plead,
  by drawing all to thee, O Prince of peace:
thus may we all one bread, one body be,
through this blest sacrament of unity.

*3

We pray thee too for wanderers from thy fold;
  O bring them back, good Shepherd of the sheep,
back to the faith which saints believed of old,
  back to the Church which still that faith doth keep:
soon may we all one bread, one body be,
through this blest sacrament of unity.

4

So, Lord, at length when sacraments shall cease,
  may we be one with all thy Church above,
one with thy saints in one unbroken peace,
  one with thy saints in one unbounded love:
more blessèd still, in peace and love to be
one with the Trinity in Unity.

W. H. Turton (1856–1938)

69 O THOU WHO CAMEST FROM ABOVE

Hereford LM S. S. WESLEY (1810–76)

O THOU who camest from above,
   the pure celestial fire to impart,
kindle a flame of sacred love
   on the mean altar of my heart.

2 There let it for thy glory burn
   with inextinguishable blaze;
and trembling to its source return,
   in humble prayer and fervent praise.

3 Jesus, confirm my heart's desire
   to work and speak and think for thee;
still let me guard the holy fire,
   and still stir up thy gift in me:

4 ready for all thy perfect will,
   my acts of faith and love repeat,
till death thine endless mercies seal,
   and make my sacrifice complete.

CHARLES WESLEY (1707–88)

70 O WORSHIP THE KING

Hanover 10 10 11 11
(55 55 65 65)

From *A Supplement to the New Version*, 1708,
probably by WILLIAM CROFT (1678–1727)

O WORSHIP the King,
  all-glorious above;
O gratefully sing
  his power and his love;
our shield and defender,
  the ancient of days,
pavilioned in splendour,
  and girded with praise.

2 O tell of his might,
  O sing of his grace,
whose robe is the light,
  whose canopy space;
his chariots of wrath
  the deep thunder-clouds form;
and dark is his path
  on the wings of the storm.

3 The earth with its store
  of wonders untold,
Almighty, thy power
  hath founded of old;
hath stablished it fast
  by a changeless decree,
and round it hath cast,
  like a mantle, the sea.

4 Thy bountiful care
  what tongue can recite?
It breathes in the air,
  it shines in the light;
it streams from the hills,
  it descends to the plain,
and sweetly distils
  in the dew and the rain.

5 Frail children of dust,
  and feeble as frail,
in thee do we trust,
  nor find thee to fail;
thy mercies how tender,
  how firm to the end,
our maker, defender,
  redeemer, and friend!

6 O measureless might,
  ineffable love,
while angels delight
  to hymn thee above,
the humbler creation,
  shall struggle to raise
with true adoration
  their songs to thy praise.

ROBERT GRANT (1779–1838)*
based on Psalm 104

71 O WORSHIP THE LORD IN THE BEAUTY OF HOLINESS

Was Lebet 13 10.13 10.

Melody from *Rheinhardt MS* (Üttingen, 1754)

v.1
v.1

O worship the Lord in the beauty of holiness;
  bow down before him, his glory proclaim;
with gold of obedience, and incense of lowliness,
  kneel and adore him: the Lord is his name.

2

Low at his feet lay thy burden of carefulness:
  high on his heart he will bear it for thee,
comfort thy sorrows, and answer thy prayerfulness,
  guiding thy steps as may best for thee be.

3

Fear not to enter his courts in the slenderness
  of the poor wealth thou wouldst reckon as
    thine:
truth in its beauty, and love in its tenderness,
  these are the offerings to lay on his shrine.

4

These, though we bring them in trembling and
    fearfulness,
  he will accept for the name that is dear;
mornings of joy give for evenings of tearfulness,
  trust for our trembling and hope for our fear.

J. S. B. MONSELL (1811–75)

The first verse may be repeated at the end

72 PRAISE MY SOUL THE KING OF HEAVEN

Praise, My Soul 8 7.8 7.8 7. John Goss (1800–80)

Unison
1 Praise, my soul, the King of hea - ven,
to his feet thy tri - bute bring;
ran - somed,
healed, re - stored, for - gi - ven,
who like me his

praise should sing?
Al - le - lu - ia, Al - le -
- lu - ia, praise the e - ver - last - ing King.
Harmony
2 Praise him for his grace and fa - vour

72 contd.

to our fa - thers in dis - tress; praise him
still the same as ev - er, slow to chide, and
swift to bless: Al - le - lu - ia, Al - le -
- lu ia, glo - rious in his faith - ful - ness.

Sopranos only
3 Fa - ther - like, he tends and spares us,
well our fee - ble frame he knows; in his
hands he gent - ly bears us, res - cues us from

72 contd.

all our foes. Al - le - lu - ia, Al - le -
- lu - ia, wide - ly as his mer - cy flows.

Descant
Leonard Blake (1907–89)
4 An - gels, help us to a - dore him;
All other voices
4 An - gels, help us to a - dore him;
ye be - hold him face to face; sun and
ye be - hold him face to face; sun and

72 contd.

moon bow down be - fore him, dwell - ers
moon bow down be - fore him, dwell - ers
all in time and space: Al - le - lu - ia,
all in time and space: Al - le - lu - ia,

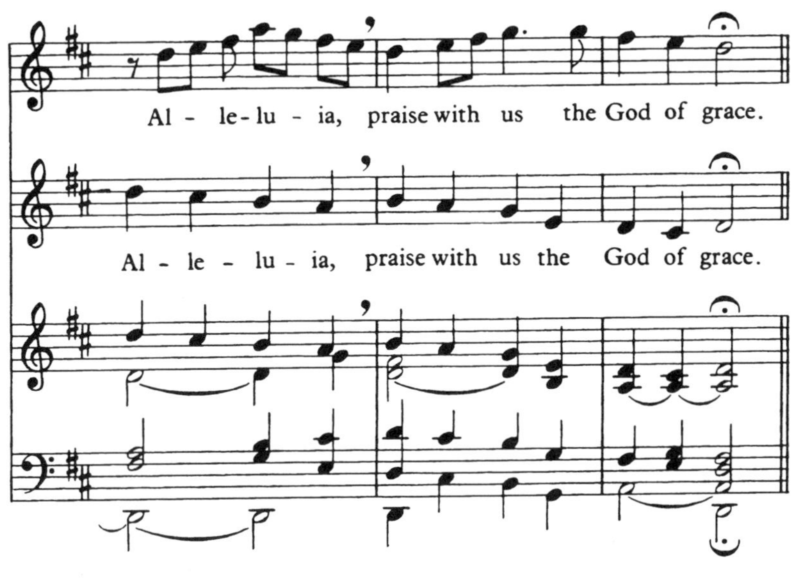
Al - le- lu - ia, praise with us the God of grace.
Al - le - lu - ia, praise with us the God of grace.

1

Praise, my soul, the King of heaven,
to his feet thy tribute bring;
ransomed, healed, restored, forgiven,
who like me his praise should sing?
Alleluia, Alleluia,
praise the everlasting King.

2

Praise him for his grace and favour
to our fathers in distress;
praise him still the same as ever,
slow to chide, and swift to bless:
Alleluia, Alleluia,
glorious in his faithfulness.

3

Father-like, he tends and spares us,
well our feeble frame he knows;
in his hands he gently bears us,
rescues us from all our foes:
Alleluia, Alleluia,
widely as his mercy flows.

4

Angels, help us to adore him;
ye behold him face to face;
sun and moon, bow down before him,
dwellers all in time and space:
Alleluia, Alleluia,
praise with us the God of grace.

H. F. LYTE (1793–1847)
Psalm 103

73 PRAISE TO THE HOLIEST

FIRST TUNE

Gerontius C.M. J. B. Dykes (1823–76)

Praise to the Holiest in the height,
  and in the depth be praise:
in all his words most wonderful,
  most sure in all his ways.

2

O loving wisdom of our God!
  when all was sin and shame,
a second Adam to the fight
  and to the rescue came.

3

O wisest love! that flesh and blood,
  which did in Adam fail,
should strive afresh against the foe,
  should strive and should prevail;

4

and that a higher gift than grace
  should flesh and blood refine,
God's presence and his very self,
  and essence all-divine.

SECOND TUNE

Somervell C.M. Arthur Somervell (1863–1937)

5

O generous love! that he, who smote‿
in Man for man the foe,
the double agony in Man
for man should undergo;

6

and in the garden secretly,
and on the cross on high,
should teach his brethren, and inspire
to suffer and to die.

7

Praise to the Holiest in the height,
and in the depth be praise:
in all his words most wonderful,
most sure in all his ways.

J. H. Newman (1801–90)

74 PRAISE TO THE LORD, THE ALMIGHTY

Lobe den Herren 14 14.4 7.8.
(Praxis pietatis)

Melody from
Praxis Pietatis Melica (1668)

Praise to the Lord, the Almighty, the King of creation;
O my soul, praise him, for he is thy health and salvation:
all ye who hear,
now to his temple draw near,
joining in glad adoration.

2

Praise to the Lord, who o'er all things so wondrously reigneth,
shieldeth thee gently from harm, or when fainting sustaineth:
hast thou not seen‿
how thy heart's wishes have been‿
granted in what he ordaineth?

3

Praise to the Lord, who doth prosper thy work and defend thee;
surely his goodness and mercy shall daily attend thee:
ponder anew
what the Almighty can do,
if to the end he befriend thee.

4

Praise to the Lord! O let all that is in me adore him!
All that hath life and breath, come now with praises before him!
let the Amen
sound from his people again:
gladly for ay we adore him.

J. NEANDER (1650–80)
tr. CATHERINE WINKWORTH (1827–78)

75 REJOICE THE LORD IS KING

Gopsal 66 66 88 G. F. HANDEL (1685–1759)

REJOICE, the Lord is King;
 your Lord and King adore;
mortals, give thanks and sing,
 and triumph evermore:

Lift up your heart, lift up your voice:
rejoice, again I say, rejoice!

2 Jesus the Saviour reigns,
 the God of truth and love;
when he had purged our stains
 he took his seat above:

3 His kingdom cannot fail;
 he rules o'er earth and heaven;
the keys of death and hell
 are to our Jesus given:

4 He sits at God's right hand
 till all his foes submit,
and bow to his command,
 and fall beneath his feet:

5 Rejoice in glorious hope;
 Jesus the judge shall come,
and take his servants up
 to their eternal home:

We soon shall hear the archangel's voice,
the trump of God shall sound, rejoice!

CHARLES WESLEY (1707–88)

76 SHALL WE GATHER AT THE RIVER

1. Shall we gath - er at the riv - er, where bright an - gel feet have trod, with its crys - tal tide for - ev - er flow - ing by the throne of God?
2. On the mar - gin of the riv - er, wash - ing up its sil - ver spray, we will walk and wor - ship ev - er, all the hap - py gold - en day.
3. Ere we reach the shin - ing riv - er, lay we ev - ery bur - den down; grace our spir - its will de - liv - er, and pro - vide a robe and crown.
4. Soon we'll reach the shin - ing riv - er, soon our pil - grim - age will cease; soon our hap - py hearts will quiv - er with the mel - o - dy of peace.
Refrain
Yes, we'll gath - er at the riv - er, the beau - ti - ful, the beau - ti - ful riv - er; gath - er with the saints at the riv - er that flows by the throne of God.

WORDS: Robert Lowry, 1864 (Rev. 22:1-5)
MUSIC: Robert Lowry, 1864

HANSON PLACE
87.87 with Refrain

77 SOUL OF MY SAVIOUR *Classical*

ANIMA CHRISTI 10 10 10 10 William Maher 1823–77

SOUL of my Saviour, sanctify my breast,
Body of Christ, be thou my saving guest,
Blood of my Saviour, bathe me in thy tide,
Wash me with water flowing from thy side.

2 Strength and protection may thy passion be,
O blessèd Jesu, hear and answer me;
Deep in thy wounds, Lord, hide and shelter me,
So shall I never, never part from thee.

3 Guard and defend me from the foe malign,
In death's dread moments make me only thine;
Call me and bid me come to thee on high
Where I may praise thee with thy saints for ay.

Latin, 14th century
Tr ANONYMOUS

78 SWEET SACRAMENT DIVINE

DIVINE MYSTERIES 66 66 886 F. Stanfield 1835–1914

A hymn to Christ in his sacramental presence.

SWEET Sacrament divine,
  Hid in thine earthly home,
Lo, round thy lowly shrine,
  With suppliant hearts we come;
Jesu, to thee our voice we raise
In songs of love and heartfelt praise:
  Sweet Sacrament divine.

2 Sweet Sacrament of peace,
  Dear home for every heart,
Where restless yearnings cease
  And sorrows all depart;
There in thine ear all trustfully
We tell our tale of misery:
  Sweet Sacrament of peace.

3 Sweet Sacrament of rest,
  Ark from the ocean's roar,
Within thy shelter blest
  Soon may we reach the shore;
Save us, for still the tempest raves,
Save, lest we sink beneath the waves:
  Sweet Sacrament of rest.

4 Sweet Sacrament divine,
  Earth's light and jubilee,
In thy far depths doth shine
  The Godhead's majesty;
Sweet light, so shine on us, we pray
That earthly joys may fade away:
  Sweet Sacrament divine.

FRANCIS STANFIELD 1835–1914

79 TEACH ME, MY GOD AND KING

Sandys SM

English traditional carol from
SANDYS' *Christmas Carols Ancient and Modern*, 1833

* ♪♪ v. 4

TEACH me, my God and King,
  in all things thee to see,
and what I do in anything
  to do it as for thee.

2 A man that looks on glass
  on it may stay his eye;
or if he pleaseth, through it pass,
  and then the heaven espy.

3 All may of thee partake:
  nothing can be so mean,
which, with this tincture, 'For thy sake',
  will not grow bright and clean.

4 A servant with this clause
  makes drudgery divine:
who sweeps a room, as for thy laws,
  makes that and the action fine.

5 This is the famous stone
  that turneth all to gold:
for that which God doth touch and own
  cannot for less be told.

GEORGE HERBERT (1593–1633)

80 THE CHURCH'S ONE FOUNDATION

Aurelia 76 76 D S. S. WESLEY (1810–76)

THE Church's one foundation
  is Jesus Christ her Lord;
she is his new creation
  by water and the word:
from heaven he came and sought her
  to be his holy bride;
with his own blood he bought her,
  and for her life he died.

2 Elect from every nation,
  yet one o'er all the earth,
her charter of salvation
  one Lord, one faith, one birth:
one holy name she blesses,
  partakes one holy food,
and to one hope she presses
  with every grace endued.

3 'Mid toil and tribulation,
  and tumult of her war,
she waits the consummation
  of peace for evermore;
till with the vision glorious
  her longing eyes are blest,
and the great Church victorious
  shall be the Church at rest.

4 Yet she on earth hath union
  with God the Three in One,
and mystic sweet communion
  with those whose rest is won:
O happy ones and holy!
  Lord, give us grace that we,
like them, the meek and lowly,
  on high may dwell with thee.

SAMUEL J. STONE (1839–1900)

81 THE DAY THOU GAVEST LORD IS ENDED

St Clement 98 98 C. C. SCHOLEFIELD (1839–1904)

THE day thou gavest, Lord, is ended,
  the darkness falls at thy behest;
to thee our morning hymns ascended,
  thy praise shall sanctify our rest.

2 We thank thee that thy Church unsleeping,
  while earth rolls onward into light,
through all the world her watch is keeping,
  and rests not now by day or night.

3 As o'er each continent and island
  the dawn leads on another day,
the voice of prayer is never silent,
  nor dies the strain of praise away.

4 The sun that bids us rest is waking
  our friends beneath the western sky,
and hour by hour fresh lips are making
  thy wondrous doings heard on high.

5 So be it, Lord; thy throne shall never,
  like earth's proud empires, pass away;
thy kingdom stands and grows for ever,
  till all thy creatures own thy sway.

JOHN ELLERTON (1826–93)

82 THE GOD OF ABRAHAM PRAISE

Leoni 6 6.8 4. D. Traditional Hebrew Melody

Classical

1

The God of Abraham praise
who reigns enthroned above,
Ancient of everlasting Days,
and God of love:
Jehovah, great I AM,
by earth and heaven confest;
we bow and bless the sacred name
for ever blest.

2

The God of Abraham praise,
at whose supreme command
from earth we rise, and seek the joys
at his right hand:
we all on earth forsake,
its wisdom, fame, and power;
and him our only portion make,
our shield and tower.

3

Though nature's strength decay,
and earth and hell withstand,
to Canaan's bounds we urge our way
at his command:
the watery deep we pass,
with Jesus in our view;
and through the howling wilderness
our way pursue.

4

The God who reigns on high
the great archangels sing,
and 'Holy, Holy, Holy,' cry,
'almighty King,
who was, and is the same,
and evermore shall be:
Jehovah, Father, great I AM,
we worship thee.'

5

Before the Saviour's face
the ransomed nations bow,
o'erwhelmed at his almighty grace
for ever new;
he shows his prints of love -
they kindle to a flame,
and sound through all the worlds above
the slaughtered Lamb.

6

The whole triumphant host
give thanks to God on high;
hail, Father, Son, and Holy Ghost,
they ever cry:
hail, Abraham's God, and mine,
(I join the heavenly lays)
all might and majesty are thine,
and endless praise.

Thomas Olivers

83 THE LORD'S MY SHEPHERD

Music used by permission of Oxford University Press

PSALM 23

Crimond CM

Melody ascribed to JESSIE IRVINE (1836–87)
but more probably by DAVID GRANT (1833–93)
harm. T. C. L. PRITCHARD (1885–1960)

THE Lord's my Shepherd, I'll not want:
he makes me down to lie
in pastures green; he leadeth me
the quiet waters by.

2 My soul he doth restore again,
and me to walk doth make
within the paths of righteousness,
ev'n for his own name's sake.

3 Yea, though I walk through death's dark vale,
yet will I fear no ill;
for thou art with me, and thy rod
and staff me comfort still.

4 My table thou hast furnishèd
in presence of my foes;
my head thou dost with oil anoint,
and my cup overflows.

5 Goodness and mercy all my life
shall surely follow me;
and in God's house for evermore
my dwelling-place shall be.

Psalm 23
Metrical version by WILLIAM WHITTINGHAM (1524–79) altd.

84 THINE BE THE GLORY

Maccabaeus 10 11 11 11 with refrain G. F. HANDEL (1685–1759)

REFRAIN

THINE be the glory, risen, conquering Son,
endless is the victory thou o'er death hast won;
angels in bright raiment rolled the stone away,
kept the folded grave-clothes where thy body lay.

Thine be the glory, risen, conquering Son,
endless is the victory thou o'er death hast won.

2 Lo, Jesus meets us, risen from the tomb;
lovingly he greets us, scatters fear and gloom;
let the Church with gladness hymns of triumph sing,
for her Lord now liveth, death hath lost its sting:

3 No more we doubt thee, glorious Prince of Life;
life is naught without thee: aid us in our strife;
make us more than conquerors through thy deathless love;
bring us safe through Jordan to thy home above:

EDMOND BUDRY (1854–1932)
R. B. HOYLE (1875–1939)

85 THROUGH ALL THE CHANGING SCENES OF LIFE

Wiltshire C.M. G. T. Smart (1776–1867)

Through all the changing scenes of life,
 in trouble and in joy,
the praises of my God shall still
 my heart and tongue employ.

2

O magnify the Lord with me,
 with me exalt his name;
when in distress to him I called,
 he to my rescue came.

3

The hosts of God encamp around‿
 the dwellings of the just;
deliverance he affords to all
 who on his succour trust.

4

O make but trial of his love:
 experience will decide‿
how blest are they, and only they,
 who in his truth confide.

5

Fear him, ye saints, and you will then‿
 have nothing else to fear;
make you his service your delight,
 your wants shall be his care.

6

To Father, Son, and Holy Ghost,
 the God whom we adore,
be glory, as it was, is now,
 and shall be evermore.

Psalm 34 in *New Version* (Tate and Brady, 1696)

86 THY HAND, O GOD, HAS GUIDED

VERSES 1 & 3
Unison

Music published by permission of the Executors of the late Dr. Basil Harwood

(Harmony version for verse 2 overleaf)

THY hand, O God, has guided
  thy flock, from age to age;
the wondrous tale is written,
  full clear, on every page;
thy people owned thy goodness,
  and we their deeds record;
and both of this bear witness:
  one Church, one Faith, one Lord.

2 Thy heralds brought glad tidings
  to greatest, as to least;
they summoned all to hasten
  and share the great King's feast;
their gospel of redemption,
  sin pardoned, earth restored,
was all in this enfolded:
  one Church, one Faith, one Lord.

3 Thy mercy will not fail us,
  nor leave thy work undone;
with thy right hand to help us,
  the victory shall be won;
and then, by all creation,
  thy name shall be adored,
and this shall be our anthem:
  one Church, one Faith, one Lord.

E. H. PLUMPTRE (1821–91)*

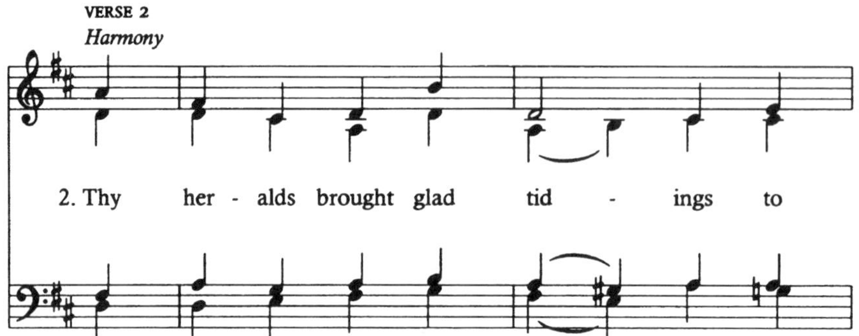
VERSE 2
Harmony
2. Thy her - alds brought glad tid - ings to

great-est, as to least; they sum-moned all to

has - ten and share the great King's feast; their

gos - pel of re - demp - tion, sin par - doned, earth re -
- stored, was all in this en - fold - ed: one
(Turn back for verse 3)
Lord.
Church, one Faith, one Lord, one Faith, one Lord.
Organ

87 THY KINGDOM COME, O GOD

St Cecilia 66 66 L. G. HAYNE (1836–83)

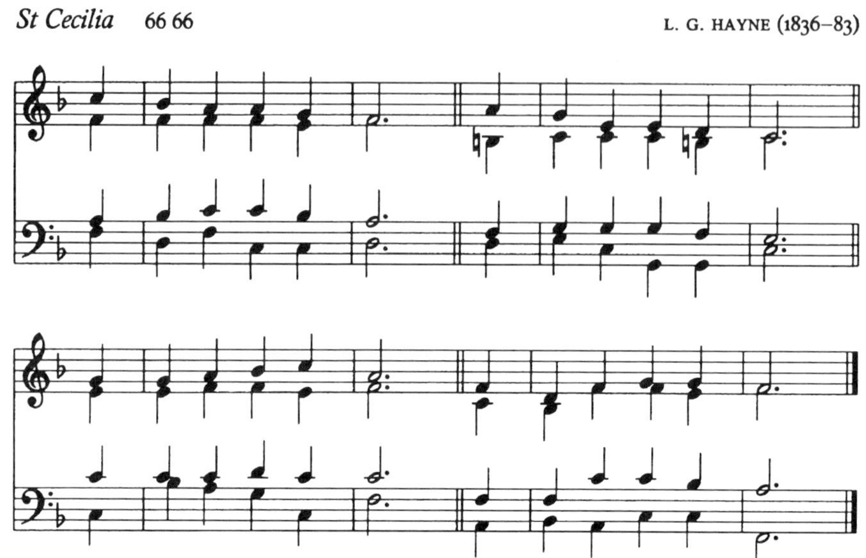

THY kingdom come, O God;
  thy rule, O Christ, begin;
break with thine iron rod
  the tyrannies of sin.

2 Where is thy reign of peace
  and purity and love?
When shall all hatred cease,
  as in the realms above?

3 When comes the promised time,
  the end of strife and war,
when lust, oppression, crime
  shall spoil the earth no more?

4 We pray thee, Lord, arise,
  and come in thy great might;
revive our longing eyes,
  which languish for thy sight.

5 O'er lands both near and far
  thick darkness broodeth yet;
arise, O Morning Star,
  arise, and never set!

LEWIS HENSLEY (1824–1905)

88 TO GOD BE THE GLORY

To God be the glory 11 11 11 11 with refrain W. H. DOANE (1832–1915)

Capo 1(G)
REFRAIN
Praise the Lord! Praise the Lord! Let the earth hear his voice!

A♭
(G)
Praise the Lord! Praise the Lord! Let the peo - ple re - joice!
E♭7
(D7)
A♭
(G)
E♭
(D)
A♭
(G)
O come__ to the Fa - ther, through Je - sus the Son;
A♭7
(G7)
D♭
(C)
A♭
(G)
E♭
(D)
A♭
(G)
E♭
(D)
A♭
(G)
and give him the glo - ry great things he has done!

TO GOD be the glory, great things he has done!
So loved he the world that he gave us his Son,
who yielded his life in atonement for sin,
and opened the life-gate that all may go in.

Praise the Lord! Praise the Lord! Let the earth hear his voice!
Praise the Lord! Praise the Lord! Let the people rejoice!
O come to the Father, through Jesus the Son;
and give him the glory—great things he has done!

2 O perfect redemption, the purchase of blood,
to every believer the promise of God!
And every offender who truly believes,
that moment from Jesus a pardon receives:

3 Great things he has taught us, great things he has done,
and great our rejoicing through Jesus the Son;
but purer and higher and greater will be
the wonder, the beauty, when Jesus we see:

FANNY CROSBY (1820–1915)

89 WE SING THE PRAISE

Bow Brickhill LM   SYDNEY H. NICHOLSON (1875–1947)

We sing the praise of him who died,
  of him who died upon the cross;
the sinner's hope though all deride,
  for this we count the world but loss.

2 Inscribed upon the cross we see
  in shining letters, 'God is Love';
he bears our sins upon the tree;
  he brings us mercy from above.

3 The cross! it takes our guilt away;
  it holds the fainting spirit up;
it cheers with hope the gloomy day,
  and sweetens every bitter cup.

4 It makes the coward spirit brave,
  and nerves the feeble arm for fight;
it takes the terror from the grave,
  and gilds the bed of death with light;

5 the balm of life, the cure of woe,
  the measure and the pledge of love,
the sinners' refuge here below,
  the angels' theme in heaven above.

THOMAS KELLY (1769–1855)

90 WHEN I SURVEY

Rockingham LM

Melody adpt. EDWARD MILLER (1735–1807)

Crucifixion to the World by the Cross of Christ (Gal. 6: 14)

WHEN I survey the wondrous Cross,
on which the Prince of glory died,
my richest gain I count but loss,
and pour contempt on all my pride.

2 Forbid it, Lord, that I should boast,
save in the death of Christ my God;
all the vain things that charm me most,
I sacrifice them to his blood.

3 See from his head, his hands, his feet,
sorrow and love flow mingled down;
did e'er such love and sorrow meet,
or thorns compose so rich a crown?

4 His dying crimson, like a robe,
spreads o'er his body on the tree;
then am I dead to all the globe,
and all the globe is dead to me.

5 Were the whole realm of nature mine,
that were a present far too small;
love so amazing, so divine,
demands my soul, my life, my all.

ISAAC WATTS (1674–1748)

91 WHO WOULD TRUE VALOUR SEE

Monks Gate 65 65 6665

Adpt. from an English traditional melody
by R. VAUGHAN WILLIAMS (1872–1958)

WHO would true valour see,
let him come hither;
one here will constant be,
come wind, come weather;
there's no discouragement
shall make him once relent
his first avowed intent
to be a pilgrim.

2 Who so beset him round
with dismal stories,
do but themselves confound;
his strength the more is.
No lion can him fright,
he'll with a giant fight,
but he will have a right
to be a pilgrim.

3 Hobgoblin nor foul fiend
can daunt his spirit;
he knows he at the end
shall life inherit.
Then fancies fly away,
he'll fear not what men say,
he'll labour night and day
to be a pilgrim.

JOHN BUNYAN (1628–88)

Bunyan's song from *The Pilgrim's Progress* is printed in its original form; but singers may prefer to alter the pronouns 'he' / 'him' / 'his' to suit the circumstances. *Music used by permission of Oxford University Press*

92 WONDERFUL WORDS OF LIFE

1. Sing them o - ver a - gain to me, won-der-ful words of life;
2. Christ, the bless-ed one, gives to all won-der-ful words of life;
3. Sweet-ly ech - o the gos - pel call, won-der-ful words of life;
let me more of their beau - ty see, won-der-ful words of life;
sin - ner, list to the lov - ing call, won-der-ful words of life;
of - fer par-don and peace to all, won-der-ful words of life;
words of life and beau - ty teach me faith and du - ty.
all so free - ly giv - en, woo - ing us to heav - en.
Je - sus, on - ly Sav - ior, sanc - ti - fy for - ev - er.
Refrain
Beau-ti - ful words, won-der-ful words, won-der-ful words of life.
Beau-ti - ful words, won-der-ful words, won-der-ful words of life.

WORDS: Philip P. Bliss, 1874
MUSIC: Philip P. Bliss, 1874

WORDS OF LIFE
86.86.66

93 YE HOLY ANGELS BRIGHT

Darwall 66 66 44 44 JOHN DARWALL (1731–89)

Ye holy angels bright
  who wait at God's right hand,
or through the realms of light
  fly at your Lord's command,
    assist our song,
      or else the theme
      too high doth seem
    for mortal tongue.

2 Ye blessed souls at rest,
who see your Saviour's face,
whose glory, ev'n the least,
is far above our grace:
God's praises sound,
as in his sight
with sweet delight
ye do abound.

3 Ye saints who toil below,
adore your heavenly King,
and onward as ye go
some joyful anthem sing;
take what he gives
and praise him still,
through good and ill,
who ever lives.

4 My soul, bear thou thy part,
triumph in God above;
and with a well-tuned heart
sing thou the songs of love.
Thou art his own,
whose precious blood
shed for thy good
his love made known.

5 Let all creation sing
and join the marvellous throng
who crowns of glory bring
and raise the Lamb's new song.
Let all our days
till life shall end,
whate'er he send
be filled with praise.

RICHARD BAXTER (1615–91)
V. 3: J. H. GURNEY (1802–62)

94 YE THAT KNOW THE LORD IS GRACIOUS

Hyfrydol 8 7.8 7. D. Melody by R. H. Prichard (1811–87)

Ye that know the Lord is gracious,
  ye for whom a Corner-stone‿
stands, of God elect and precious,
  laid that ye may build thereon,
see that on that sure foundation
  ye a living temple raise,
towers that may tell forth salvation,
  walls that may re-echo praise.

2

Living stones, by God appointed
  each to his allotted place,
kings and priests, by God anointed,
  shall ye not declare his grace?
Ye, a royal generation,
  tell the tidings of your birth,
tidings of a new creation
  to an old and weary earth.

3

Tell the praise of him who called you
  out of darkness into light,
broke the fetters that enthralled you,
  gave you freedom, peace and sight:
tell the tale of sins forgiven,
  strength renewed and hope restored,
till the earth, in tune with heaven,
  praise and magnify the Lord.

C. A. ALINGTON (1872–1955)

95 YE WATCHERS AND YE HOLY ONES

Lasst uns erfreuen 8 8.4 4.8 8. and Alleluias
Melody from *Geistliche Kirchengesang* (Cologne, 1623)
arr. R. Vaughan Williams (1872–1958)

Unison
Harmony
Al - le - lu - ia.
Unison
Harmony
Al - le - lu - ia, Al - le - lu - ia, Al - le -

Unison
lu - ia, Al - le - lu - ia, Al - le - lu - ia.

Music used by permission of Oxford University Press

With angels and archangels

Ye watchers and ye holy ones,
bright Seraphs, Cherubim and Thrones,
raise the glad strain, Alleluia.
Cry out, Dominions, Princedoms, Powers,
Virtues, Archangels, Angels' choirs,
Alleluia.

2

O higher than the Cherubim,
more glorious than the Seraphim,
lead their praises, Alleluia.
Thou Bearer of the eternal Word,
most gracious, magnify the Lord.
Alleluia.

3

Respond, ye souls in endless rest,
ye Patriarchs and Prophets blest,
Alleluia, alleluia.
Ye holy Twelve, ye Martyrs strong,
all Saints triumphant, raise the song
Alleluia.

4

O friends, in gladness let us sing,
supernal anthems echoing,
Alleluia, alleluia.
To God the Father, God the Son,
and God the Spirit, Three in One,
Alleluia.

ATHELSTAN RILEY (1858–1945)
Words used by permission of Oxford University Press

96 YE WHO OWN THE FAITH

DAILY, DAILY 87 87 87 6

Melody 'from a French Paroissien'
Composer unidentified

Hail Ma- ry, hail Ma- ry, hail — Ma - ry full of grace.

Suitable for use in Procession

YE who own the faith of Jesus
  Sing the wonders that were done,
When the love of God the Father
  O'er our sin the victory won,
When he made the Virgin Mary
  Mother of his only Son.
    Hail Mary, full of grace.

2 Blessèd were the chosen people
  Out of whom the Lord did come,
Blessèd was the land of promise
  Fashioned for his earthly home;
But more blessèd far the Mother
  She who bare him in her womb.

3 Wherefore let all faithful people
  Tell the honour of her name,
Let the Church in her foreshadowed
  Part in her thanksgiving claim;
What Christ's Mother sang in gladness
  Let Christ's people sing the same.

4 Let us weave our supplications,
  She with us and we with her,
For the advancement of the faithful,
  For each faithful worshipper,
For the doubting, for the sinful,
  For each heedless wanderer.

5* May the Mother's intercessions
  On our homes a blessing win,
That the children all be prospered,
  Strong and fair and pure within,
Following our Lord's own footsteps,
  Firm in faith and free from sin.

6*

For the sick and for the agèd,
  For our dear ones far away,
For the hearts that mourn in secret,
  All who need our prayers today,
For the faithful gone before us,
  May the holy Virgin pray.

7

Praise, O Mary, praise the Father,
  Praise thy Saviour and thy Son,
Praise the everlasting Spirit,
  Who hath made thee ark and throne;
O'er all creatures high exalted,
  Lowly praise the Three in One.

V. Stuckey. S. Coles 1845–1929

Contemporary Hymnody

97 AFFIRM ANEW THE THREEFOLD NAME

Kingsfold D.C.M. **English Traditional Melody**

Contemporary

1

Affirm anew the threefold Name
of Father, Spirit, Son,
our God whose saving acts proclaim
a world's salvation won.
In him alone we live and move
and breath and being find,
the wayward children of his love
who cares for humankind.

2

Declare in all the earth his grace,
to every heart his call,
the living Lord of time and place
whose love embraces all.
So shall his endless praise be sung,
his teaching truly heard,
and every culture, every tongue,
receive his timeless word.

3

Confirm our faith in this our day
amid earth's shifting sand,
with Christ as Life and Truth and Way,
the one eternal Son and Lord
by God the Father given,
the true and life-imparting Word,
the Way that leads to heaven.

4

Renew once more the ancient fire,
let love our hearts inflame;
renew, restore, unite, inspire
the church that bears your Name;
one Name exalted over all,
one Father, Spirit, Son,
O grant us grace to heed your call
and in that Name be one.

Timothy Dudley-Smith

98 AMONG US AND BEFORE US

GATEHOUSE 10 10 10 10

Unison 1. A - mong us and be - fore us, Lord, you stand with
G Em Am D

arms out - stretched and bread and wine at hand. Con - front - ing those un -
G Em Am7 D7 G

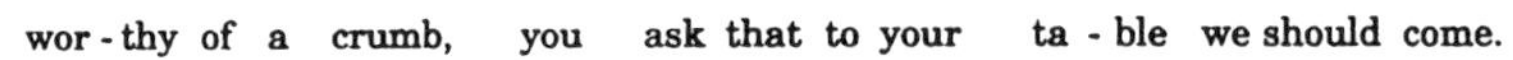
wor - thy of a crumb, you ask that to your ta - ble we should come.

Em Am D G Em Am7 D7 G

2. Who dare say No, when such is your resolve
our worst to witness, suffer and absolve,
our best to raise in lives by God forgiv'n,
our souls to fill on earth with food from heav'n?

3. Who dare say No, when such is your intent
to love the selves we famish and resent,
to cradle our uncertainties and fear,
to kindle hope as you in faith draw near?

4. Who dare say No, when such is your request
that each around your table should be guest,
that here the ancient word should live as new
'Take, eat and drink – all this is meant for you.'?

5. No more we hesitate and wonder why;
no more we stand indiff'rent, scared or shy.
Your invitation leads us to say Yes,
to meet you where you nourish, heal and bless.

99 AN UPPER ROOM

Music used by permission of Oxford University Press

Folksong 98 98

English traditional melody
arr. JOHN WILSON (1905–1992)

INTRODUCTION*
Man.
VERSES
Unison
Ped. ad lib.

1

An Upper Room did our Lord prepare
For those he loved until the end:
And his disciples still gather there
To celebrate their Risen Friend.

2

A lasting gift Jesus gave his own:
To share his bread, his loving cup.
Whatever burdens may bow us down,
He by his Cross shall lift us up.

3

And after Supper he washed their feet
For service, too, is sacrament.
In him our joy shall be made complete -
Sent out to serve, as he was sent.

4

No end there is! We depart in peace,
He loves beyond the uttermost:
In every room in our Father's house
He will be there, as Lord and Host.

Frederick Pratt Green

100 AS MAN AND WOMAN

Music used by permission of Oxford University Press

Sussex Carol 88 88 88

English traditional melody
harm. R. VAUGHAN WILLIAMS (1872–1958)

Unison
Harmony (ad lib.)
Unison
Harmony (ad lib.)

Love 1

As man and woman were made one
that love be found and life begun:
the likeness of the living God,
unique, yet called to live as one.
Through joy or sadness, calm or strife,
come, praise the love that gives us life.

Joy 2

Now Jesus lived and gave his love
to make our life and loving new
so celebrate with him today
and drink the joy he offers you
that makes the simple moment shine
and changes water into wine.

Hope 3

And Jesus died to live again
so praise the love that, come what may,
can bring the dawn and clear the skies,
and waits to wipe all tears away
and let us hope for what shall be
believing where we cannon see.

Peace 4

Then spread the table, clear the hall
and celebrate till day is done;
let peace go deep between us all
and joy be shared by everyone:
laugh and make merry with your friends
and praise the love that never ends!

Brian Arthur Wren

101 CHRIST IS ALIVE

Truro LM

Melody from T. WILLIAMS'S
Psalmodia Evangelica, 1789

1

Christ is alive! Let Christians sing.
The cross stands empty to the sky.
Let streets and homes with praises ring.
Love, drowned in death, shall never die.

2

Christ is alive! No longer bound
to distant years in Palestine,
but saving, healing, here and now,
and touching every place and time.

3

In every insult, rift and war,
where colour, scorn or wealth divide,
Christ suffers still, yet loves the more,
and lives, where even hope has died.

4

Women and men, in age and youth,
can feel the Spirit, hear the call,
and find the way, the life, the truth,
revealed in Jesus, freed for all.

5

Christ is alive, and comes to bring
good news to this and every age,
till earth and sky and ocean ring
with joy, with justice, love and praise.

Brian Arthur Wren

102 CHRIST IS THE KING

Words and music used by permission of Oxford University Press

Vulpius 888 with alleluias

Melody by MELCHIOR VULPIUS (*c.*1570–1615)
harm. ERIK ROUTLEY (1917–82)

CHRIST is the King! O friends rejoice;
brothers and sisters, with one voice
tell all the earth he is your choice:

Alleluia! Alleluia! Alleluia!

2 O magnify the Lord, and raise
anthems of joy and holy praise
for Christ's brave saints of ancient days:

3 Christ through all ages is the same:
place the same hope in his great name,
with the same faith his word proclaim:

4 Let Love's unconquerable might
your scattered companies unite
in service to the Lord of light:

5 So shall God's will on earth be done,
new lamps be lit, new tasks begun,
and the whole Church at last be one:

G. K. A. BELL (1883–1958)*

103 CHRIST IS THE WORLD'S LIGHT

Melody from Paris *Antiphoner*, 1681
harm. DAVID EVANS (1874–1948)

Christe sanctorum 10 11 11 6

Unison

CHRIST is the world's Light, he and none other;
born in our darkness, he became our Brother.
If we have seen him, we have seen the Father:
Glory to God on high.

2 Christ is the world's Peace, he and none other;
no one can serve him and despise a brother.
Who else unites us, one in God the Father?
Glory to God on high.

3 Christ is the world's Life, he and none other;
sold once for silver, murdered here, our Brother—
he, who redeems us, reigns with God the Father:
Glory to God on high.

4 Give God the glory, God and none other;
give God the glory, Spirit, Son and Father;
give God the glory, God in Man my brother:
Glory to God on high.

F. PRATT GREEN (1903–)*

104 CHRIST TRIUMPHANT

Used by permission of Hope Publishing Co., Carol Steam, IL 60188 USA

GUITING POWER 85 85 and Refrain
Unison 1. Christ tri - um - phant, ev - er reign - ing, Sav - iour, Mas - ter,
Capo 3 C Am F G C Am
King, Lord of heav'n, our lives sus - tain - ing,
G C Am F♯dim B7
hear us as we sing: *Refrain* Yours the glo - ry
Em D7 G7 C C7

and the crown, the high re - nown, th'e - ter - nal name.
F E Am Em Dm7 G7 C

2. Word incarnate, truth revealing,
   Son of Man on earth!
   Pow'r and majesty concealing
   by your humble birth:

3. Suff'ring servant, scorned, ill-treated,
   victim crucified!
   Death is through the cross defeated,
   sinners justified:

4. Priestly King, enthroned for ever
   high in heav'n above!
   Sin and death and hell shall never
   stifle hymns of love:

5. So, our hearts and voices raising
   through the ages long,
   ceaselessly upon you gazing,
   this shall be our song:

Text: Michael Saward (b. 1932)
Music: John Barnard (b. 1948)

105 COME, LIVING GOD

Spiritus Vitae 98 98 MARY J. HAMMOND (1878–1964)

1

Come, living God, when least expected,
When minds are dull and hearts are cold,
Through sharpening word and warm affection
Revealing truths as yet untold.

2

Break from the tomb in which we hide you
To speak again in startling ways;
Break through the words in which we bind you
To resurrect our lifeless praise.

3
Come now, as once you came to Moses
Within the bush alive with flame,
Or to Elijah on the mountain,
By silence pressing home your claim.

4
So, let our minds be sharp to read you
In sight or sound or printed page,
And let us greet you in our neighbours,
In ardent youth or mellow age.

5
Then, through our gloom, your Son will meet us
As vivid truth and living Lord,
Exploding doubt and disillusion
To scatter hope and joy abroad.

6
Then we will share his radiant brightness
And, blazing through the dread of night,
Illuminate by love and reason,
For those in darkness, faith's delight.

Alan Gaunt

106 DEAR LORD, TO YOU AGAIN

Words used by permission of Oxford University Press

Song 24 10 10.10 10.10 10. Orlando Gibbons (1583–1625)

(♮ in
repeat)

Bread and Wine

He took

Dear Lord, to you again our gifts we bring,
this bread our toil, this wine our ecstasy,
poor and imperfect though they both must be;
yet you will take a heart-free offering.
Yours is the bounty, ours the unfettered will
to make or mar, to fashion good or ill.

He blessed 2

Yes, you will take and bless, and grace impart
to make again what once your goodness gave,
what we half crave, and half refuse to have,
a sturdier will, a more repentant heart.
You have on earth no hands, no hearts but ours;
bless them as yours, ourselves, our will, our powers.

He broke 3

Break bread, O Lord, break down our wayward wills,
break down our prized possessions, break them down;
let them be freely given as your own
to all who need our gifts, to heal their ills.
Break this, the bread we bring, that all may share
in your one living body, everywhere.

He gave 4

Our lips receive your wine, our hands your bread;
you give us back the selves we offered you,
won by the Cross, by Calvary made new,
a heart enriched, a life raised from the dead.
Grant us to take and guard your treasure well,
that we in you, and you in us may dwell.

H. C. A. Gaunt (1902–83)

107 FATHER ALL-LOVING

Was lebet 12 10.12 10. *Rheinhardt MS.* (Üttingen, 1754)

2

Father all-loving, thou rulest in majesty,
  judgment is thine, and condemneth our pride;
stir up our rulers and peoples to penitence,
  sorrow for sins that for vengeance have cried.

4

Blessèd Lord Jesus, thou camest in poverty,
  sharing a stable with beasts at thy birth;
stir us to work for thy justice and charity,
  truly to care for the poor upon earth.

6

Come, Holy Spirit, create in us holiness,
  lift up our lives to thy standard of right;
stir every will to new ventures of faithfulness,
  flood the whole Church with thy glorious light.

7

Holiest Trinity, perfect in Unity,
  bind in thy love every nation and race:
may we adore thee for time and eternity,
  Father, Redeemer, and Spirit of grace.

PATRICK APPLEFORD (b. 1924)

108 FATHER, LORD OF ALL CREATION

Music used by permission of Oxford University Press

Abbot's Leigh 8 7.8 7.D. Cyril V. Taylor (1907–91)

Father, Lord of all Creation,
Ground of Being, Life and Love;
height and depth beyond description
only life in you can prove:
you are mortal life's dependence:
thought, speech, sight are ours by grace;
yours is every hour's existence,
sovereign Lord of time and space.

2

Jesus Christ, the Man for Others,
we, your people, make our prayer:
help us love-as sisters, brothers-
all whose burdens we can share.
Where your name binds us together
you, Lord Christ, will surely be;
where no selfishness can sever
there your love the world may see.

3

Holy Spirit, rushing, burning-
wind and flame of Pentecost,
fire our hearts afresh with yearning-
to regain what we have lost.
May your love unite our action,
nevermore to speak alone:
God in us abolish faction,
God, through us your love make known.

Stewart Cross (1928-89)

109 FATHER, WHO IN JESUS FOUND US

Quem pastores 8 8 8.7. German Mediaeval Melody

1
God, whose love is all around us,
who in Jesus sought and found us,
who to freedom new unbound us,
keep our hearts with joy aflame.

2
For the sacramental breaking,
for the honour of partaking,
for our life and lives re-making,
young and old, we praise your name.

3
From the service of this table
lead us to a life more stable
for our witness make us able;
blessings on our work we claim.

4
Through our calling closely knitted,
daily to your praise committed,
for a life of service fitted,
let us now your love proclaim.

Frederick Herman Kaan

110 FILLED WITH THE SPIRIT'S POWER

Farley Castle 10 10.10 10. Henry Lawes (1596–1662)

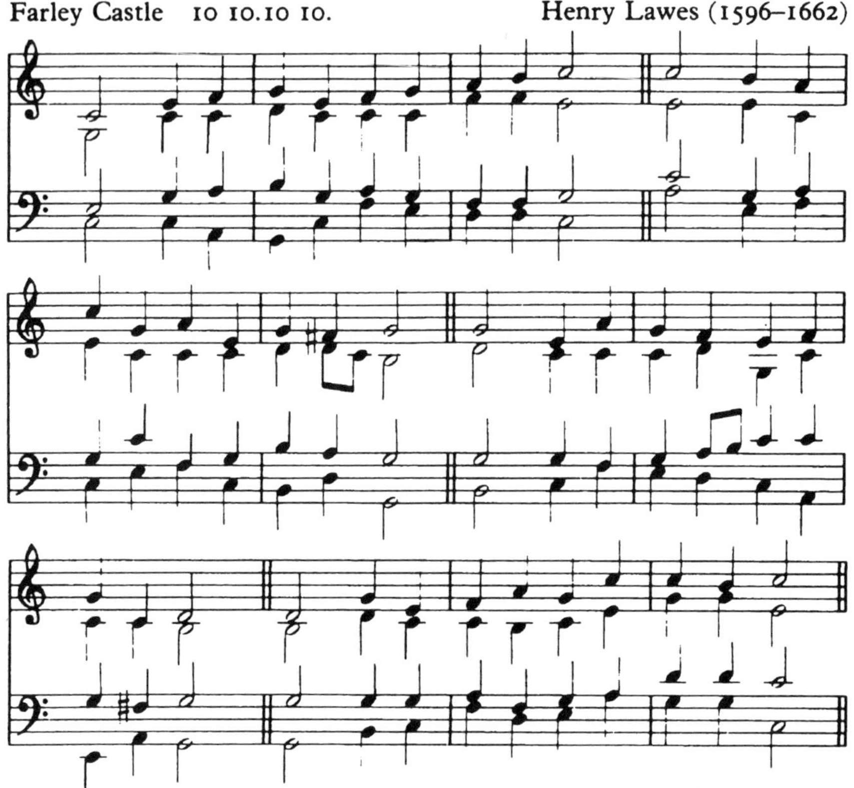

Fellowship in the Holy Spirit

1 Filled with the Spirit's power, with one accord
the infant Church confessed its risen Lord.
O Holy Spirit, in the Church to-day
no less your power of fellowship display.

2 Now with the mind of Christ set us on fire,
that unity may be our great desire.
Give joy and peace; give faith to hear your call,
and readiness in each to work for all.

3 Widen our love, good Spirit, to embrace
in your strong care the men of every race.
Like wind and fire with life among us move,
till we are known as Christ's, and Christians prove.

J. R. Peacey (1896–1971)

111 FOR THE HEALING OF THE NATIONS

Für die Heilung aller Völker

England

1 For the heal - ing of the na - tions, Lord, we pray with
2 Für die Hei - lung al - ler Völ - ker bit - ten wir mit
one ac - - cord; for a just and e - qual shar - ing
ei-nem Mund um ge - rech - tes, glei - ches Tei - len
of the things that earth af - fords. To a life, of
auf dem glei - chen Er - den - rund. Hilf, daß wir in

love in ac - tion help us rise and pledge our word.
tät' - ger Lie- be wu-chern mit dem eig - nen Pfund.

2

Lead your people into freedom,
from despair your world release;
that redeemed from war and hatred,
all may come and go in peace.
Show us how through care and goodness
fear will die and hope increase.

3

All that kills abundant living,
let if from the earth be banned;
pride of status, race or schooling,
dogmas that obscure your plan.
In our common quest for justice
may we hallow life's brief span.

4

You, creator-God, have written
your great name on humankind;
for our growing in your likeness
bring the life of Christ to mind;
that by our response and service
earth its destiny may find.

Frederick Herman Kaan

2

Fuhr uns, Vater, in die Freiheit,
mach uns von Verzweiflung frei,
daB erlost von HaB und Kriegen
Friede mit uns allen sei.
Zeig uns, wie durch Hilf und Gute
Angst stirbt, Hoffnung wachst herbei.

3

Alles, was das Leben totet,
stelle unter deinen Bann:
Stolz auf Stellung, Farbe, Klasse,
Lehren gegen deinen Plan.
Noch im Kampf fur das, was recht ist,
she'n wir Leben heilig an.

4

Schopfer, du schreibst deinen Namen
tief ins Buch der Menschheit ein:
LaB in uns dein Bildnis wachsen,
hilf uns, Christus naher sein,
daB durch unsres Lebens Antwort
Erde glanzt in deinem Schein.

1=englisch, 2=deutsch
Melodie: nach Henry Purcell. Satz: Hartmut Bietz. Text: 1 Fred Kaan, 2: Dieter Trautwein.

112 FORTH IN THE PEACE OF CHRIST

Hymn by James Quinn,

PSALM 145

Duke Street LM

Melody from BOYD's *Psalm & Hymn Tunes*, 1793
Later attrib. JOHN HATTON (d. 1793)

FORTH in the peace of Christ we go;
  Christ to the world with joy we bring;
Christ in our minds, Christ on our lips,
  Christ in our hearts, the world's true King.

2 King of our hearts, Christ makes us kings;
  kingship with him his servants gain;
with Christ, the Servant-Lord of all,
  Christ's world we serve to share Christ's reign.

3 Priests of the world, Christ sends us forth,
  this world of time to consecrate,
our world of sin by grace to heal,
  Christ's world in Christ to recreate.

4 Prophets of Christ, we hear his Word:
  he claims our minds, to search his ways,
he claims our lips, to speak his truth,
  he claims our hearts, to sing his praise.

5 We are his Church, he makes us one:
  here is one hearth for all to find,
here is one flock, one Shepherd-King,
  here is one faith, one heart, one mind.

JAMES QUINN (1919–)

113 FROM THE SUN'S RISING

Words and music: Graham Kendrick
Psalm 50.1, Isaiah 45.6, Matthew 28.19
Capo 2(C)
Steadily
D (C) G (F) D (C) A (G) D (C) G (F)
1. From the sun's ris - ing un - to the sun's setting Je - sus our Lord shall be
2. From ev - ery tongue, tribe, and na - tion he's called us, to be his peo - ple - the
3. To ev - ery tongue, tribe, and na - tion he sends us, to make di - sci - ples, to
4. Come let us join with the church from all nations, cross ev - ery bor - der, throw
D (C) Asus (Gsus) A (G) D (C) G (F) D (C) A (G)
great in the earth; and all earth's kingdom shall be his do - minion -
church with one face; called by his Spir - it to forge a new wit- ness
teach and bap - tize; for all au - tho - ri - ty to him is gi- ven -
wide ev - ery door: wor - kers with him as he ga - thers his har - vest,
D (C) G (F) Bm (Am) G/A (F) A7 (G7) D (C) Dsus (Csus) D (C)
all of cre - a - tion shall sing of his worth.
and build a king - dom of just - ice and peace.
now as his wit - nes - ses we shall a - rise.
till earth's far cor - ners our sav - iour a - dore.
Chorus
Bm (Am) F♯m (Em) G (F) D (C) Em (Dm)
Let ev - ery heart, ev - ery voice, ev - ery tongue join with spi - rits a -

Asus (Gsus) A (G) Bm (Am) F#m (Em) G (F) D (C)
blaze: one in his love we will cir - cle the world with the
Em (Dm) F#sus (Esus) F# (E) Em7 (Dm7) A (G)
song of his praise. O let all his peo - ple re -
last time to Coda
Bm (Am) G (F) A (G) D (C) Dsus (Csus) D (C) Asus (Gsus) A (G)
joice, and let all the earth hear his voice!
CODA
Bm (Am) Em (Dm) A (G) Bm (Am)
voice! Let all his peo - ple re - joice,
G (F) A (G) D (C) Dsus (Csus) D (C)
and let all the earth hear his voice!

114 GATHER AROUND

SKYE BOAT SONG Irregular
Unison
Ga - ther a - round, for the ta - ble is spread, wel - come the food and
G Em Am D G C
rest! Wide is our cir - cle, with Christ at the head,
G Em Am D
he is the ho - noured guest. Learn of his love,
G C G Em
grow in his grace, pray for the peace he gives;
Am Em B Em

here at this meal, here in this place, know that his spi - rit
Am Em B

lives! Once he was known in the break - ing of bread,
Em G Em Am D

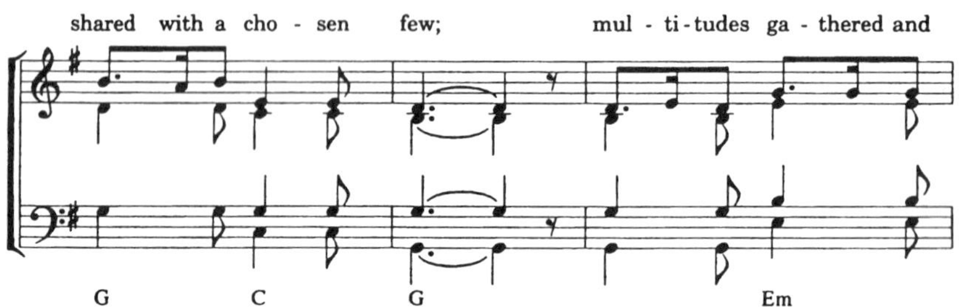
shared with a cho - sen few; mul - ti - tudes ga - thered and
G C G Em

by him were fed, so will he feed us too.
Am D G C G

Text: Jean Holloway (*b.* 1939)
Music: traditional Scottish melody arr. Colin Hand (*b.* 1929)

115 GATHERED HERE FROM MANY NATIONS

NEANDER 8787 87 (UNSER HERRSCHER)

Neander's *Alpha and Omega 1680*

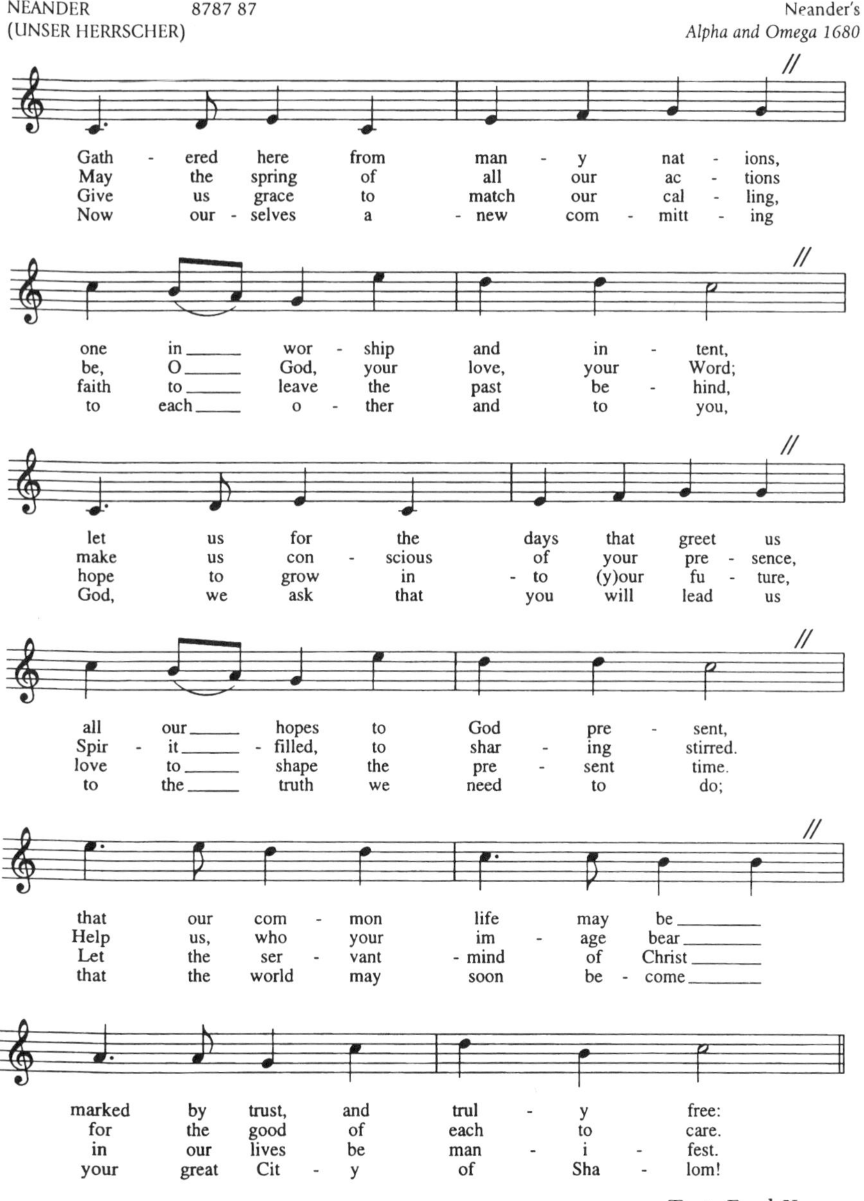

Gath - ered here from man - y nat - ions,
May the spring of all our ac - tions
Give us grace to match our cal - ling,
Now our - selves a - new com - mitt - ing
one in wor - ship and in - tent,
be, O God, your love, your Word;
faith to leave the past be - hind,
to each o - ther and to you,
let us for the days that greet us
make us con - scious of your pre - sence,
hope to grow in - to (y)our fu - ture,
God, we ask that you will lead us
all our hopes to God pre - sent,
Spir - it - filled, to shar - ing stirred.
love to shape the pre - sent time.
to the truth we need to do;
that our com - mon life may be
Help us, who your im - age bear
Let the ser - vant - mind of Christ
that the world may soon be - come
marked by trust, and trul - y free:
for the good of each to care.
in our lives be man - i - fest.
your great Cit - y of Sha - lom!

Text: Fred Kann

Written in 1971 and subsequently widely used at ecumenical / international gatherings.

116 GO FORTH AND TELL

Used by permission of Hope Publishing Co., Carol Steam, IL 60188 USA

Yanworth 10 10 10 10 JOHN BARNARD (1948–)

Unison

Go forth and tell! O Church of God, awake!
God's saving news to all the nations take:
proclaim Christ Jesus, Saviour, Lord and King,
that all the world his glorious praise may sing.

2 Go forth and tell! God's love embraces all;
he will in grace respond to all who call:
how shall they call if they have never heard
the gracious invitation of his word?

3 Go forth and tell! The doors are open wide:
share God's good gifts—let no one be denied;
live out your life as Christ your Lord shall choose,
your ransomed powers for his sole glory use.

4 Go forth and tell! O Church of God, arise!
Go in the strength which Christ your Lord supplies;
go till all nations his great name adore
and serve him, Lord and King for evermore.

JAMES E. SEDDON (1915–83)*

117 GOD IS HERE

Blaenwern 8 7.8 7.D. William P. Rowlands (1860–1937)

1

God is here! As we his people
Meet to offer praise and prayer,
May we find in fuller measure
What it is in Christ we share.
Here, as in the world around us,
All our varied skills and arts
Wait the coming of his Spirit
Into open minds and hearts.

2

Here are symbols to remind us
Of our lifelong need of grace;
Here are table, font and pulpit;
Here the cross has central place.
Here in honesty of preaching,
Here in silence, as in speech,
Here, in newness and renewal,
God in Spirit comes to each.

3

Here our children find a welcome
In the Shepherd's flock and fold,
Here as bread and wine are taken,
Christ sustains us as of old,
Here the servants of the Servant
Seek in worship to explore
What it means in daily living
To believe and to adore.

4

Love of all, of Church and Kingdom,
In an age of change and doubt,
Keep us faithful to the gospel,
Help us to work your purpose out.
Here, in this day's dedication,
All we have to give, receive:
We, who cannot live without you,
We adore you! we believe!

Frederick Pratt Green

118 GOD OF FREEDOM, GOD OF JUSTICE

Rhuddlan 87 87 87 Welsh traditional melody

Used by permission of Hope Publishing Co., Carol Stream, IL 60188 USA.

For Prisoners of Conscience

GOD of freedom, God of justice,
  God whose love is strong as death,
God who saw the dark of prison,
  God who knew the price of faith:
touch our world of sad oppression
  with your Spirit's healing breath.

2 Rid the earth of torture's terror,
  God whose hands were nailed to wood;
hear the cries of pain and protest,
  God who shed the tears and blood;
move in us the power of pity,
  restless for the common good.

3 Make in us a captive conscience
  quick to hear, to act, to plead;
make us truly sisters, brothers,
  of whatever race or creed:
teach us to be fully human,
  open to each other's need.

SHIRLEY ERENA MURRAY (1931–)*
Written in 1981 for *Amnesty International*

119 GOD WITH HUMANITY

Music used by permission of Oxford University Press.

Gonfalon Royal LM PERCY BUCK (1871–1947)

Unison
Harmony
A - - - - - men.

GOD with humanity made one
is seen in Christ, God's only Son:
in you, Lord Christ, the Son of Man,
we see God's reconciling plan.

2 To save a broken world you came,
and from chaotic depths reclaim
your whole creation, so we share
your reconciling work and care.

3 In you all humankind can see
the people God would have us be.
In you we find how God forgives,
through you, the Spirit in us lives.

4 Through us God calls the world again;
and constantly his love remains
with arms outstretched, to heal and bless
the refugees of emptiness.

5 Where race or creed or hate divide,
the Church, like God, must stand beside
and stretch out reconciling hands
to join, through suffering, every land.

6 Then give us strength, great Lord of life,
to work until all human strife
is reconciled, and all shall praise
your endless love, your glorious ways.
(Amen.)

DAVID FOX (1956–)

120 GREAT GOD, YOUR LOVE HAS CALLED US HERE

Abingdon 88 88 88

ERIK ROUTLEY (1917–82)

1

Great God, your love has called us here,
as we, by love for love were made.
Your living likeness still we bear,
though marred, dishonoured, disobeyed.
 We come, with all our heart and mind
 your call to hear, your love to find.

2

We come with self-inflicted pains
of broken trust and chosen wrong,
half-free, half-bound by inner chains,
by social forces swept along,
 by powers and systems close confined
 yet seeking hope for humankind.

3

Great God, in Christ you call our name
and then receive us as your own,
not through some merit, right or claim,
but by your gracious love alone.
 We strain to glimpse your mercy seat
 and find you kneeling at our feet.

4

Then take the towel, and break the bread,
and humble us, and call us friends.
Suffer and serve till all are fed,
and show how grandly love intends
 to work till all creation sings,
 to fill all worlds, to crown all things.

5

Great God, in Christ you set us free
your life to live, your joy to share.
give us your Spirit's liberty
to turn from guilt and dull despair
 and offer all that faith can do
 while love is making all things new.

Brian Arthur Wren

121 HYMNE POUR L'EGLISE

(French Translation)

BRIGGS 7676D

Patrick Wedd

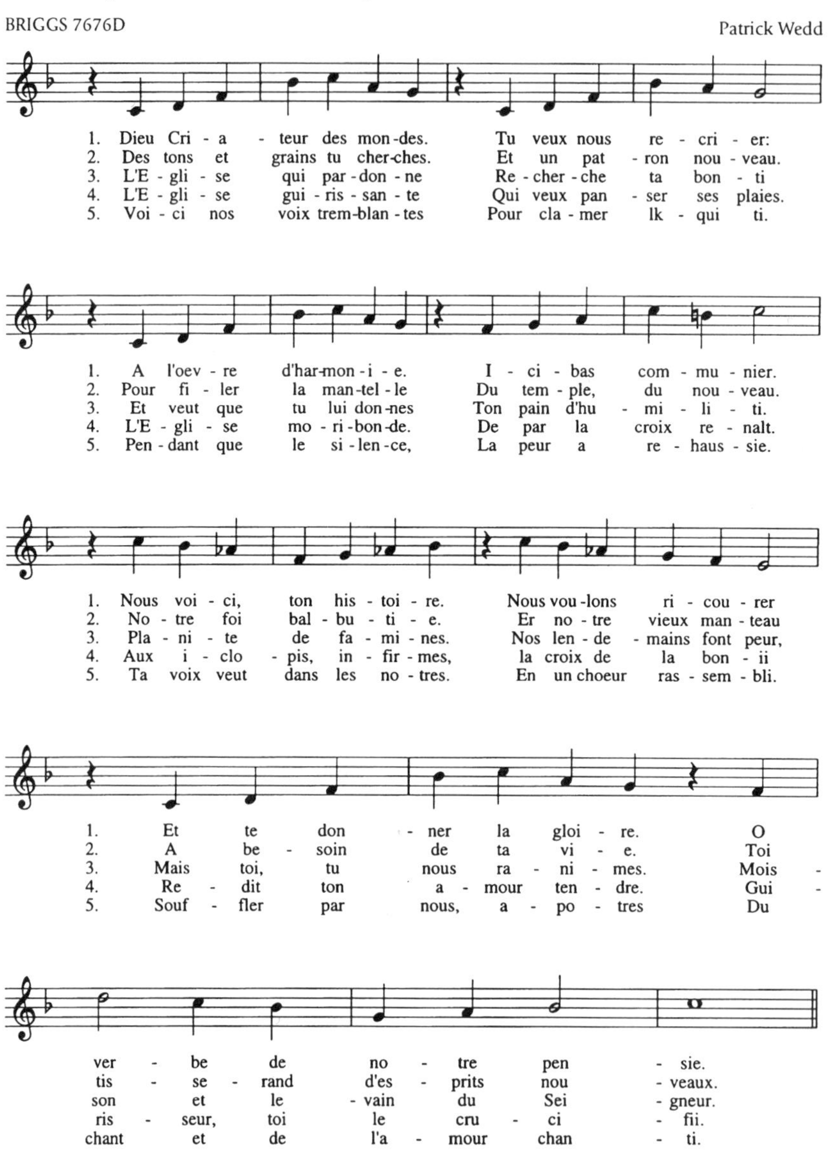
1. Dieu Cri - a - teur des mon-des. Tu veux nous re - cri - er:
2. Des tons et grains tu cher-ches. Et un pat - ron nou - veau.
3. L'E - gli - se qui par - don - ne Re - cher - che ta bon - ti
4. L'E - gli - se gui - ris - san - te Qui veux pan - ser ses plaies.
5. Voi - ci nos voix trem-blan - tes Pour cla - mer lk - qui ti.
1. A l'oev - re d'har-mon - i - e. I - ci - bas com - mu - nier.
2. Pour fi - ler la man-tel - le Du tem - ple, du nou - veau.
3. Et veut que tu lui don-nes Ton pain d'hu - mi - li - ti.
4. L'E - gli - se mo - ri - bon-de. De par la croix re - nalt.
5. Pen - dant que le si - len - ce, La peur a re - haus - sie.
1. Nous voi - ci, ton his - toi - re. Nous vou - lons ri - cou - rer
2. No - tre foi bal - bu - ti - e. Er no - tre vieux man - teau
3. Pla - ni - te de fa - mi - nes. Nos len - de - mains font peur,
4. Aux i - clo - pis, in - fir - mes, la croix de la bon - ii
5. Ta voix veut dans les no - tres. En un choeur ras - sem - bli.
1. Et te don - ner la gloi - re. O
2. A be - soin de ta vi - e. Toi
3. Mais toi, tu nous ra - ni - mes. Mois -
4. Re - dit ton a - mour ten - dre. Gui -
5. Souf - fler par nous, a - po - tres Du
ver - be de no - tre pen - sie.
tis - se - rand d'es - prits nou - veaux.
son et le - vain du Sei - gneur.
ris - seur, toi le cru - ci - fii.
chant et de l'a - mour chan - ti.

Anna Briggs, 1992
Adaption francise: le Reverend Louis-Marie Gallant

HYMN FOR THE CHURCH

(English Translation)

BRIGGS 7676D
Patrick Wedd
1. You call us out to praise you, The God who gave us birth;
2. For var - ied hues and tex - tures New pat - terns, still you search
3. The church that speaks for-give - ness Con - fes - ses its own need;
4. The church that of - fers heal - ing Dis - cerns its wounds and loss;
5. Our fee - ble voic - es strug - gle To sing your jus - tice clear;
1. To gath - er in com-mun-ion, And treas - ure your whole earth;
2. To weave your seam-less gar-ment, The fab - ric of your church;
3. The church that feels its hung - er Finds grace to care and feed;
4. The church that fac - es dy - ing Shares life be - yond the cross;
5. The world has sunk in si - lence, Each dis - cord ech - oes fear;
1. We are your li - ving sto - ry, To hear and to be heard;
2. Our tat - tered faith you che - rish Re-claim from wear and moth;
3. Our fam - ished world is cry - ing, Its fu - ture filled with dread;
4. To peo - ple torn and bro - ken Your mer - cy is re - vealed;
5. One voice a - lone is rag - ged, To-geth - er we are strong;
1. We praise your name, who writes us, The Au___ - thor and___ the Word.
2. We praise your name, who twines us, The Weav___ - er and___ the Cloth.
3. We praise your name, who fills us, The Bak___ - er and___ the Bread.
4. We praise your name, who loves us, The Heal___ - er and___ the Healed.
5. We praise your name, who breathes us, The Sing___ - er and___ the Song.

Anna Briggs, 1992

122 I COME WITH JOY

Unison or harmony

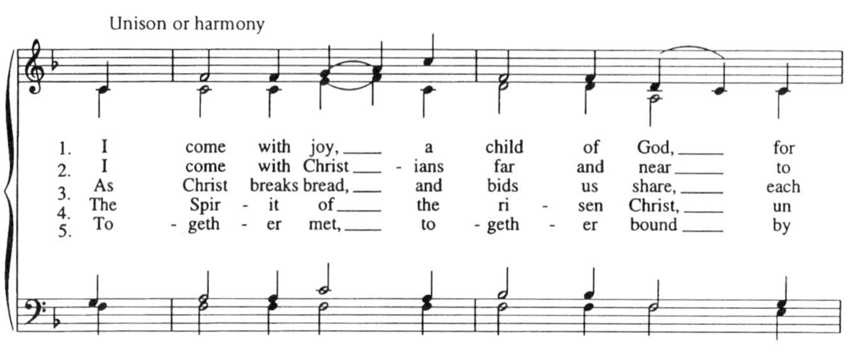
1. I come with joy, a child of God, for
2. I come with Christ - ians far and near to
3. As Christ breaks bread, and bids us share, each
4. The Spir - it of the ri - sen Christ, un
5. To - geth - er met, to - geth - er bound by

giv - en, loved and free, the life of Je - sus
find, as all are fed, the new com - mun - it
proud di - vi - sion ends. The love that made us,
seen, but e - ver near, is in such friend - ship
all that God has done, we'll go with joy, to

to re - call, in love laid down for me.
y of love in Christ's com - mun - ion bread.
makes us one, and strang - ers now are friends.
bet - ter known, a - live a - mong us here.
give the world the love that makes us one.

Words: Brian A. Wren (b. 1936). alt.
Music: Land of Rest, American folk melody; adapt. and harm. Annabel Morri Buchanan (1889-1983)

Second Tune

St Botolph CM GORDON SLATER (1896–1979)

1
I come with joy, a child of God,
forgiven, loved and free,
the life of Jesus to recall,
in love laid down for me.

2
I come with Christians far and near
to find, as all are fed,
the new community of love
in Christ's communion bread.

3
As Christ breaks bread, and bids us share,
each proud division ends.
The love that made us, makes us one,
and strangers now are friends.

4
The Spirit of the risen Christ,
unseen, but ever near,
is in such friendship better known,
alive among us here.

5
Together met, together bound
by all that God has done,
we'll go with joy, to give the world
the love that makes us one.

123 I, THE LORD OF SEA AND SKY

Unison
1. I, the Lord of sea and sky, I have heard my peo-ple cry.
G C G C G D
All who dwell in dark and sin my hand will save.
G Em Am7 G C Am Am7 D G/B D/A
I who made the stars of night, I will make their dark-ness bright.
G C G C G D
Who will bear my light to them? Whom shall I send?
G Em Am7 G C Am G C D

Refrain
Here I am, Lord. Is it I, Lord? I have
G Gsus4 G Gmaj7/F♯ C/E G Gsus4
heard you call-ing in the night. I will go, Lord,
G Am7 G/B C D G
if you lead me. I will hold your peo-ple in my
Gmaj7/F♯ C/E G Am7 D
heart.
vs. 1&2
D.C.
last time
G Gsus4 Gmaj7/F♯ C/E D G

2. I, the Lord of snow and rain,
I have borne my people's pain.
I have wept for love of them.
They turn away.
I will break their hearts of stone,
give them hearts for love alone.
I will speak my word to them.
Whom shall I send?

3. I, the Lord of wind and flame,
I will tend the poor and lame.
I will set a feast for them.
My hand will save.
Finest bread I will provide
till their hearts be satisfied.
I will give my life to them.
Whom shall I send?

Text: Dan Schutte, based on Isaiah 6
Music: Dan Schutte

124 I WAITED PATIENTLY FOR GOD

Tune: Amazing Grace (Scottish trad.)
Tenderly
A B C D
1. I wait - ed pa - tient - ly for God, for God to hear my pray'r; and God bent down to where I sank and lis - tened to me there.
2. God raised me from a mir - y pit, from mud and sink - ing sand, and set my feet up - on a rock where I can firm - ly stand.
3. And on my lips a song was put, a new song to the Lord. Man - y will mar - vel o - pen- eyed and put their trust in God.
(Hum)

1. I waited patiently for God,
for God to hear my prayer;
and God bent down to where I sank
and listened to me there.

2. God raised me from a miry pit,
from mud and sinking sand,
and set my feet upon a rock
where I can firmly stand.

G
Bm
Am7
4. Great won - ders you have done, O
D
Em
Am7
D
Lord, all pur - posed for our good.
D7
G
Bm
C
Un - a - ble ev - 'ry one to
D
G/B
G/D
D7
G
name, I bow in grat - i - tude.

3. And on my lips a song was put,
a new song to the Lord.
Many will marvel, open-eyed
and put their trust in God.

4. Great wonders you have done, O Lord,
all purposed for our good.
Unable every one to name,
I bow in gratitude.

125 JESUS CHRIST IS WAITING

Words & arrangement by John L. Bell & Graham Maule; Copyright © 1988 WGRG, Iona Community, 840 Govan Road, Glasgow G51 3UU Scotland; Melody "Noel nouvelet" French traditional.

NOEL NOUVELET 11 11 10 11
1. Je - sus Christ is wait - ing, wait - ing in the streets:
Em A Em D C Em
no - one is his neigh - bour, all a - lone he eats.
A Em D C Em
Lis - ten, Lord Je - sus, I am lone - ly too;
B7 Em B7
make me, friend or strang - er, fit to wait on you.
Em A Em D C Em

2. Jesus Christ is raging,
raging in the streets
where injustice spirals
and all hope retreats.
Listen, Lord Jesus,
I am angry too;
in the kingdom's causes
let me rage with you.

3. Jesus Christ is healing,
healing in the streets;
curing those who suffer,
touching those he greets.
Listen, Lord Jesus,
I have pity too;
let my care be active,
healing just like you.

4. Jesus Christ is dancing,
dancing in the streets,
where each sign of hatred
his strong love defeats.
Listen, Lord Jesus,
I feel triumph too;
on suspicion's graveyard,
let me dance with you.

5. Jesus Christ is calling,
calling in the streets,
'Come and walk faith's tightrope,
I will guide your feet.'
Listen, Lord Jesus,
let my fears be few;
walk one step before me,
I will follow you.

126 LET US BREAK BREAD TOGETHER

Let us break bread together 10 10 with refrain

Afro–American folk-song
harm. GERRE HANCOCK (1934–)

Unison
E♭ Fm7 E♭ Fm
E♭ Fm7 E♭ Gm E♭ Cm F7
B♭ E♭ B♭
REFRAIN
E♭ Gm B♭7 C7
When I fall on my knees, with my
Fm A♭m6 B♭7 E♭ E♭+5 A♭ B♭7 E♭
face to the ris - ing sun, O Lord, have mer - cy on me.

LET us break bread together in the Lord;
let us break bread together in the Lord:

when I fall on my knees,
with my face to the rising sun,
O Lord, have mercy on me.

2 Let us drink wine together in the Lord;
let us drink wine together in the Lord:

3 Let us praise God together in the Lord;
let us praise God together in the Lord:

based on an Afro-American Spiritual

Other verses or variations may be improvised; for example, when the hymn is sung during communion where a common loaf is shared: 'Let us break bread together, hand to hand . . . '.

127 LET US LIGHT A CANDLE

Words: Robert Willis

Music: Richard Shepard

Crotchet = c. 96
Optional Intro
In a world where peo - ple walk in
dark-ness Let us turn our fa-ces to the light To the
light of God re-vealed in Je - sus To the Day - star scatt - e - ring our

Chorus
night For the light is stron-ger than the dark - ness And the
day will ov - er come the night Though the shad - ows lin-ger all a -
round us Let us turn our fac-es to the light.

2. In a world where suffering of the helpless
Casts a shadow all along the way,
Let us bear the Cross of Christ with gladness
And proclaim the dawning of the day.

Chorus: For the light........

3. Let us light a candle in the darkness,
In the face of death a sign of life;
As a sign of hope where all seemed hopeless
As a sign of peace in place of strife.

Chorus: For the light........

128 LET US TALENTS AND TONGUES EMPLOY

Auf, bringt Gaben und Lob herbei

Jamaika/England

C F C
1. Let us tal - ents and tongues em - ploy.
2. Auf, bringt Ga - ben und Lob her - bei.
Dm C G7 C
reach - ing out with a shout of joy: bread is bro - ken, the
daß die Freu - de weit hör - bar sei: Brot und Wein hat er
F C F G C G7 C
wine is poured. Christ is spo - ken and seen and heard.
aus - ge - teilt. Chri - stus gibt, was uns hilft und heilt.
Refrain
C7 F Dm
Je - sus lives a - gain earth can breathe a - gain,
Je - sus lebt und spricht: Seht, ich bin das Licht,
G 7 C F C
pass the Word a - round: Loaves a - bound!
tragt das Brot hin - aus, kommt, teilt aus!

1 2. Christ is able to make us one. / at his table he sets the tone, / teaching people to live, to bless, / love in word and in deed express. / Jesus lives again . . .

3. Jesus calls us in, send us out / bearing fruit in a world of doubt, / gives us love to tell, bread to share: / God Immanuel everywhere! / Jesus lives again . . .

---

2 *2. Christus hilft uns zur Einigkeit, / spricht am Tisch das Gebot der Zeit, / lehrt das Leben als Segen sehn, / Liebe muß in der Tat bestehn. / Jesus lebt und spricht . . .*

3. Jesus ruft uns und sendet aus, / Frucht zu tragen in jedes Haus, / Brot der Liebe für jeden Fall: / Gott ist mit uns überall. / Jesus lebt und spricht . . .

1 = englisch, 2 = deutsch

129 LIVING GOD

Music used by permission of Oxford University Press

Abbot's Leigh 87 87 D CYRIL V. TAYLOR (1907–91)

Living God, your joyful Spirit
 breaks the bounds of time and space,
rests in love upon your people,
 drawn together in this place.
Here we join in glad thanksgiving,
 here rejoice to pray and praise:
Lord of all our past traditions,
 Lord of all our future days.

2 As your bread may we be broken,
 scattered in community;
we who know your greatest blessings
 called to share Christ's ministry.
May we gently lead each other,
 share our hunger and our thirst;
learn that only through our weakness
 shall we know the strength of Christ.

3 Lord, when we grow tired of giving,
 feel frustration, hurt and strain,
by your Spirit's quiet compulsion,
 draw us back to you again.
Guide us through the bitter searching
 when our confidence is lost;
give us hope from desolation,
 arms outstretched upon a cross.

4 Living God, your power surrounds us,
 as we face the way Christ trod,
challenge us to fresh commitment
 to the purposes of God:
called to share a new creation,
 called to preach a living word,
promised all the joys of heaven,
 through the grace of Christ our Lord.

JILL JENKINS (1937–)*

130 LORD, BRING THE DAY TO PASS

Rawthorpe 66 66 88 PETER CUTTS (1937–)

Unison

Contemporary

1

Lord, bring the day to pass
When forest, rock and hill,
The beasts, the birds, the grass,
Will know thy finished will:
When man attains his destiny
And nature its lost unity.

2

Forgive our careless use
Of water, ore and soil -
The plenty we abuse
Supplied by other's toil:
Save us from making self our creed,
Turn us towards our brother's need.

3

Give us, when we release
Creation's secret powers,
To harness them for peace
Our children's peace and ours;
Teach us the art of mastering
Which makes life rich and draws death's sting.

4

Creation groans, travails,
Futile its present plight,
Bound - till the hour it hails
The newfound sons of light
Who enter on their true estate.
Come, Lord: new heavens and earth create.

Ian Masson Fraser

131 LORD JESUS CHRIST

Living Lord 4 55 3 888 3

PATRICK APPLEFORD (1925–)
arr. JOHN BIRCH (1929–) altd.

Unison
3
3
3
1,3
(interlude)
2,4

LORD Jesus Christ,
you have come to us,
you are one with us,
Mary's Son—
cleansing our souls from all their sin,
pouring your love and goodness in;
Jesus, our love for you we sing,
living Lord.

2 Lord Jesus Christ,
now and every day
teach us how to pray,
Son of God.
You have commanded us to do
this, in remembrance, Lord, of you;
into our lives your power breaks through,
living Lord.

3 Lord Jesus Christ,
you have come to us,
born as one of us,
Mary's Son—
led out to die on Calvary,
risen from death to set us free;
living Lord Jesus, help us see
you are Lord.

4 Lord Jesus Christ,
we would come to you,
live our lives for you,
Son of God;
all your commands we know are true,
your many gifts will make us new;
into our lives your power breaks through,
living Lord.

PATRICK APPLEFORD (1925–)

132 LORD OF ALL POWER

Music used by permission of Oxford University Press

Slane 10 11.11 11. Irish Traditional Melody

Contemporary

Self-giving

Lord of all power, I give you my will,
in joyful obedience your tasks to fulfil.
  Your bondage is freedom, your service is song,
  and, held in your keeping, my weakness is strong.

2

Lord of all wisdom, I give you my mind,
rich truth that surpasses man's knowledge to find.
  What eye has not seen and what ear has not heard
  is taught by your Spirit and shines from your Word.

3

Lord of all bounty, I give you my heart;
I praise and adore you for all you impart:
  your love to inspire me, your counsel to guide,
  your presence to cheer me, whatever betide.

4

Lord of all being, I give you my all;
if e'er I disown you I stumble and fall;
  but, sworn in glad service your word to obey,
  I walk in your freedom to the end of the way.

JACK C. WINSLOW* (1882–1974)

133 LORD OF LORDS

Rhuddlan 8 7.8 7.8 7. Welsh Traditional Melody

Contemporary

For the Church and Nation

Lord of lords and King eternal,
  down the years in wondrous ways
you have blessed our land and guided,
  leading us through darkest days.
For your rich and faithful mercies,
  Lord, accept our thankful praise.

2

Speak to us and every nation,
  bid our jarring discords cease;
to the starving and the homeless
  bid us bring a full release;
and on all this earth's sore turmoil
  breathe the healing of your peace.

3

Love that binds us all together‿
  be upon the Church outpoured;
shame our pride and quell our factions,
  smite them with your Spirit's sword;
till the world, our love beholding,
  claims your power and calls you Lord.

4

Brace the wills of all your people
  who in every land and race
know the secrets of your kingdom,
  share the treasures of your grace;
till the summons of your Spirit
  wakes new life in every place.

5

Saviour, by your mighty Passion
  once you turned sheer loss to gain,
wresting in your risen glory
  victory from your cross and pain;
now in us be dead and risen,
  in us triumph, live, and reign.

JACK C. WINSLOW* (1882–1974)

134 LORD OF THE BOUNDLESS CURVES OF SPACE

San Rocco CM DEREK WILLIAMS (1945–)

Unison
Optional interlude between verses

Words used by permission of Oxford University Press

LORD of the boundless curves of space
and time's deep mystery,
to your creative might we trace
all nature's energy.

2 Your mind conceived the galaxy,
each atom's secret planned,
and every age of history
your purpose, Lord, has spanned.

3 Your Spirit gave the living cell
its hidden, vital force:
the instincts which all life impel
derive from you, their source.

4 Yours is the image humans bear,
though marred by human sin;
and yours the liberating care
again our souls to win.

5 Science explores your reason's ways,
and faith can this impart
that in the face of Christ our gaze
looks deep within your heart.

6 In Christ the human race has heard
your strong compassion plead:
he is your wisdom's perfect word,
your mercy's crowning deed.

A. F. BAYLY (1901–84)

135 LORD OF THE CHURCH

Words copyright by Timothy Dudley-Smith. Used by permission.

LONDONDERRY AIR Irregular

Words: Timothy Dudley-Smith
Music: Irish traditional melody
arranged Roland Fudge

G C Dm Am Em F
Lord of the church, we pray for our re - new - ing: Christ o - ver
C/E Dm Em Am Dm/F Dm7 G C Dm Am Em
all, our un - di - vid - ed aim; Fire of the Spi - rit, burn for our en -
F C/G F/A Em/G G C Dm/C C G
- du - ing, wind of the Spi - rit, fan the liv - ing flame! We turn to
C F Cmaj7/G Am7 Am7/G F
Christ a - mid our fear and fail - ing, the will that

C/E F Cmaj7/G Dm7/F Em7 Dm7 G7 C C7 Dm7
lacks the cour-age to be free,___ the wea-ry la - bours, all but un-a -
Em C/E Fmaj7 Cmaj7/G Dm7/G G7 C
- vail - ing,___ to bring us near-er what a church___ should be.___

1 Lord of the church, we pray for our renewing:
Christ over all, our undivided aim;
Fire of the Spirit, burn for our enduing,
wind of the Spirit, fan the living flame!
We turn to Christ amid our fear and failing,
the will that lacks the courage to be free,
the weary labours, all but unavailing,
to bring us nearer what a church should be.

2 Lord of the church, we seek a Father's blessing,
a true repentance and a faith restored,
a swift obedience and a new possessing,
filled with the Holy Spirit of the Lord!
We turn to Christ from all our restless striving,
unnumbered voices with a single prayer –
the living water for our souls' reviving,
in Christ to live, and love and serve and care.

3 Lord of the church, we long for our uniting,
true to one calling, by one vision stirred;
one cross proclaiming and one creed reciting,
one in the truth of Jesus and His word!
So lead us on; till toil and trouble ended,
one church triumphant one new song shall sing,
to praise His glory, risen and ascended,
Christ over all, the everlasting King!

136 LORD, FOR THE YEARS

LORD OF THE YEARS 11 10 11 10

1. Lord, for the years your love has kept and guid - ed,
C Dm7 C F Em7 G7 C
urged and in - spired us, cheered us on our way,
B7 Em Cm(E♭) G D7 G
sought us and saved us, par - doned and pro - vi - ded:
C F A7 D G G7
Lord of the years, we bring our thanks to - day.
Am Em F Am7 Dm G7 C

2
Lord, for that Word, the Word of life which fires us,
Speaks to our hearts and sets our souls ablaze;
Teaches and trains, rebukes us and inspires us;
Lord of the Word, receive your people's praise.

3
Lord, for our land, in this our generation,
Spirits oppressed by pleasure, wealth and care;
For young and old, for commonwealth and nation,
Lord of our land, be pleased to hear our prayer.

4
Lord, for our world; when we disown and doubt him,
Loveless in strength, and comfortless in pain;
Hungry and helpless, lost indeed without him;
Lord of the world, we pray that Christ may reign.

5
Lord, for ourselves; in living power remake us -
Self on the cross and Christ upon the throne,
Past put behind us, for the future take us,
Lord of our lives, to live for Christ alone.

Timothy Dudley-Smith

137 LORD, THY CHURCH ON EARTH

Music used by permission of Oxford University Press

Abbot's Leigh 87 87 D

CYRIL V. TAYLOR (1907–91)

LORD, thy Church on earth is seeking
thy renewal from above;
teach us all the art of speaking
with the accent of thy love.
We would heed thy great commission:
'Go now into every place—
preach, baptize, fulfil my mission,
serve with love and share my grace'.

2 Freedom give to those in bondage,
lift the burdens caused by sin.
Give new hope, new strength and courage,
grant release from fears within.
Light for darkness; joy for sorrow;
love for hatred; peace for strife:
these and countless blessings follow
as the Spirit gives new life.

3 In the streets of every city
where the bruised and lonely dwell,
let us show the Saviour's pity,
let us of his mercy tell;
to all lands and peoples bringing
all the richness of thy word,
till the world, thy praises singing,
hails thee Christ, Redeemer, Lord.

HUGH SHERLOCK (1905–)

138 LORD, WE COME TO ASK

AR HYD Y NOS 84 84 88 84

1. Lord, we come to ask your heal - ing, teach us of love;
all un-spo - ken shame re-veal - ing, teach us of love.
Take our self - ish thoughts and ac - tions, pet - ty feuds, di - vi - sive fac-tions,
hear us now to you ap-peal-ing, teach us of love.
G C Am D C D7 G
C Am D C D7 G
C E7 Am D7
G C Am D C D7 G

2. Soothe away our pain and sorrow,
hold us in love;
grace we cannot buy or borrow,
hold us in love.
Though we see but dark and danger,
though we spurn both friend and stranger,
though we often dread tomorrow,
hold us in love.

3. When the bread is raised and broken,
fill us with love;
words of consecration spoken,
fill us with love.
As our grateful prayers continue,
make the faith that we have in you
more than just an empty token,
fill us with love.

4. Help us live for one another,
bind us in love;
stranger, neighbour, father, mother –
bind us in love.
All are equal at your table,
through your Spirit make us able
to embrace as sister, brother,
bind us in love.

Text: Jean Holloway
Music: trad. Welsh Melody arr. Colin Hand

139 LOVE IS HIS WORD

CRESSWELL 88 97 and Refrain

Unison 1. Love is his word, love is his way, feast - ing with all,

C G7 F Am G F

fast - ing a - lone, liv - ing and dy - ing, ri - sing a - gain,
G C D7 G Bm

Refrain
love, on - ly love, is his way. Rich - er than gold is the
Am D7 G C

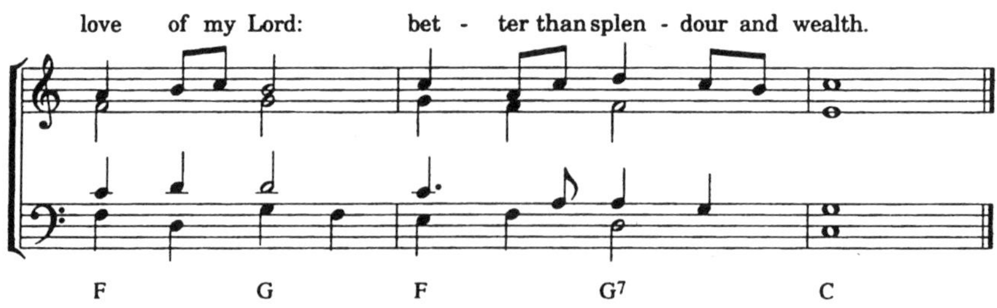

love of my Lord: bet - ter than splen - dour and wealth.
F G F G7 C

2. Love is his way, love is his mark,
   sharing his last Passover feast,
   Christ at the table, host to the twelve,
   love, only love, is his mark.

3. Love is his mark, love is his sign,
   bread for our strength, wine for our joy,
   'This is my body, this is my blood.'
   Love, only love, is his sign.

4. Love is his sign, love is his news,
   'Do this,' he said, 'lest you forget
   all my deep sorrow, all my dear blood.'
   Love, only love, is his news.

5. Love is his news, love is his name,
   we are his own, chosen and called,
   family, brethren, cousins and kin.
   Love, only love, is his name.

6. Love is his name, love is his law,
   hear his command, all who are his,
   'Love one another, I have loved you.'
   Love, only love, is his law.

7. Love is his law, love is his word:
   love of the Lord, Father and Word,
   love of the Spirit, God ever one,
   love, only love, is his word.

Text: Luke Connaughton
Music: Anthony Milner

140 MORNING GLORY

Song 13 7 7.7 7.

Melody and bass by Orlando Gibbons (1583–1625)

1
Morning glory, starlit sky,
Leaves in springtime, swallows' flight,
Autumn gales, tremendous seas,
Sounds and scents of summer night;

2
Soaring music, tow'ring words,
Art's perfection, scholar's truth,
Joy supreme of human love,
Memory's treasure, grace of youth;

3

Open, Lord, are these, Thy gifts,
Gifts of love to mind and sense;
Hidden is love's agony,
Love's endeavour, love's expense.

4

Love that gives gives ever more,
Gives with zeal, with eager hands,
Spares not, keeps not, all outpours,
Ventures all, its all expends.

5

Drained is love in making full;
Bound in setting others free;
Pour in making many rich;
Weak in giving power to be.

6

Therefore He Who Thee reveals
Hangs, O Father, on that Tree
Helpless; and the nails and thorns
Tell of what Thy love must be.

7

Thou are God; no monarch Thou
Thron'd in easy state to reign;
Thou are God, Whose arms of love
Aching, spent, the world sustain.

W. H. Vanstone

141 NOT HERE FOR HIGH AND HOLY THINGS

*1

Not here for high and holy things we render thanks to thee, but for the common things of earth, the purple pageantry of dawning and of dying days, the splendor of the sea,

*2

the royal robes of autumn moors the golden gates of spring, the velvet of soft summer nights, the silver glistering of all the million million stars, the silent song they sing,

*3
of faith and hope and love undimmed, undying still through
death, the resurrection of the world, what
time there comes the breath of dawn that rustles
through the trees, and that clear voice that saith:

4
Awake, awake to love and work! The lark is in the
sky, the fields are wet with diamond dew, the
worlds awake to cry their blessings on the
Lord of life, as he goes meekly by.

5
Come, let thy voice be one with theirs, shout with their shout of
praise; see how the giant sun soars up, great
lord of years and days! So let the love of
Jesus come and set thy soul ablaze,

6
to give and give, and give again, what God hath given
thee; to spend thyself nor count the cost; to
serve right gloriously the God who gave all
worlds that are, and all that are to be.

Words: Geoffrey Anketel Studdert-Kennedy (1883-1929)
Music: Morning Song, melody att. Elkanah Kelsay Dare (1782-1826)

142 NOW IS ETERNAL LIFE

Words used by permission of Oxford University Press

Eastview **66 66 88** J. VERNON LEE (1892–1959)

Now is eternal life,
  if risen with Christ we stand,
in him to life re-born,
  and held within his hand;
no more we fear death's ancient dread,
in Christ arisen from the dead.

2 The human mind so long
  brooded o'er life's brief span;
was it, O God, for naught,
  for naught that life began?
Thou art our hope, our vital breath;
shall hope undying end in death?

3 And God, the living God,
  stooped down to share our state;
by death destroying death
  Christ opened wide life's gate.
He lives, who died; he reigns on high;
who live in him shall never die.

4 Unfathomed love divine,
  reign thou within my heart;
from thee nor depth nor height,
  nor life nor death can part;
my life is hid in God with thee,
now and through all eternity.

5 Thee will I love and serve
  now in time's passing day;
thy hand shall hold me fast
  when time is done away,
in God's unknown eternal spheres
to serve him through eternal years.

G. W. BRIGGS (1875–1959)*

143 NOW LET US FROM THIS TABLE RISE

First Tune

Warrington LM

RALPH HARRISON (1748–1810)

Second Tune

Solothurn LM

Swiss traditional melody
harm. R. VAUGHAN WILLIAMS (1872–1958) altd.

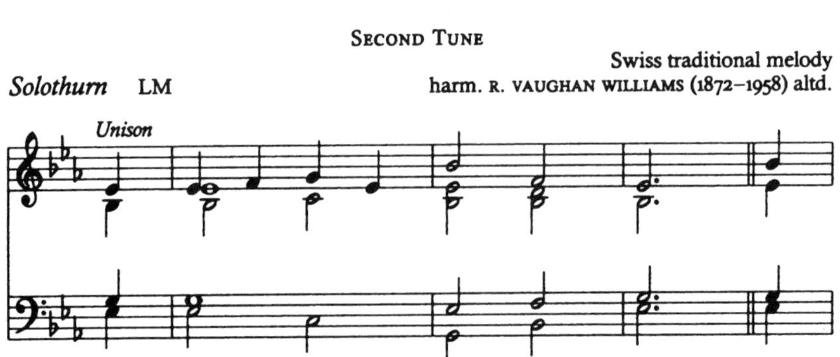
Unison

Music used by permission of Oxford University Press

1
Now let us from this table rise
renewed in body, mind and soul;
with Christ we die and live again,
his selfless love has made us whole.

2
With minds alert, upheld by grace,
to spread the Word in speech and deed,
we follow in the steps of Christ,
at one with all in hope and need.

3
To fill each human house with love,
it is the sacrament of care;
the work that Christ began to do
we humbly pledge ourselves to share.

4
Then grant us courage, Father-God,
to choose again the pilgrim way,
and help us to accept with joy
the challenge of tomorrow's day.

Frederick Herman Kaan

144 NOW THE GREEN BLADE RISES

Words used by permission of Oxford University Press

Noël nouvelet 11 11 10 11

French melody
arr. GEOFFREY LAYCOCK (1927–86)

Now the green blade rises from the buried grain,
wheat that in the dark earth many days has lain;
Love lives again, that with the dead has been:
Love is come again, like wheat that springs up green.

2 In the grave they laid him, Love whom we had slain,
thinking that he never would awake again,
laid in the earth like grain that sleeps unseen:
Love is come again, like wheat that springs up green.

3 Forth he came at Easter, like the risen grain,
he that for the three days in the grave had lain,
quick from the dead my risen Lord is seen:
Love is come again, like wheat that springs up green.

4 When our hearts are wintry, grieving, or in pain,
then your touch can call us back to life again,
fields of our hearts that dead and bare have been:
Love is come again, like wheat that springs up green.

J. M. C. CRUM (1872–1958)

145 O GOD YOUR LOVE'S UNDYING FLAME

Sussex Carol 88 88 88

English traditional melody
harm. R. VAUGHAN WILLIAMS (1872–1958)

Unison
Harmony (ad lib.)
Unison
Harmony (ad lib.)

Music used by permission of Oxford University Press

O GOD, your love's undying flame
  was seen in desert bush ablaze,
when Moses learned your secret name,
  the Lord of past and future days;
Lord, we would learn what you require,
and burn for you with living fire.

2 O Lord of fire, your love a flame
  that longed to set the earth ablaze:
to bring the Kingdom's joy you came
  and freed us, trapped in earth-bound ways;
Lord, we would share your love's desire,
and burn for you with living fire.

3 O Holy Spirit, tongues of flame
  that set the new-born Church ablaze;
to each believer then you came,
  and lives were filled with power and praise;
O Spirit, come, our lives inspire
to burn for you with living fire.

BASIL E. BRIDGE (1927–)*
(Exodus 3: 2, Luke 12: 49, Acts 2: 3)

146 O LORD, WE LONG TO SEE YOUR FACE

Surrey 8 8.8 8.8 8. Henry Carey (c. 1690–1743)

Walking by faith

O Lord, we long to see your face,
to know you risen from the grave,
but we have missed the joy and grace‿
of seeing you, as others have.
  Yet in your company we'll wait,
  and we shall see you, soon or late.

2

O Lord, we do not know the way,
nor clearly see the path ahead;
so often, therefore, we delay
and doubt your power to raise the dead.
  Yet with you we will firmly stay;
  you are the Truth, the Life, the Way.

3

We find it hard, Lord, to believe;
all habit makes us want to prove;
we would with eye and hand perceive‿
the truth and person whom we love.
  Yet, as in fellowship we meet,
  you come yourself each one to greet.

4

You come to us, our God, our Lord;
you do not show your hands and side;
but faith has its more blest reward;
in love's assurance we confide.
  Now we believe, that we may know,
  and in that knowledge daily grow.

J. R. Peacey (1896–1971)

147 O MATCHLESS BEAUTY OF OUR GOD

Melody by CHARLES HUTCHESON (1792–1860)
Stracathro CM harm. ERIC H. THIMAN (1900–75)

O MATCHLESS beauty of our God
so ancient and so new,
kindle in us your fire of love,
fall on us as the dew!

2 How late we came to love you, Lord,
how strong the hold of sin!
Your beauty speaks from all that is,
your likeness pleads within.

3 You called and cried, yet we were deaf;
our stubborn wills you bent;
you shed your fragrance, and we caught
a moment of its scent.

4 You blazed and sparkled, yet our hearts
to lesser glories turned;
your radiance touched us far from home,
your beauty in us burned!

5 And should our faith grow weak and fall,
tried in the wilderness,
let beauty blossom out of ash,
and streams of water bless!

6 O matchless beauty of our God
so ancient and so new,
enfold in us your fire of love,
anoint us with your dew!

COLIN THOMPSON (1945–)
based on ST AUGUSTINE (354–430), *Confessions*

148 PRAY FOR THE CHURCH

Song 1 10 10 10 10 10 10 ORLANDO GIBBONS (1583–1625)

1

Pray for the Church, afflicted and oppressed,
For all who suffer for the gospel's sake,
That Christ may show us how to serve them best
In that one Kingdom Satan cannot shake.
But how much more than us they have to give,
Who by their dying show us how to live.

2

Pray for Christ's dissidents, who daily wait,
As Jesus waited in the olive grove,
The unjust trial, the pre-determined fate,
The world's contempt for reconciling love.
Shall all they won for us, at such a cost,
Be by our negligence or weakness lost?

3

Pray that if times of testing should lay bare
What sort we are, who call ourselves his own,
We may be counted worthy then to wear,
With quiet fortitude, Christ's only crown:
The crown that in his saints he wears again -
The crown of thorns that signifies his reign.

Frederick Pratt Green

149 PUT PEACE INTO EACH OTHER'S HANDS

Ancient Irish hymn melody
St Columba 87 87 (Iambic) harm. ERIC H. THIMAN (1900–75)

PUT peace into each other's hands
  and like a treasure hold it,
protect it like a candle-flame,
  with tenderness enfold it.

2 Put peace into each other's hands
  with loving expectation;
be gentle in your words and ways,
  in touch with God's creation.

3 Put peace into each other's hands
  like bread we break for sharing;
look people warmly in the eye:
  our life is meant for caring.

4 As at communion, shape your hands
  into a waiting cradle;
the gift of Christ receive, revere,
  united round the table.

5 Put Christ into each other's hands,
  he is love's deepest measure;
in love make peace, give peace a chance,
  and share it like a treasure.

FRED KAAN (1929–)

150 SPIRIT OF GOD WITHIN ME

Words © Timothy Dudley-Smith. Used by permission.

Deben 76 86 86 86 GORDON HAWKINS (1911–)

1

Spirit of God within me,
possess my human frame;
fan the dull embers of my heart,
stir up the living flame.
Strive till that image Adam lost,
new minted and restored,
in shining splendour brightly bears
the likeness of the Lord.

2

Spirit of truth within me,
possess my thought and mind;
lighten anew the inward eye
by Satan rendered blind;
shine on the words that wisdom speaks,
and grant me power to see
the truth made known to all in Christ,
and in that truth be free.

3

Spirit of love within me,
possess my hands and heart;
break through the bonds of self-concern
that seeks to stand apart;
grant me the love that suffers long,
that hopes, believes and bears,
the love fulfilled in sacrifice
that cares as Jesus cares.

4

Spirit of life within me,
possess this life of mine;
come as the wind of heaven's breath,
come as the fire divine!
Spirit of Christ, the living Lord,
reign in this house of clay,
till from its dust with Christ I rise
to everlasting day.

Timothy Dudley-Smith

151 TELL OUT MY SOUL

Woodlands 10 10.10 10. Walter Greatorex (1877–1949)

Unison

Magnificat

Tell out, my soul, the greatness of the Lord:
  unnumbered blessings, give my spirit voice;
tender to me the promise of his word;
  in God my Saviour shall my heart rejoice.

2

Tell out, my soul, the greatness of his name:
  make known his might, the deeds his arm has done;
his mercy sure, from age to age the same;
  his holy name, the Lord, the Mighty One.

3

Tell out, my soul, the greatness of his might:
  powers and dominions lay their glory by;
proud hearts and stubborn wills are put to flight,
  the hungry fed, the humble lifted high.

4

Tell out, my soul, the glories of his word:
  firm is his promise, and his mercy sure.
Tell out, my soul, the greatness of the Lord
  to children's children and for evermore.

TIMOTHY DUDLEY-SMITH (b. 1926)
based on Luke I. 46–55
in *The New English Bible*

152 THE KINGDOM IS UPON YOU

Music used by permission of Oxford University Press

Wolvercote 7 6.7 6.D.
W. H. Ferguson (1874–1950)
Unison

1

'The kingdom is upon you!'
  the voice of Jesus cries,
fulfilling with its message
  the wisdom of the wise;
it lightens with fresh insight
  the striving human mind,
creating new dimensions
  of faith for all to find.

2

'God's kingdom is upon you!'
  the message sounds today,
it summons every pilgrim
  to take the questing way,
with eyes intent on Jesus,
  our leader and our friend,
who trod faith's road before us,
  and trod it to the end.

3

The kingdom is upon us!
  Stirred by the Spirit's breath,
we glory in its freedom
  from emptiness and death;
we celebrate its purpose,
  its mission and its goal,
alive with the conviction
  that Christ can make us whole.

Robert Willis (b. 1947)

153 THE LOVE OF GOD COMES CLOSE

Rhosymedre 66 66 888

JOHN DAVID EDWARDS (1805–85)

Words by John L. Bell & Graham Maule. Copyright © 1988 WGRG, Iona Community, 840 Govan Road, Glasgow G51 3UU Scotland; melody "Rhosymedre"

THE love of God comes close
  where stands an open door
to let the stranger in,
  to mingle rich and poor.
The love of God is here to stay;
embracing those who walk his way,
the love of God is here to stay.

2 The peace of God comes close
  to those caught in the storm,
forgoing lives of ease
  to ease the lives forlorn.
The peace of God is here to stay;
embracing those who walk his way,
the peace of God is here to stay.

3 The joy of God comes close
  where faith encounters fears,
where heights and depths of life
  are found through smiles and tears.
The joy of God is here to stay;
embracing those who walk his way,
the joy of God is here to stay.

4 The grace of God comes close
  to those whose grace is spent,
when hearts are tired or sore
  and hope is bruised and bent.
The grace of God is here to stay;
embracing those who walk his way,
the grace of God is here to stay.

5 The Son of God comes close
  where people praise his name,
where bread and wine are blest
  and shared as when he came.
The Son of God is here to stay;
embracing those who walk his way,
the Son of God is here to stay.

JOHN BELL (1949–)
and GRAHAM MAULE (1958–)

154 THE SERVANT

Who would ev - er have be - lieved it?
Who could ev - er have con - ceived it?
Who dared trace God's hand be - hind it
when a ser - vant came a - mong us?

1 Who would ever have believed it?
Who could ever have conceived it?
Who dared trace God's hand behind it
When a servant came among us?

2 Like a sapling in dry soil,
He was rooted in our presence;
Lacking beauty, grace and splendour,
No one felt attracted to him.

3 We despised him, we disowned him,
Though he clearly hurt and suffered:
We, believing he was worthless,
Never turned our eyes towards him.

4 Yet it was the pain and torment
We deserved which he accepted,
While we reckoned his afflictions
Must have come by heaven's instruction.

5 Though our sins let him be wounded,
Though our cruelty left him beaten,
Yet, through how and why he suffered,
God revealed our hope of healing.

6 We, like sheep despite our wisdom,
All had wandered from God's purpose;
And our due in pain and anger
God let fall on one among us.

7 Who would ever have believed it?
Who could ever have conceived it?
Who dared trace God's hand behind it
When a servant came among us?

Isaiah, chapter 53, contains the passage which identified God's 'suffering servant'. These words, here paraphrased, are evocative both of how Christ, at the Last Supper, took the servant's place and of how, at his death, there was little about him which seemed godly.

155 THE SERVANT KING

Unison
1. From heav'n you came, help - less babe,
Capo 3 Am E Fmaj7
en - tered our world, your glo - ry veiled; not to be served but to
G C F C G Am E
serve, and give your life that we might
Fmaj7 G C F C
live. Refrain This is our God, the Ser - vant
G C G

King, he calls us now to fol - low
Am Am7 F G

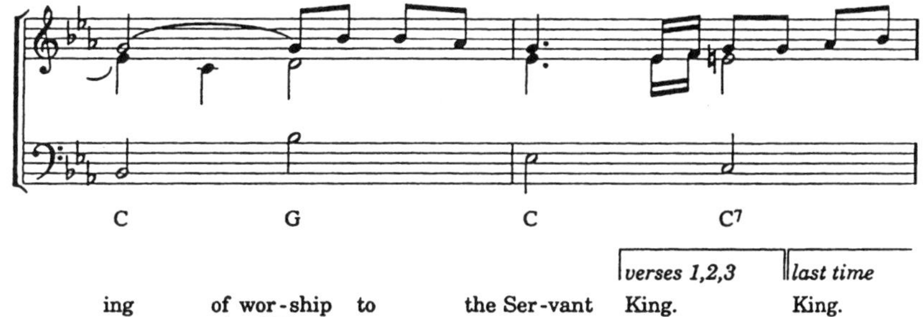
him, to bring our lives as a dai - ly of - fer -
C G C C7

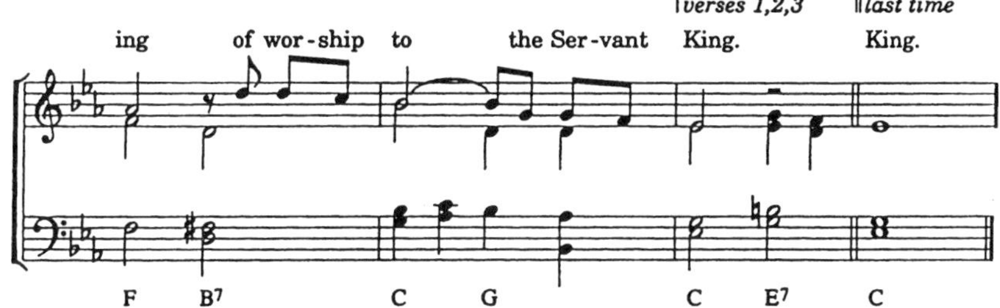
verses 1,2,3
last time
ing of wor-ship to the Ser-vant King. King.
F B7 C G C E7 C

2. There in the garden of tears,
my heavy load he chose to bear;
his heart with sorrow was torn,
'Yet not my will but yours,' he said.

3. Come see his hands and his feet,
the scars that speak of sacrifice,
hands that flung stars into space
to cruel nails surrendered.

4. So let us learn how to serve,
and in our lives enthrone him;
each other's needs to prefer,
for it is Christ we're serving.

Text: Graham Kendrick (b. 1950)
Music: Graham Kendrick (b. 1950) arr. Christopher Tambling (b. 1964)

156 THE SERVANT SONG

1. Bro - ther, sis - ter, let me serve you, let me be as
Capo 1 D G A7 D Bm
Christ to you; pray that I may have the grace to
Em A G D G A7 Bm
let you be my ser - vant, too.
Em G A7 D

2. We are pilgrims on a journey,
fellow trav'llers on the road;
we are here to help each other
walk the mile and bear the load.

3. I will hold the Christlight for you
in the night-time of your fear;
I will hold my hand out to you,
speak the peace you long to hear.

4. I will weep when you are weeping;
when you laugh, I'll laugh with you.
I will share your joy and sorrow
till we've seen this journey through.

5. When we sing to God in heaven,
we shall find such harmony,
born of all we've known together
of Christ's love and agony.

6. Brother, sister, let me serve you,
let me be as Christ to you;
pray that I may have the grace to
let you be my servant, too.

157 THE SPIRIT LIVES TO SET US FREE

WALK IN THE LIGHT 85 85 and Refrain

1. The Spi rit lives to set us free,
G Bm C G
walk, walk in the light. He binds us all in
Am7 D7 G Bm
u - ni - ty, walk, walk in the light.
C G Am7 D7 G
Refrain
Walk in the light, walk
C D

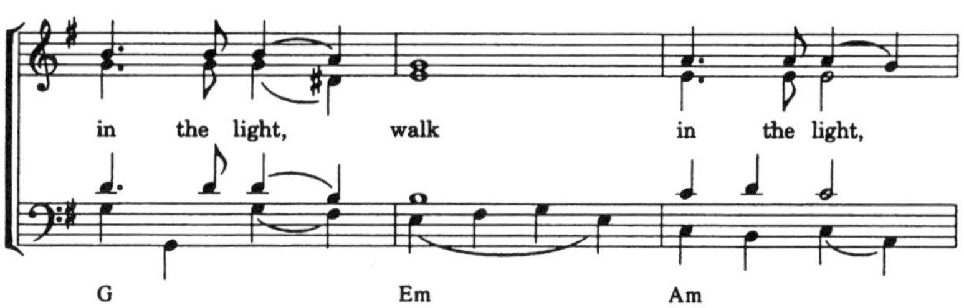
in the light, walk in the light,
G Em Am

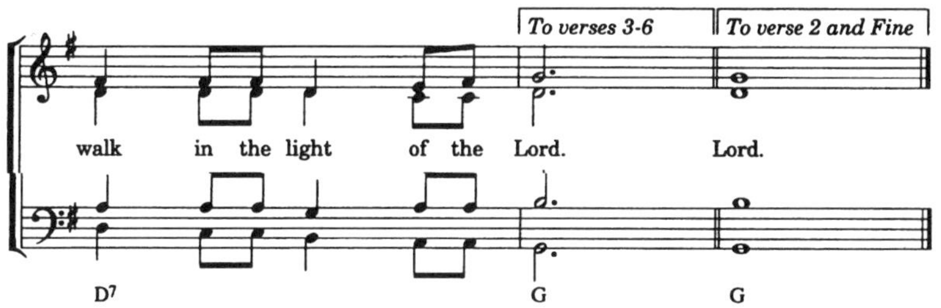
To verses 3-6
To verse 2 and Fine
walk in the light of the Lord. Lord.
D7 G G

2. Jesus promised life to all,
   walk, walk in the light.
   The dead were wakened by his call,
   walk, walk in the light.

3. He died in pain on Calvary,
   walk, walk in the light,
   to save the lost like you and me,
   walk, walk in the light.

4. We know his death was not the end,
   walk, walk in the light.
   He gave his Spirit to be our friend,
   walk, walk in the light.

5. By Jesus' love our wounds are healed,
   walk, walk in the light.
   The Father's kindness is revealed,
   walk, walk in the light.

6. The Spirit lives in you and me,
   walk, walk in the light.
   His light will shine for all to see,
   walk, walk in the light.

Text: Damian Lundy (*b*. 1944)
Music: unknown arr. Christopher Tambling (*b*. 1964)

158 THERE'S A SPIRIT IN THE AIR

Music used by permission of Oxford University Press

Lauds 7 7.7 7.
John Wilson (b. 1905)
Optional descant for verses 4 and 7
Praise the love!
Praise the love!
Al le lu ia!
Al le lu ia!

(*small notes organ only*)

1
There's a spirit in the air,
telling Christians everywhere:
"Praise the love that Christ revealed,
living, working in our world!"

2
Lose your shyness, find your tongue,
tell the world what God has done:
God in Christ has come to stay.
Live tomorrow's life today!

3
When believers break the bread,
when a hungry child is fed,
praise the love that Christ revealed,
living, working, in our world.

4
Still the Spirit gives us light,
seeing wrong and setting right:
God in Christ has come to stay.
Live tomorrow's life today!

5
When a stranger's not alone,
where the homeless find a home,
praise the love that Christ revealed,
living, working, in our world.

6
May the Spirit fill our praise,
guide our thoughts and change or ways.
God in Christ has come to stay.
Live tomorrow's life today!

7
There's a Spirit in the air,
calling people everywhere:
Praise the love that Christ revealed,
living, working, in our world.

Brian Wren

159 THIS DAY GOD GIVES ME

Bunessan **55 54 D** **Gaelic melody**

Unison

THIS day God gives me
  strength of high heaven,
sun and moon shining,
  flame in my hearth;
flashing of lightning,
wind in its swiftness,
deeps of the ocean,
  firmness of earth.

2 This day God sends me
strength to sustain me,
might to uphold me,
  wisdom as guide.
Your eyes are watchful,
your ears are listening,
your lips are speaking,
  Friend at my side.

3 God's way is my way,
God's shield is round me,
God's host defends me,
  saving from ill;
angels of heaven,
drive from me always
all that would harm me,
  stand by me still.

4 Rising, I thank you,
mighty and strong one,
King of creation,
  giver of rest,
firmly confessing
Threeness of Persons,
Oneness of Godhead,
  Trinity blest.

JAMES QUINN (1919–)
based on 'St Patrick's Breastplate'
5th–7th cent. Gaelic

160 WE CANNOT MEASURE HOW YOU HEAL

Tune: YE BANKS AND BRAES (Scottish Trad.)

WE cannot measure how you heal
  or answer every sufferer's prayer,
yet we believe your grace responds
  where faith and doubt unite to care.

2 The pain that will not go away,
  the guilt that clings from things long past,
the fear of what the future holds
  are present as if meant to last.

3 But present too is love which tends
  the hurt we never hoped to find,
the private agonies inside,
  the memories that haunt the mind.

4 Your hands, though bloodied on the cross,
  survive to hold and heal and warn,
to carry all through death to life
  and cradle children yet unborn.

5 So some have come who need your help,
  and some have come to make amends:
your hands which shaped and saved the world
  are present in the touch of friends.

6 Lord, let your Spirit meet us here
  to mend the body, mind and soul,
to disentangle peace from pain
  and make your broken people whole.

JOHN BELL (1949–)
and GRAHAM MAULE (1958–)

161 WE PRAY FOR PEACE

Herstmonceux 4 666 68

EBENEZER PROUT (1835–1909)
adpt. ERIC H. THIMAN (1900–75)

1
We pray for peace,
But not the easy peace,
Built on complacency
And not the truth of God.
We pray for real peace,
The peace God's love alone can seal.

2
We pray for peace,
But not the cruel peace,
Leaving God's poor bereft
And dying in distress,
We pray for real peace,
Enriching all the human race.

3
We pray for peace,
And not the evil peace,
Defending unjust laws
And nursing prejudice,
But for the real peace
Of justice, mercy, truth and love.

4
We pray for peace:
Holy communion
With Christ our risen Lord
And every living thing;
God's will fulfilled on earth
And all creation reconciled.

5
We pray for peace,
And for the sake of peace,
Look to the risen Christ
Who gives the grace we need,
To serve the cause of peace
And make our own self-sacrifice.

6
God, give us peace:
If you withdraw your love,
There is no peace for us
Nor any hope of it.
With you to lead us on,
Through death or tumult, peace will come.

Alan Gaunt

162 WE TURN TO YOU

Intercessor 11 10 11 10 C. H. H. PARRY (1848–1918)

*B♮ in last verse only.

WE turn to you, O God of every nation,
  giver of good and origin of life;
your love is at the heart of all creation,
  your hurt is people's pain in war and death.

2 We turn to you that we may be forgiven
  for crucifying Christ on earth again.
We know that we have never wholly striven
  to share with all the promise of your reign.

3 Free every heart from pride and self-reliance,
  our ways of thought inspire with simple grace;
break down among us barriers of defiance,
  speak to the soul of all the human race.

4 On all who work on earth for right relations
  we pray the light of love from hour to hour.
Grant wisdom to the leaders of the nations,
  the gift of carefulness to those in power.

5 Teach us, good Lord, to serve the need of others,
  help us to give and not to count the cost.
Unite us all to live as sisters, brothers,
  defeat our Babel with your Pentecost!

FRED KAAN (1929–)*

163 WE UTTER OUR CRY

Uppsala 10 10 11 11 PETER CUTTS (1937–)

Unison

Contemporary

1

We utter our cry: that peace may prevail!
That earth will survive and faith must not fail.
We pray with our life for the world in our care,
for people diminished by doubt and despair.

2

We cry from the fright of our daily scene
for strength to say 'No' to all that is mean:
designs bearing chaos, extinction of life,
all energy wasted on weapons of death.

3

We lift up our hearts for children unborn:
give wisdom, O God, that we may hand on,
re-plenished and tended, this good planet earth,
preserving the future and wonder of birth.

4

Creator of life, come, share out, we pray,
your Spirit on earth, revealing the Way
to statesmen conferring 'round tables for peace,
that they may from bias and guile be released.

5

Come with us, Lord-Love, in protest and march,
and help us to fire with passion your church,
to match all our statements and lofty resolve
with being - unresting - in action involved.

6

Whatever the ill or pressure we face,
Lord, hearten and heal, give insight and grace
to think and make peace with each heartbeat and breath,
choose Christ before Caesar and life before death!

Frederick Herman Kaan

164 WHEN I NEEDED A NEIGHBOUR

NEIGHBOUR 13 10 and Refrain
Unison 1. When I need - ed a neigh-bour, were you there, were you there? When I
(B7) Em G B7
need - ed a neigh - bour, were you there? *Refrain* And the
Em D7
creed and the col - our and the name won't mat-ter, were you there?
(last verse) I'll be there.
G G (C) B7 Em

1

When I needed a neighbour were you there, were you there?
When I needed a neighbour were you there?
And the creed and the colour and the name won't matter,
Were you there?

2

I was hungry and thirsty, were you there, were you there?
I was hungry and thirsty, were you there?
Chorus

3

I was cold, I was naked, were you there, were you there?
I was cold, I was naked, were you there?
Chorus

4

When I needed a shelter were you there, were you there?
When I needed a shelter were you there?
Chorus

5

When I needed a healer were you there, were you there?
When I needed a healer were you there?
Chorus

6

Wherever you travel I'll be there, I'll be there,
Wherever you travel I'll be there.
And the creed and the colour and the name won't matter,
I'll be there.

Sydney Bertram Carter

165 WHERE LOVE AND LOVING KINDNESS DWELL

Maisemore C.M. John Dykes Bower (1905–1981)

Serving Christ in one another

Where love and loving-kindness dwell,
  there God will ever be:
One Father, Son, and Holy Ghost
  in perfect charity.

2

Brought here together into one
  by Christ our Shepherd-king,
now let us in his love rejoice,
  and of his goodness sing.

3

Here too let God, the living God,
  both loved and honoured be;
and let us each the other love
  with true sincerity.

4

Brought here together by Christ's love,
  let no ill-will divide,
nor quarrels break the unity
  of those for whom he died.

5

Let envy, jealousy and strife
  and all contention cease,
for in our midst serves Christ the Lord,
  our sacrament of peace.

6

Together may we with the saints
  thy face in glory see,
and ever in thy kingdom feast,
  O Christ our God, with thee.

From the Latin Liturgy of Maundy Thursday
tr. GEOFFREY PRESTON (1936–77)

166 WILL YOU COME AND FOLLOW ME

Kelvingrove 76 76 7776

Scottish traditional melody
arr. compilers

Unison

Will you come and follow me,
  if I but call your name?
Will you go where you don't know
  and never be the same?
Will you let my love be shown,
will you let my name be known,
will you let my life be grown
  in you and you in me?

2 Will you leave your self behind
  if I but call your name?
Will you care for cruel and kind
  and never be the same?
Will you risk the hostile stare
should your life attract or scare,
will you let me answer prayer
  in you and you in me?

3 Will you love the 'you' you hide
  if I but call your name?
Will you quell the fear inside
  and never be the same?
Will you use the faith you've found
to reshape the world around
through my sight and touch and sound
  in you and you in me?

4 Lord, your summons echoes true
  when you but call my name.
Let me turn and follow you
  and never be the same.
In your company I'll go
where your love and footsteps show.
Thus I'll move and live and grow
  in you and you in me.

JOHN BELL (1949–) and
GRAHAM MAULE (1958–)

World Church Songs

167 ALL WHO ARE THIRSTY

PHILIPPINES

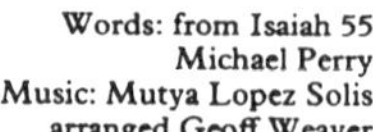
Words: from Isaiah 55
Michael Perry
Music: Mutya Lopez Solis
arranged Geoff Weaver

Steadily ♩ = 92
Dm
A
1 All who are thirs - ty, come to the Lord,
2 Why spend your mon - ey, yet have no bread;
3 Call on God's mer - cy while he is near,
4 Where once were bri - ers, flo-wers will grow,

A7
Dm
all who are hun - gry, feed on his word;
why work for noth - ing? Trust God in-stead!
turn from your e - vil, come with-out fear;
where lives were bar - ren, riv - ers will flow:

D
Gm
buy with-out pay - ing, food with-out price,
He will pro-vide you rich-est of food:
ask him for par - don – grace will a-bound!
praise to our Sav - iour: grace and re-nown –

Typically Filipino in its blend of joy and melancholy, this song speaks of the hope that Filipino Christians, so often hit by suffering and oppression, have in Christ. A guitar accompaniment is very effective here.

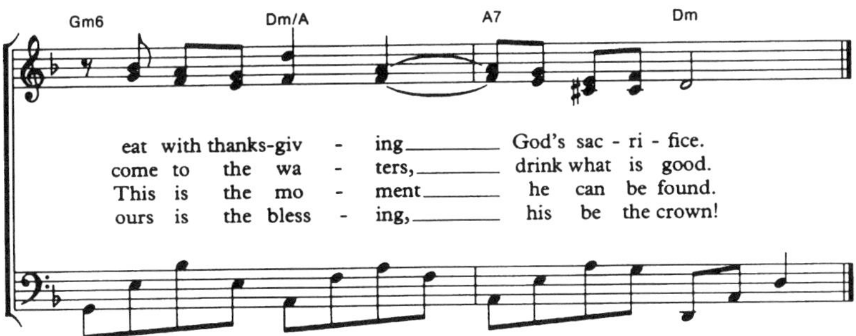
Gm6
Dm/A
A7
Dm
eat with thanks-giv - ing God's sac - ri - fice.
come to the wa - ters, drink what is good.
This is the mo - ment he can be found.
ours is the bless - ing, his be the crown!

1 All who are thirsty, come to the Lord,
all who are hungry, feed on his word;
buy without paying, food without price,
eat with thanksgiving God's sacrifice.

2 Why spend your money, yet have no bread;
why work for nothing? Trust God instead!
He will provide you richest of food:
come to the waters, drink what is good.

3 Call on God's mercy while he is near,
turn from your evil, come without fear;
ask him for pardon – grace will abound!
This is the moment he can be found.

4 Where once were briers, flowers will grow,
where lives were barren, rivers will flow:
praise to our Saviour: grace and renown –
ours is the blessing, his be the crown!

168 AMEN! SIAKUDUMISA

SOUTH AFRICA

Words: unknown
Music: attributed to S. C. Molefe,
as taught by George Mxadana
arranged Dave Dargie

At a steady pace ♩ = 120
Capo 3(D)
F
(D)
C
(A)
LEADER
Ma - si thi!
Sing prai - ses!
Ma - si thi!
Sing prai - ses!
S. A.
A-men, si - a - ku - du - mi - sa!
A-men, we praise your name, O God!
T. B.
DESCANT
A-men, si - a - ku - du - mi - sa!
A-men, we praise your name, O God!
ECHO
A - men, si - a - ku - du - mi - sa!
A - men, we praise your name, O God!
ECHO

This exuberant song of praise was written by S. C. Molefe at a workshop in South Africa. The harmonies are rich and the 'masithi' from the leader is an encouragement to the congregation. It is very effective in procession, either at the start or at the end of a service.

Gm
(Em)
F
(D)
Ma - si thi!
Sing prai-ses!
A-men, si - a - ku - du - mi - sa!
A-men, we praise your name, O God!
A-men, ba-wo.
A-men, a-men.
A-men, ba-wo, A-men.
A-men, a-men, a-men.
A-men,
si - a - ku - du - mi - sa!
we praise your name, O God!
Bb
(G)
F/C
(D)
C7
(A7)
A-men, ba-wo.
A-men, a-men.
A-men, A - men, ba-wo.
A-men, a - men, a-men.

169 BEAR THE WEIGHT OF THE CROSS

Solo
♩= ca. 92
Pa - sa - nin mo ang krus, lan - da - sin ang kal - bar - yo, i - ta -
Bear the weight of the Cross. Cal - va - ry's where we're go - ing, Let us
yo ang ban - ta - yog ng ta - o. Da - ma - hin mo ang hi - rap, a - la -
show we're not al - ways a bur - den. With the thorns on our fore - head we'll en-
min ang li - wa - nag at sa bu - kas ang ba - go'y mas - dan.
count - er a bright - ness and to - mor - row a new sun will rise.
Chorus
Sa ga - bi'y may li - wa - nag, a - la - min ang pag - al - kat sa pag - ba - ngon mag ba -
E - ven dark - ness that gath - ers can be part - ed like cur - tains when we rise, dawn will be
kang li - way - wag. Lu - ba mo'y 'yong pa - hi - rin, ang mat - wid ay ha -
wait - ing for us. E - ven tears will all dry up in a world of the

1.
ma - kan, ga- pi - in la - bat ng ka - a - wag.
right - eous, all our foes will be van - quished at last.
2.
ng ka - a - wag.
van - quished at last.
Descant (to be sung with first two lines in the last repetiton)
Na - larg ma i - ta - ta - yo kung hin - di ma - i - gu - gu - po, lu -
No har - vest can fill the land if we don't de - va - state the weeds, burn
ka - hoy na da - ho'y tu - yo. Ang ap - do ay hin - di pi - pi - gil, sa
old trees with parched leaves and twigs. Though the stones leave our feet with bruis - es we
nik ay hin - di ti - ti - gil, lak - bay tu - ngo sa ka - la - ya - an.
climb up the hill of sor - rows, there we'll un - cru - ci - fy our free - dom.

Words: Aloysius Baes, Philippines; para. Rolando S. Tindo Mark 8:34-
Music: PASANIN; Aloysius and Jonas Baes, Philippines II Timothy

170 BY THE BABYLONIAN RIVERS

Used by permission of Hope Publishing Co., Carol Stream, IL 60188 USA

LATVIA

Words: from Psalm 137
Ewald Bash
Music: Latvian melody
arranged Geoff Weaver

With expression ♩ = 80
Capo 3(D) Dm (Bm) Dm7 (Bm7) G7 (E7)
1 By the Ba - by - lon - ian ri - vers we sat
2 There our cap - tors, in de - ri - sion, did re -
3 How__ shall we sing the Lord's song in a
4 Let your cross be be - ne - dic - tion for all

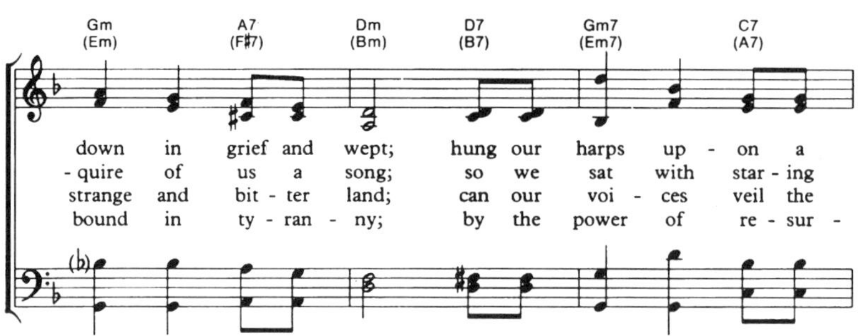
Gm (Em) A7 (F♯7) Dm (Bm) D7 (B7) Gm7 (Em7) C7 (A7)
down in grief and wept; hung our harps up - on a
- quire of us a song; so we sat with star - ing
strange and bit - ter land; can our voi - ces veil the
bound in ty - ran - ny; by the power of re - sur -

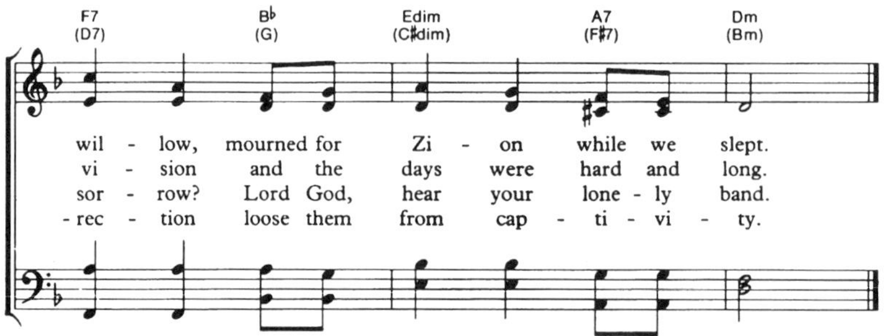
F7 (D7) B♭ (G) Edim (C♯dim) A7 (F♯7) Dm (Bm)
wil - low, mourned for Zi - on while we slept.
vi - sion and the days were hard and long.
sor - row? Lord God, hear your lone - ly band.
- rec - tion loose them from cap - ti - vi - ty.

This melancholy Latvian folk melody reflects beautifully the desolation of the exiles. This is very effective when sung unaccompanied or with simple guitar accompaniment.

171 BY THE WATERS OF BABYLON

Used by permission of Hope Publishing Co., Carol Steam, IL 60188 USA

ISRAEL

Words: from Psalm 137
Music: Israeli folk melody
arranged Geoff Weaver

Flowing ♩ = 112

①
Bm
A
G
F♯
Bm
• By ___ the wa - ters, the wa - ters of Ba - by - lon,

②
A
G
F♯
Bm
we sat down and wept, and wept_ for you, Zi - on;

③
A
G
F♯
Bm
we re-mem-ber, we re-mem-ber, we re-mem-ber you, Zi-on.

The source of this very effective canon is uncertain. As with all canons, ensure that it is well known before dividing the congregation.

172 CANCAO DA CHEGADA

E♭ B♭ E♭ A♭ E♭
1.Es - ta - mos a - qui, Se - nhor. Vi - e - mos de to - do lu -
A♭ B♭
gar tra - zen-do um pou - co do que so - mos pra
E♭ B♭ E♭ E♭
nos - sa fi par - ti - lhar, tra - zen - do o nos - so lou -
A♭ B♭ E♭
vor, um can - to de a - le - gri - a, tra -
Cm Fm B♭ E♭
zen-do a nos-sa von - ta - de de ver rai - ar um no - vo di - a.

Cancao da chegada

1. Estamos aqui, Senhor./ Viemos de todo lugar/ trazendo um pouco do que somos/ pra nossa fi partilhar,/ trazendo o nosso louvor,/ um canto de alegria,/ trazendo a nossa vontade/ de ver raiar um novo dia.

2. Estamos aqui, Senhor,/ cercando esta mesa comum,/ trazendo idiias diferentes,/ mas em Cristo somos um./ E quando sairmos daqui/ nss vamos para voltar,/ na forga da esperanga/ e na coragem de lutar.

173 CANTAI AO SENHOR

BRAZIL

Words: anonymous
translated Gerhard Cartford
Music: Brazilian folksong
arranged Christopher Norton

Brightly ♩. = 70

Am Em/B B7 Em
1 Can -
1 O

Em B7
- tai ao Sen - hor um cân - ti - co no - vo, can -
(2) - que el - e fez, el - e faz mar - avil - has, por -
sing to the Lord, O sing God a new song, O
(2) God is the Lord and God has done won - ders, for

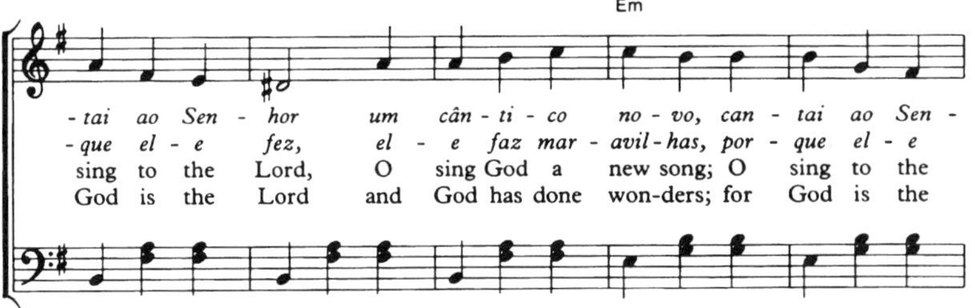
Em
- tai ao Sen - hor um cân - ti - co no - vo, can - tai ao Sen -
- que el - e fez, el - e faz mar - avil - has, por - que el - e
sing to the Lord, O sing God a new song; O sing to the
God is the Lord and God has done won-ders; for God is the

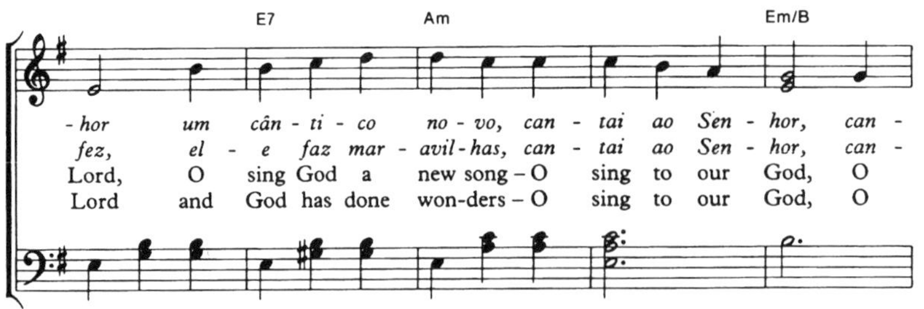
E7 Am Em/B
- hor um cân - ti - co no - vo, can - tai ao Sen - hor, can -
fez, el - e faz mar - avil - has, can - tai ao Sen - hor, can -
Lord, O sing God a new song – O sing to our God, O
Lord and God has done won-ders – O sing to our God, O

A lively Brazilian worship song that can be enhanced by a range of percussive sounds and joyful dancing.

B7
1–4.
Em
5.
Em
- tai ao Sen - hor!
2 Por -
- or!
- tai ao Sen - hor!
3 Can -
sing to our God!
2 For
God.
sing to our God!
3 So

1 *Cantai ao Senhor um cântico novo,*
cantai ao Senhor um cântico novo,
cantai ao Senhor um cântico novo,
cantai ao Senhor, cantai ao Senhor!

2 *Porque ele fez, ele faz maravilhas,*
porque ele fez, ele faz maravilhas,
porque ele fez, ele faz maravilhas,
cantai ao Senhor, cantai ao Senhor!

3 *Cantai ao Senhor, bendizei o seu nome,*
cantai ao Senhor, bendizei o seu nome,
cantai ao Senhor, bendizei o seu nome,
cantai ao Senhor, cantai ao Senhor!

4 *É ele quem dá o Espíritu Santo,*
é ele quem dá o Espíritu Santo,
é ele quem dá o Espíritu Santo,
cantai ao Senhor, cantai ao Senhor!

5 *Jesus é o Senhor! Amén, aleluia!*
Jesus é o Senhor! Amén, aleluia!
Jesus é o Senhor! Amén, aleluia!
cantai ao Senhor, cantai ao Senhor!

1 O sing to the Lord, O sing God a new song,
O sing to the Lord, O sing God a new song;
O sing to the Lord, O sing God a new song –
O sing to our God, O sing to our God!

2 For God is the Lord and God has done wonders,
for God is the Lord and God has done wonders;
for God is the Lord and God has done wonders –
O sing to our God, O sing to our God!

3 So dance for our God and blow all the trumpets,
so dance for our God and blow all the trumpets;
so dance for our God and blow all the trumpets –
O sing to our God, O sing to our God!

4 O shout to our God, who gave us the Spirit,
O shout to our God, who gave us the Spirit;
O shout to our God, who gave us the Spirit –
O sing to our God, O sing to our God!

5 For Jesus is Lord, Amen! Alleluia!
For Jesus is Lord, Amen! Alleluia!
For Jesus is Lord, Amen! Alleluia!
O sing to our God, O sing to our God!

174 CHRIST IS ALL TO ME

Used by permission of Hope Publishing Co., Carol Stream, IL 60188 USA

INDIA

Words: after Y. Gnanamani
D. T. Niles
Music: Tamil melody
arranged Geoff Weaver

Expressively ♩ = 104

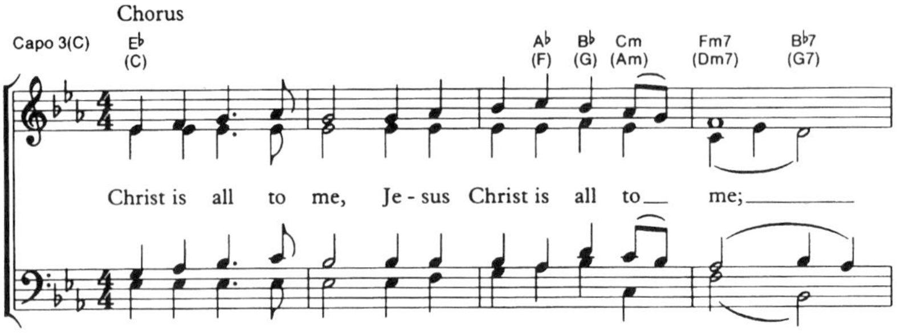

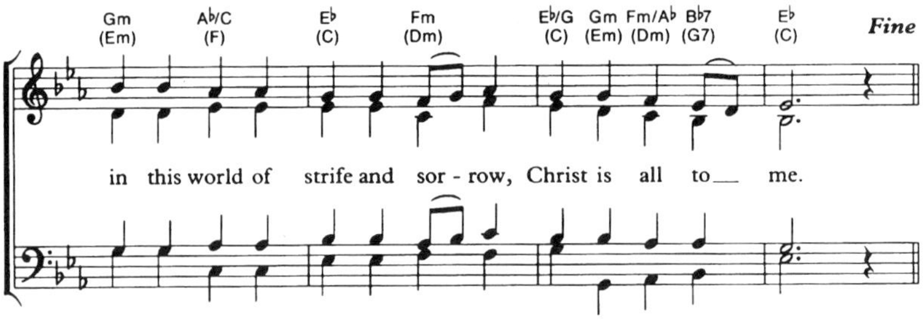

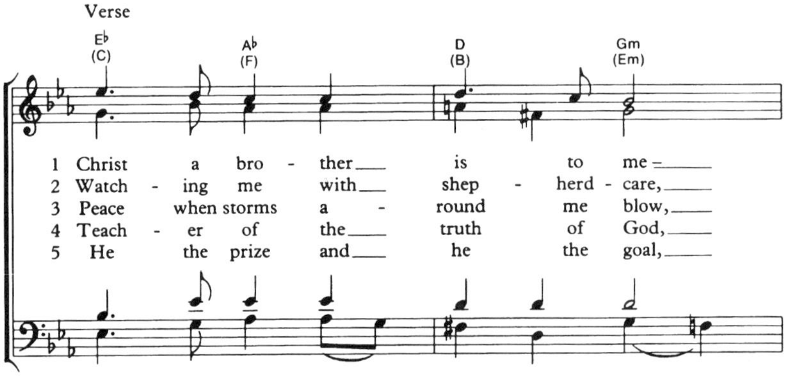

Chorus

Capo 3(C)

Christ is all to me, Je - sus Christ is all to__ me;______
in this world of strife and sor - row, Christ is all to__ me. *Fine*

Verse

1 Christ a bro - ther__ is to me -____
2 Watch - ing me with__ shep - herd - care,____
3 Peace when storms a - round me blow,____
4 Teach - er of the__ truth of God,____
5 He the prize and__ he the goal,____

The great Sri Lankan Christian leader, D. T. Niles, based this hymn of commitment and trust in Christ upon a Tamil text, and appropriately set it to a Tamil melody.

C/E (A) Fm (Dm) Fm7/E♭ B♭/D (G) Fm (D) B♭ (G) E♭/G (C) A♭ (F) Fm6 (Dm)
bride - groom he, the Church his bride; pa - rent, teach - er,
lov - ing - ly my needs at - tends, my com - pan - ion
joy in sor - row, calm in strife; health in sick - ness,
pro - phet of God's heaven - ly reign; sent by God that
and by him the race be - gun; he the run - ner
Cm (Am) Fm (Dm) Fm7/A♭ B♭6 (G) B♭7 E♭ (C) D.C.
mas - ter, sav - iour, and to each a friend and guide.
all the way till even - ing falls and jour - ney ends.
wealth in want, the noon - day sun, the light of life.
we may find in serv - ing him e - ter - nal gain.
of the team who will com-plete the race I run.

Christ is all to me,
Jesus Christ is all to me;
in this world of strife and sorrow,
Christ is all to me.

1 Christ a brother is to me –
bridegroom he, the Church his bride;
parent, teacher, master, saviour,
and to each a friend and guide.
Christ is all to me . . .

2 Watching me with shepherd-care,
lovingly my needs attends,
my companion all the way
till evening falls and journey ends.
Christ is all to me . . .

3 Peace when storms around me blow,
joy in sorrow, calm in strife;
health in sickness, wealth in want,
the noonday sun, the light of life.
Christ is all to me . . .

4 Teacher of the truth of God,
prophet of God's heavenly reign;
sent by God that we may find
in serving him eternal gain.
Christ is all to me . . .

5 He the prize and he the goal,
and by him the race begun;
he the runner of the team
who will complete the race I run.
Christ is all to me . . .

175 COME NOW O PRINCE OF PEACE

KOREA

Words: Geonyong Lee;
paraphrased by Marion Pope; altered
Music: Geonyong Lee

Steadily ♩ = 104

Capo 3(Em)
Gm (Em)
Gm7/F
E♭ (C)
Am/D (F♯m)
D(no 3rd) B(no 3rd)
1 Come now, O___ Prince of peace, make us one__ bo - dy,
2 Come now, O___ God of love, make us one__ bo - dy,
3 Come now and__ set us free, O God, our__ Sav - iour,
4 Come, Hope of___ u - ni - ty, make us one__ bo - dy,

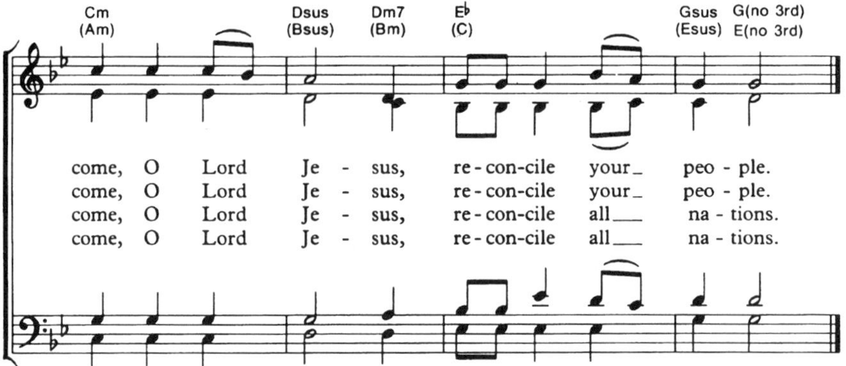

Cm (Am)
Dsus (Bsus)
Dm7 (Bm)
E♭ (C)
Gsus (Esus)
G(no 3rd) E(no 3rd)
come, O Lord Je - sus, re-con-cile your_ peo - ple.
come, O Lord Je - sus, re-con-cile your_ peo - ple.
come, O Lord Je - sus, re-con-cile all___ na - tions.
come, O Lord Je - sus, re-con-cile all___ na - tions.

For most Korean Christians reunification of North and South Korea is their priority, and their urgent prayer. Geonyong Lee, one of the leading contemporary composers in Korea, has long identified himself with this struggle. Note how the dissonant harmonies paint the discord within the nation. This is very effective when sung unaccompanied.

1 Come now, O Prince of peace,
make us one body,
come, O Lord Jesus,
reconcile your people.

2 Come now, O God of love,
make us one body,
come, O Lord Jesus,
reconcile your people.

3 Come now and set us free,
O God, our Saviour,
come, O Lord Jesus,
reconcile all nations.

4 Come, Hope of unity,
make us one body,
come, O Lord Jesus,
reconcile all nations.

176 DI AKO KARAPAT-DAPAT

D G D Bm A
1. Di a - ko ka - ra - pat - da - pat na sa I - yo'y tu - mang - gap,
2. Ang ling - kod mo'y di man da - pat na sa I - yo'y tu - mang - gap,

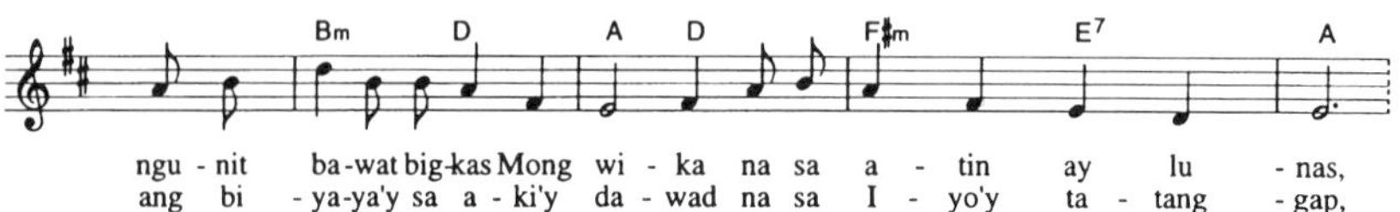
Bm D A D F♯m E7 A
ngu - nit ba - wat big - kas Mong wi - ka na sa a - tin ay lu - nas,
ang bi - ya - ya'y sa a - ki'y da - wad na sa I - yo'y ta - tang - gap,

D G Bm Em D A7 D
ngu - nit ba-wat big-kas Mong wi - ka na sa a - tin ay lu - nas.
ang bi - ya-ya'y sa a - ki'y ga - wad na sa I - yo'y ta - tang - gap.

3 O Hesus ako'y di dapat, O Hesus naming mahal,
ngunit sa Isa Mong wika, kalul'wa ko ay ligtas,
ngunit sa Isa Mong wika, kalul'wa ko ay ligtas.

177 EL CIELO CANTA ALEGRIA

ARGENTINA

Words and music: Pablo D. Sosa
arranged Geoff Weaver

With joy and movement ♩ = 112
Dm
B♭
C
F
1 El cie-lo can-ta a-le - grí - a, ¡A - le - lu - ya!
2 El cie-lo can-ta a-le - grí - a, ¡A - le - lu - ya!
1 Hea-ven is sing-ing for joy. Al - le - lu - ia!
2 Hea-ven is sing-ing for joy. Al - le - lu - ia!
Dm
B♭
A7
Dm
por-que en tu vi-da y la mi - a bri - lla la glo - ria de Dios.
por-que a tu vi-da y la mí - a las une el a - mor de Dios.
For in your life and mine is shin-ing the glo - ry of God.
For your life and mine are one in the love of God.
C7
F
C7
F
¡A - le - lu - ya, a - le - lu - ya,
Al - le - lu - ia, al - le - lu - ia,

Pablo Sosa is one of the most prolific of Argentinian hymn and songwriters, and this joyful dance song should be sung with rhythm and with abandon! A percussion accompaniment helps to highlight its dance-like character.

C7
F
Gm
A7
Dm
a - le - lu - ya, a - le - lu - ya!
al - le - lu - ia, al - le - lu - ia!

1 El cielo canta alegría, ¡Aleluya!
porque en tu vida y la mía brilla la gloria de Dios.
¡Aleluya, aleluya, aleluya, aleluya!

2 El cielo canta alegría, ¡Aleluya!
porque a tu vida y la mía las une el amor de Dios.
¡Aleluya, aleluya, aleluya, aleluya!

3 El cielo canta alegría, ¡Aleluya!
porque a tu vida y la mía proclamarán al Señor.
¡Aleluya, aleluya, aleluya, aleluya!

1 Heaven is singing for joy. Alleluia!
For in your life and mine is shining the glory of God.
Alleluia, alleluia, alleluia, alleluia!

2 Heaven is singing for joy. Alleluia!
For your life and mine are one in the love of God.
Alleluia, alleluia, alleluia, alleluia!

3 Heaven is singing for joy. Alleluia!
For your life and mine will always proclaim the Lord.
Alleluia, alleluia, alleluia, alleluia!

178 FATHER IN HEAVEN

PHILIPPINES

HALAD

Words: D. T. Niles
Music: Elena G. Maquiso
arranged Geoff Weaver

Unhurried ♩ = 88
Em
1 Fa-ther in hea - ven, grant to your child - ren mer - cy and
(2) - deem - er, may we re - mem - ber your gra-cious
(3) - cend - ing, whose is the bless - ing, strength for the
F♯m7
B7
Em
E7
bless - ing, songs ne - ver ceas - ing; love to u -
pas - sion, your re - sur - rec - tion: wor - ship we
wea - ry, help for the nee - dy: seal - ing Christ's
Am
Em
- nite us, grace to re - deem us, Fa - ther in
bring you, praise we shall sing you, Je - sus re -
Lord - ship, bless - ing our wor - ship, Spi - rit des -
B7
1.2.
Em
3.
Em
hea - ven, Fa-ther, our God. 2 Je - sus re -
- deem - er, Je - sus, our Lord. 3 Spi - rit des -
- cend - ing, Spi - rit a - - dored.

A beautiful hymn to the Trinity based on a Filipino folk song.
The words are by D. T. Niles, the great Sri Lankan Christian leader.

179 HALLE, HALLE, HALLELUJAH

Used by permission of Hope Publishing Co., Carol Stream, IL 60188 USA

CARIBBEAN

Words: traditional
Music: unknown
arranged Geoff Weaver

Lively ♩ = 112
G G D/F♯ Em
Hal - le, hal - le, hal - le - lu - jah!
C Am D
Hal - le, hal - le, hal - le - lu - jah!
hal - le - lu - jah
G D/F♯ Em
Hal - le, hal - le, hal - le - lu - jah! Hal - le -
Am7 G/D D7
to repeat
G C G/B Am7
last time
G
- lu - jah, hal - le - lu - jah! - jah!
hal - le - lu - jah

A song from the Caribbean, where many people are uninhibited in expressing their worship.

180 HE CAME DOWN

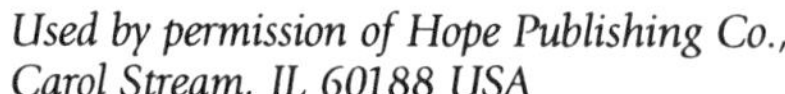
Used by permission of Hope Publishing Co., Carol Stream, IL 60188 USA

CAMEROON

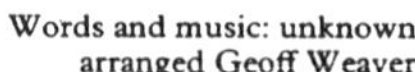
Words and music: unknown
arranged Geoff Weaver

Brightly 𝅗𝅥 = 60

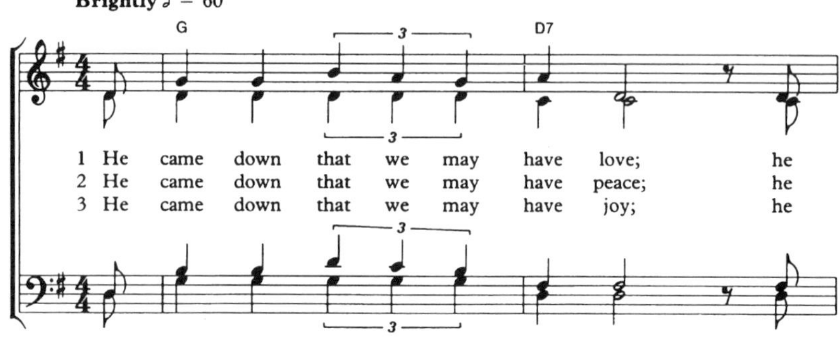
G
D7
1 He came down that we may have love; he
2 He came down that we may have peace; he
3 He came down that we may have joy; he

G
G7
came down that we may have love; he came down that we may
came down that we may have peace; he came down that we may
came down that we may have joy; he came down that we may

C
Cm/A
G/D
D7
G
3
have love;
have peace; hal - le - lu - jah for ev - er - more.
have joy;
(LEADER Why did he come?)

4 He came down that we may have power . . .

5 He came down that we may have hope . . .

A traditional Cameroonian song, which is often performed as a circle dance with sweeping movements to suggest Christ's coming down. The leader calls and encourages the congregation to respond.

181 HE CAME SINGING LOVE

Aotearoa New Zealand

Colin Gibson

Tune: SINGING LOVE
Colin Gibson

E♭ E♭/D Cm
He came sing-ing love and he lived sing - ing love; he
E♭/G A♭ 3 E♭ B♭/D Cm
died sing _ -ing love. He a - rose in
Gm E♭ A♭ B♭7
si - lence. For the love to go on we must
Gm Cm A♭ B♭7 E♭ A♭ E♭
make it our song; you and I be the sing-ers.

1. He came singing love
And he lived singing love;
He died singing love.
He arose in silence.
For the love to go on
We must make it our song:
You and I be the singers.

2. He came singing faith
And he lived singing faith;
He died singing faith.
He arose in silence.
For the faith to go on
We must make it our song:
You and I be the singers.

3. He came singing hope
And he lived singing hope;
He died singing hope.
He arose in silence.
For the hope to go on
We must make it our song:
You and I be the singers.

4. He came singing peace
And he lived singing peace;
He died singing peace.
He arose in silence.
For the peace to go on
We must make it our song:
You and I be the singers.

182 HUMBLY IN YOUR SIGHT

MALAWI

Words and music: Tom Colvin
arranged Geoff Weaver

Easy movement ♩ = 96
Capo 3(D) F (D) C/E (A) F (D) C (A) Dm (Bm) Gm (Em) C (A)
1 Hum - bly in your sight we come to - ge - ther, Lord:
2 These our hearts are yours– we give them to you, Lord:
3 These our ears are yours, we give them to you, Lord:
4 These our eyes are yours, we give them to you, Lord:

F (D) C (A) Dm (Bm) Gm/B♭ (Em) C6 (A) C7 F (D)
grant us now the bless - ing of your pre - sence here.
pu - ri - fy our love to make it like your own.
o - pen them to hear the gos - pel straight from you.
may we al - ways see this world as with your sight.

Alternative setting for verses 3 and 7.
Sopranos sing the words, lower voices hum

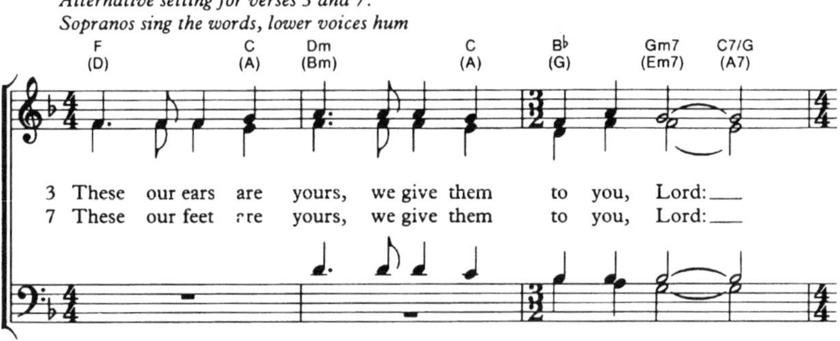

F (D) C (A) Dm (Bm) C (A) B♭ (G) Gm7 (Em7) C7/G (A7)
3 These our ears are yours, we give them to you, Lord:
7 These our feet are yours, we give them to you, Lord:

A simple Malawian folk song with straightforward harmonies, effective when sung as people gather for worship

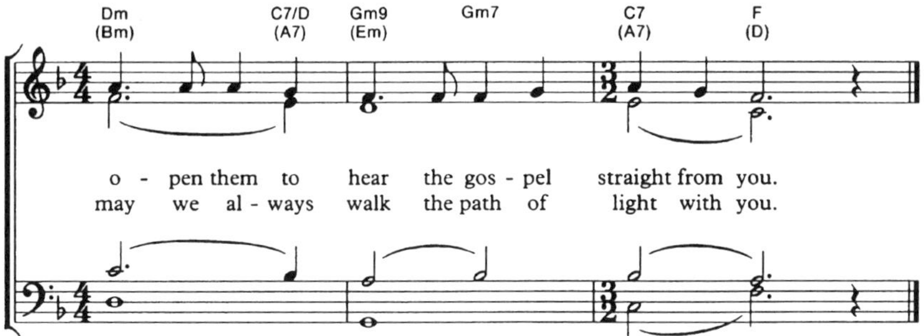
Dm
(Bm)
C7/D
(A7)
Gm9
(Em)
Gm7
C7
(A7)
F
(D)
o - pen them to hear the gos - pel straight from you.
may we al - ways walk the path of light with you.

1 Humbly in your sight we come together, Lord:
grant us now the blessing of your presence here.

2 These our hearts are yours – we give them to you, Lord:
purify our love to make it like your own.

3 These our ears are yours, we give them to you, Lord:
open them to hear the gospel straight from you.

4 These our eyes are yours, we give them to you, Lord:
may we always see this world as with your sight.

5 These our hands are yours, we give them to you, Lord:
give them strength and skill to work and build for you.

6 These our tongues are yours, we give them to you, Lord:
may we speak your healing words of light and truth.

7 These our feet are yours, we give them to you, Lord:
may we always walk the path of light with you.

8 Our whole selves are yours, we give them to you, Lord:
take us now and keep us safe for evermore.

183 IN SILENT STILLNESS

Used by permission of Hope Publishing Co., Carol Stream, IL 60188 USA

PAKISTAN

Words: from Psalm 62
translated from the Punjabi
by Alison Blenkinsop
Music: unknown
arranged Geoff Weaver

Confidently ♩. = 68

Chorus
Capo 3(Em)
Gm (Em) F/G (D) Gm (Em) F/G (D) Cm (Am) D (B)
In si - lent still-ness, wait for God and rest, my soul, in peace: in

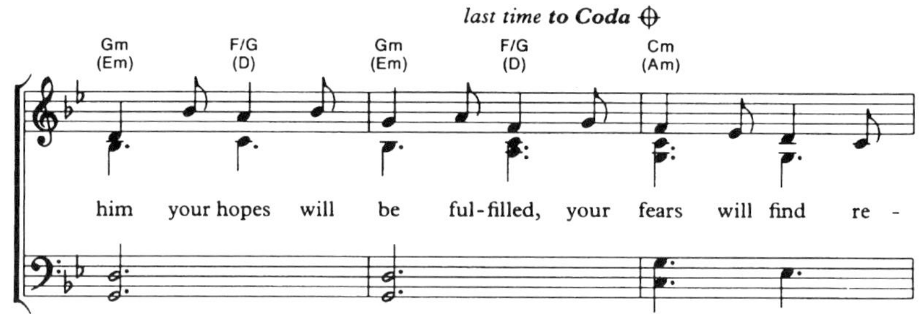

last time to **Coda**
Gm (Em) F/G (D) Gm (Em) F/G (D) Cm (Am)
him your hopes will be ful-filled, your fears will find re -

Verse
D (B) Gm (Em) F/G (D) Gm (Em) Dm (Bm)
1 He is the for-tress of my soul, he is the for-tress
- lease. 2 He is my strong de - liv - er - er, he is my strong de -
3 Let all the na-tions trust in him, let all the na-tions

This expressive Punjabi setting of words from Psalm 62 is sung by Pakistani Christians who are a very small minority in an Islamic state. Although in the minor key, it should be sung with rhythm and conviction. When changing from 6/8 to 3/4, the speed of the dotted crotchet is equal to the crotchet of the new pattern.

Gm
(Em)
B♭
(G)
Cm
(Am)
Gm
(Em)
of my soul – my Rock, my hid - ing - place, my
- liv - er - er – I'm safe with - in his hand, I'm
trust in him and bow be - fore his throne, and
Cm
(Am)
F
(D)
B♭
(G)
Rock, my hid - ing - place; so I shall not be o - ver-come, de -
safe with-in his hand, the Lord is my de-fend-er and the
bow be-fore his throne, and wor-ship him with hum-ble hearts – for
Cm
(Am)
D
(B)
Gm
(Em)
- feat I'll ne - ver face, so I shall not be o - ver-come, de -
rock on which I stand, the Lord is my de-fend-er and the
he is God a - lone, and wor-ship him with hum-ble hearts – for
Cm
(Am)
D
(B)
- feat I'll ne-ver face!
rock on which I stand. In
he is God a-lone.
CODA
Cm
(Am)
Gm
(Em)
fears will find re-lease.

184 ISA MASIH

PAKISTAN

Words: translated from the original
by Alison Blenkinsop
Music: unknown

Unhurried ♩. = 48
I - sa ma - sih ma la - ta - vi ma da gu - nah na tcha
la - sa - vi.
Chorus
Je - sus the Lord is seek - ing me,
and from my sin he will set me free.
Fine
Verse
1 Who is the one who
2 Why does he care so
3 This is the rea - son –
looks_ for me, who is the one who is call - ing me?
much_ for me, why is he call - ing so pa - tient - ly?
Je - sus loves me, com-forts and heart-ens and strength - ens me.
D.S.

4 How can he give such comfort to me –
there is such weakness and sin in me.
Jesus the Lord . . .

5 He gave his life in sacrifice
and for my sin he has paid the price.
Jesus the Lord . . .

6 I am so glad he set me free –
I'll live with God for eternity.
Jesus the Lord . . .

This haunting song comes from the North-West Frontier province of Pakistan, and is best sung unaccompanied. Christians in Pakistan are in a small minority. It is good that we remember them and identify with them as we sing this song.

185 JEHOVAH THOU HAST PROMISED

Ceylon
Arr. Surya Sena, 1950
Je - ho - vah, Thou hast promised The lands shall wait for Thee;
The lands by ev - ery o - cean, The is - lands of the sea;
Lo! we, our peo - ples' watch - men, Would give and take no rest,
For thus hast Thou com - man - ded, Till our dear lands be blessed.
For thus hast Thou com - man - ded, Till our dear lands be blessed.

Courtesy of Christian Conference of Asia

1. Jehovah, Thou hast promised
 The lands shall wait for Thee;
The lands by every ocean,
 The islands of the sea;
Lo! we, our peoples' watchmen,
 Would give and take no rest,
For thus hast Thou commanded,
 Till our dear lands be blessed.

2. Then bless them, mighty Father,
 With blessings needed most,
In every verdant village,
 By every palmy coast;
On every soaring mountain,
 O'er every spreading plain,
May all Thy sons and daughters
 Thy righteousness attain.

3. Give peace between their borders,
 'Twixt man and man goodwill,
The love all unsuspicious,
 The love that works no ill;
In loyal, lowly service
 Let each from other learn,
The guardian and the guarded,
 Till Christ Himself return.

4. To Him our lands shall listen,
 To Him our peoples kneel,
All rule be on His shoulder,
 All wrong beneath His heel;
O consummation glorious
 Which now by faith we sing!
Come, cast we up the highway
 That brings us back the King.

W. S. Senior

(adapted for general use from his "Song of Lanka")

186 JESU, JESU FILL US WITH YOUR LOVE

Used by permission of Hope Publishing Co., Carol Stream, IL 60188 USA

GHANA

Words: Tom Colvin
Music: Ghanaian melody
arranged Geoff Weaver

With a gentle lilt ♩. = 63
Chorus PARTS
Capo 1(E) F (E)
Am (G♯m)
Gm (F♯m)
Je - su, Je - su, fill us with your love; show
Je - su, Je - su

Gm/C
F (E)
Dm7 (C♯m)
Gm (F♯m)
C7 (B7)
F (E)
Fine
us how to serve the neigh-bours we have from you.

UNISON
Dm7 (C♯m7)
Gm (F♯m)
C7 (B7)
1 Kneels at the feet of his friends, si - lent - ly wash - es their
2 Neigh-bours are rich folk and poor; neigh-bours are black, brown and
3 These are the ones we should serve, these are the ones we should
4 Lov - ing puts us on our knees, serv - ing as though we were

One of the many hymns from Ghana originally collected by Tom Colvin. This 'song of service' has been included in many modern hymn books in recent years.
Suggested drum pattern:

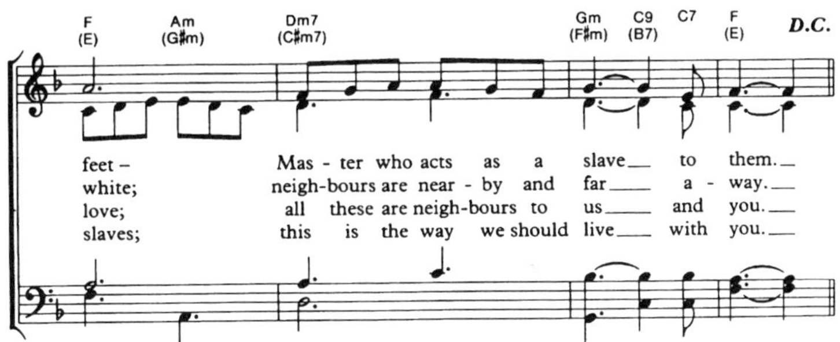
F (E)
Am (G#m)
Dm7 (C#m7)
Gm (F#m)
C9 (B7)
C7
F (E)
D.C.
feet – Mas - ter who acts as a slave to them.
white; neigh-bours are near - by and far a - way.
love; all these are neigh-bours to us and you.
slaves; this is the way we should live with you.

Jesu, Jesu, fill us with your love;
show us how to serve the neighbours we have from you.

1 Kneels at the feet of his friends,
silently washes their feet –
Master who acts as a slave to them.
Jesu, Jesu . . .

2 Neighbours are rich folk and poor;
neighbours are black, brown and white;
neighbours are nearby and far away.
Jesu, Jesu . . .

3 These are the ones we should serve,
these are the ones we should love;
all these are neighbours to us and you.
Jesu, Jesu . . .

4 Loving puts us on our knees,
serving as though we were slaves;
this is the way we should live with you.
Jesu, Jesu . . .

187 JESU TAWA PANO

ZIMBABWE

Words and music: Patrick Matsikenyiri

With expression ♩ = 100

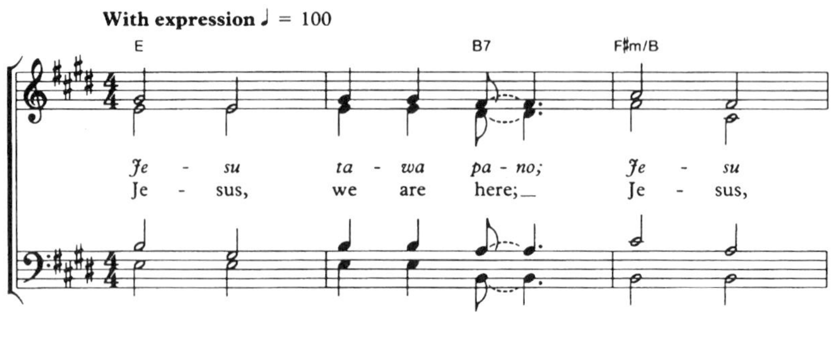

E
B7
F♯m/B
Je - su ta - wa pa - no; Je - su
Je - sus, we are here; Je - sus,

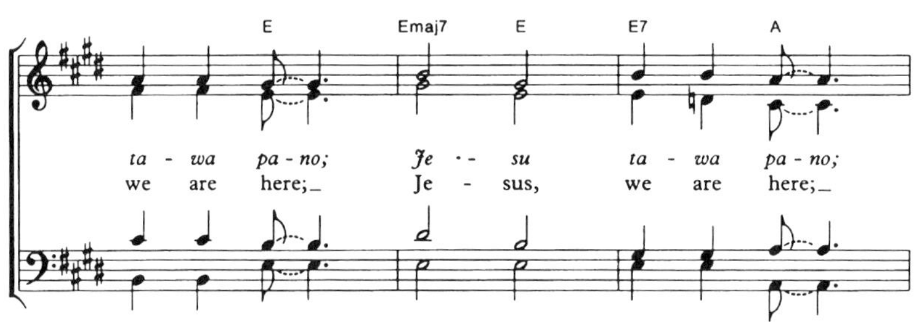

E
Emaj7
E
E7
A
ta - wa pa - no; Je - su ta - wa pa - no;
we are here; Je - sus, we are here;

A9
A6
E/B
B9
B7
E
(except last time)
Mam - bo Je - su.
ta - wa pa - no mu zi - ta re - nyu.
we are here for you.

A gathering song, originally from Shona, and composed by Patrick Matsikenyiri, a primary school headmaster and a leading composer of African Church music. The harmonic clash in bar five is deliberate. Patrick said to John Bell of the Iona Community, 'If you knew the history of our country, you would know that we have had so many clashes that a little difficulty in the harmony will cause us no problem.' Other verses may be added e.g. We are here *with* you, . . . *in* you.

188 JESUS CRISTO IDO DO MUNDO

Words used by permission of World Council of Churches

Portuguese Words: Jaci C. Maraschin
English Words: © Len Lythgoe
Music: Herbert Beuerle

C
1. Não é vi - da a vi - da que se vi - ve por en - ga - no,
1. It's no life, no life at all, that's root- ed in de - cep - tion,
G7 C
es - sa tris - te vi - da que não tem ca - lor hu - ma - no.
it's no life when hu - man warmth is miss-ing from per - cep - tion.
F G
Pois vi - ver a vi - da é mui - to mais do que a a - pa - rên - cia.
Liv - ing is a whole lot more than scram-bling for sur - vi - val,
G C
de vi - ver a vi - da que só é so - bre - vi - vên - cia.
go - ing through the mo - tions with your neigh-bour as a ri - val.
Refrain
F G C F G C
Je - sus Cris - to é a vi - da, é a vi - da do mun - do.
Je - sus Christ, he is the life, he is the life of the world___.

2. Não é vida a vida que se vive como escravo / sem ter voz ou vez, sem lar, abrigo nem centavo. / Pois viver a vida é como a busca da aventura: / só é vida a vida enquanto a liberdade dura.

3. Não é vida a vida que se vive sem futuro, / que só tem memória, só passado vago e escuro. / Pois viver a vida é muito mais do que a lembrança: / só é vida a vida que ressurge da esperança.

4. Essa vida é a vida que em Jesus nós alcançamos / quando junto a ele o mundo injusto transformamos, / e vencendo a morte, as opressões e a tirania, / viveremos sempre no seu Reino de alegria.

2. It's no life, no life at all, in slavery to suffer, / with no shelter or a voice or money for a buffer. / Living ought to be more like a wonderful adventure, / with the freedom to move out in any kind of venture.

3. It's no life, no life at all, when there's no future showing, / memory is not enough to keep a person going. / Living cannot be reliving of the past, discouraged, / life must be attainable and real for hope to flourish.

4. It is life, authentic life, that Jesus has to offer, / working with us to transform our world where people suffer. / Tyranny shall be no more and all oppression vanish; / in his kingdom full of joy the fear of death is banished.

189 JESUS THE LORD SAID

INDIA

Words: anonymous
translated Dermott Monahan
Music: Urdu melody
arranged Geoff Weaver

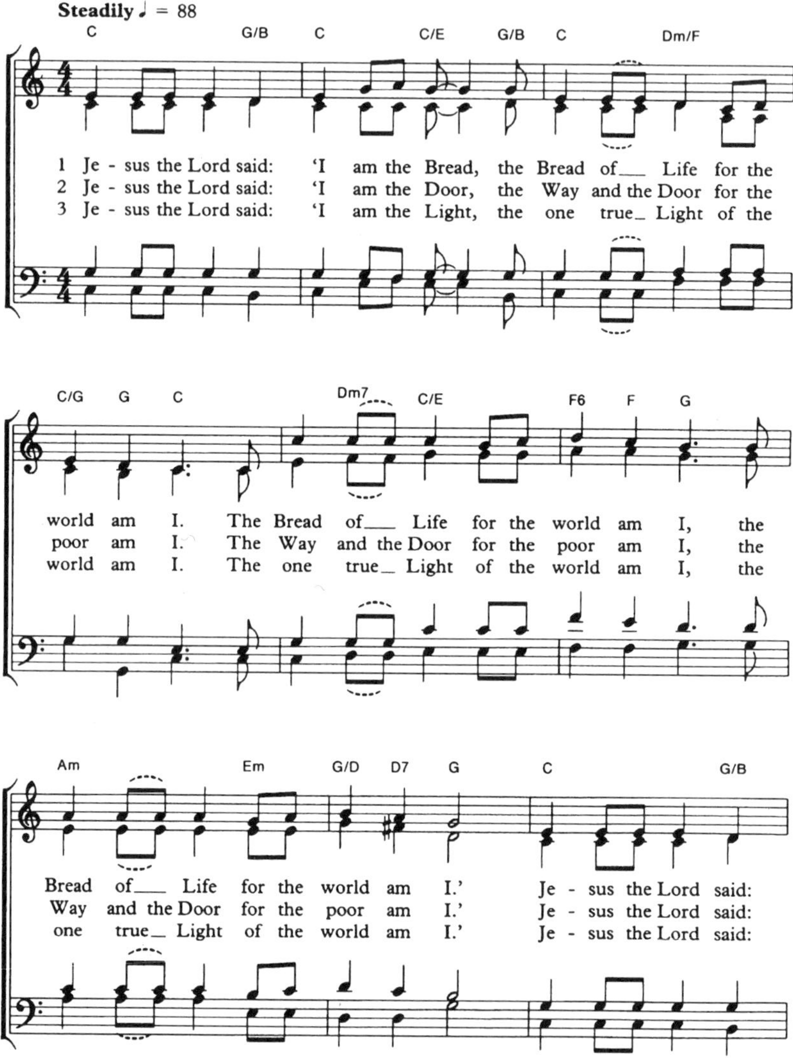

Steadily ♩ = 88
C G/B C C/E G/B C Dm/F
1 Je - sus the Lord said: 'I am the Bread, the Bread of__ Life for the
2 Je - sus the Lord said: 'I am the Door, the Way and the Door for the
3 Je - sus the Lord said: 'I am the Light, the one true_ Light of the
C/G G C Dm7 C/E F6 F G
world am I. The Bread of__ Life for the world am I, the
poor am I. The Way and the Door for the poor am I, the
world am I. The one true_ Light of the world am I, the
Am Em G/D D7 G C G/B
Bread of__ Life for the world am I.' Je - sus the Lord said:
Way and the Door for the poor am I.' Je - sus the Lord said:
one true_ Light of the world am I.' Je - sus the Lord said:

One of the most widely travelled of Indian hymns, this haunting melody is Urdu in origin. It makes an ideal vehicle through which to teach many of Jesus' sayings about himself, and may be expanded ad lib.

C
Em
Am
Dm
Dm/F
G6
G7
C
'I am the Bread, the Bread of___ Life for the world am I.'
'I am the Door, the Way and the Door for the poor am I.'
'I am the Light, the one true_ Light of the world am I.'

1 Jesus the Lord said: 'I am the Bread,
the Bread of Life for the world am I.
The Bread of Life for the world am I,
the Bread of Life for the world am I.'
Jesus the Lord said: 'I am the Bread,
the Bread of Life for the world am I.'

2 Jesus the Lord said: 'I am the Door,
the Way and the Door for the poor am I . . .'

3 Jesus the Lord said: 'I am the Light,
the one true Light of the world am I . . .'

4 Jesus the Lord said: 'I am the Shepherd,
the one Good Shepherd of the sheep am I . . .'

5 Jesus the Lord said: 'I am the Life,
the Resurrection and the Life am I . . .'

190 JESUS WHERE CAN WE FIND YOU

Jamaica

Doreen Potter

Doreen Potter

F
C
Am
Dm
C
Je- sus, where can we find you In our world to- day?
Je- sus in hand of the heal-er, Can we feel you there?
Am
Dm
G
G7
C
Je- sus where can we find you, In- car- nate Word to- day?
Je- sus in word of the preach-er, Can we hear you there?
CHORUS
F
B♭
Gm
LOOK AT YOUR BRO- THER BE- SIDE YOU; LOOK AT YOUR SIS- TER BE-
(slower)
F/C
C
Gm7
C7
F
SIDE YOU; LOOK! LIS- TEN! CARE!

World

1. Jesus, where can we find you,
   In our world today?
   Jesus, where can we find you,
   Incarnate Word today?

   Chorus
   Look at your brother beside you;
   Look at your sister beside you;
   Look! Listen! Care!

2. Jesus, in hand of the healer,
   Can we feel you there?
   Jesus, in word of the preacher,
   Can we hear you there?

3. Jesus, in mind of the leader,
   Can we know you there?
   Jesus, in aims of the planner,
   Can we find you there?

4. Jesus, in thought of the artist,
   Can we sense you there?
   Jesus, in work of the builder,
   Can we see you there?

5. Jesus, in face of the famished,
   Can we see you there?
   Jesus, in face of the prisoner,
   Can we see you there?

6. Jesus, in faces of children,
   Can we see you there?
   Jesus, in all of creation,
   Can we see you there?

191 KATA KU NA NI MO SHU O KOBA MI NU

JAPAN

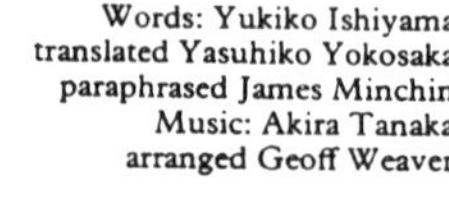
Words: Yukiko Ishiyama
translated Yasuhiko Yokosaka
paraphrased James Minchin
Music: Akira Tanaka
arranged Geoff Weaver

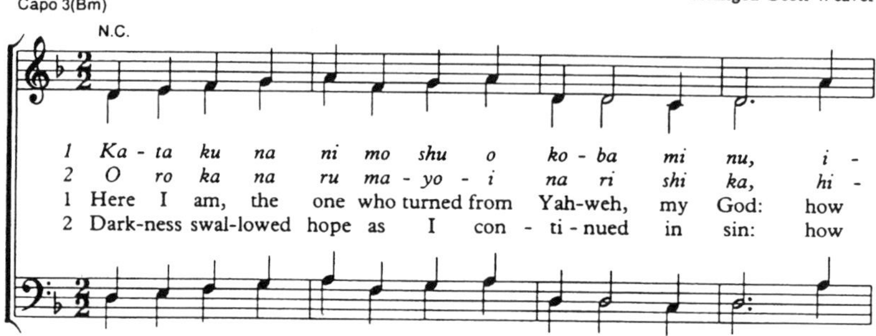

Flowing 𝅗𝅥 = 69
Capo 3(Bm)
N.C.
1 Ka - ta ku na ni mo shu o ko - ba mi nu, i -
2 O ro ka na ru ma - yo - i na ri shi ka, hi -
1 Here I am, the one who turned from Yah-weh, my God: how
2 Dark-ness swal-lowed hope as I con - ti - nued in sin: how

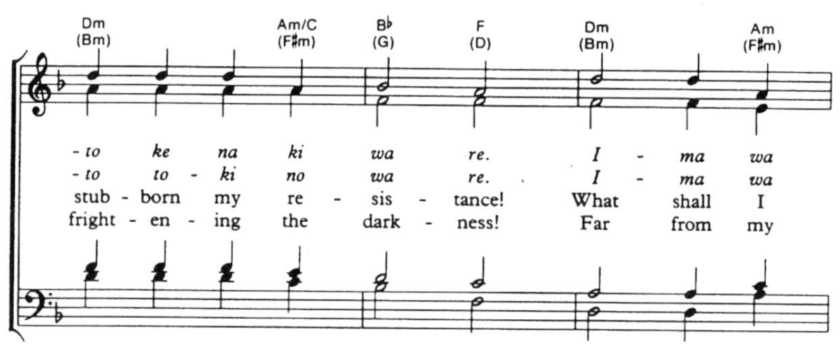

Dm (Bm) Am/C (F♯m) B♭ (G) F (D) Dm (Bm) Am (F♯m)
- to ke na ki wa re. I - ma wa
- to to - ki no wa re. I - ma wa
stub - born my re - sis - tance! What shall I
fright - en - ing the dark - ness! Far from my

Gm (Em) Am (F♯m) Gm/B (Em) Dm/A (Bm) Gm7 (Em7) Gm/E A (F♯) N.C.
shú no mi - ko - ko - ro o, mo - to - me tsu -
shú no mi - ko - ko - ro o, a - o - gi tsu -
do to find for - give - ness now? I will pray and
home, I was be - wil - dered, lost. Now I go forth

There is an austere joy in this song of repentance and new life, perhaps reflecting the often turbulent history of the small Christian community in Japan.

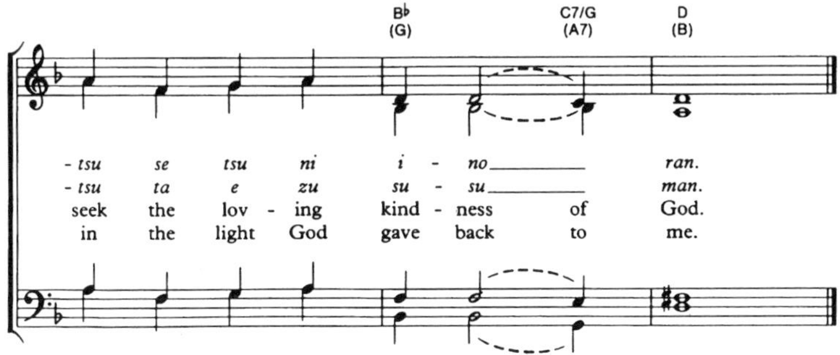
B♭
(G)
C7/G
(A7)
D
(B)
-tsu se tsu ni i - no ran.
-tsu ta e zu su - su man.
seek the lov - ing kind - ness of God.
in the light God gave back to me.

1 *Kata ku na ni mo shu o koba mi nu,*
ito ke na ki wa re.
Ima wa shú no mikokoro o,
motome tsutsu se tsu ni ino ran.

2 *O ro ka na ru mayoi na ri shi ka,*
hito toki no wa re.
Ima wa shú no mikokoro o,
aogi tsutsu ta e zu susu man.

3 *No ni yama ni hikari ahure te,*
suku wa re shi wa re.
Ima wa shú no mimegumi o,
Taka raka ni tatae uta wan.

1 Here I am, the one who turned from Yahweh, my God:
how stubborn my resistance!
What shall I do to find forgiveness now?
I will pray and seek the loving kindness of God.

2 Darkness swallowed hope as I continued in sin:
how frightening the darkness!
Far from my home, I was bewildered, lost.
Now I go forth in the light God gave back to me.

3 All around, the landscape shines with new light and life,
the fields and mountains glisten!
Jesus' salvation fills the world with joy.
I will praise and sing God's goodness while I have breath.

192 KAY YAHWEH AKO

Used by permission of Hope Publishing Co., Carol Stream, IL 60188 USA

PHILIPPINES

Words: from the Tagalog
in this version Word & Music
Music: unknown
arranged Geoff Weaver

Relaxed, easy flow ♩ = 88

Bm
F♯m
G
D
Kay Yah - weh a - ko, kay Yah - weh a - ko Kay
I'll fol - low my Lord, I'll fol - low my Lord, I'll

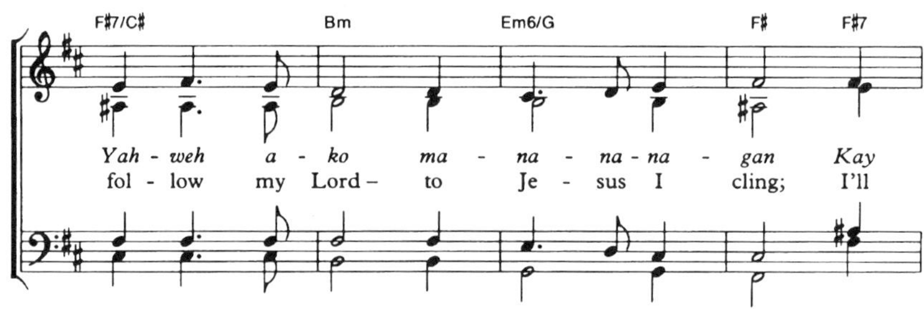
F♯7/C♯
Bm
Em6/G
F♯
F♯7
Yah - weh a - ko ma - na - na - na - gan Kay
fol - low my Lord – to Je - sus I cling; I'll

Bm
F♯m
G
D
Yah - weh a - ko, kay Yah - weh a - ko, Kay
fol - low my Lord, I'll fol - low my Lord, I'll
F♯7/C♯
Bm
F♯7
Bm
Yah - weh a - ko ma - na - na - gan.
fol - low my Lord – my love I will bring!

The arranger heard this beautiful song sung by Filipino Christians who had recently suffered devastation from earthquake, volcanic eruption and typhoon. In that context, to sing, 'to Jesus I cling', has tremendous power and relevance. Its folk-song character is well served by a guitar accompaniment.

193 LA VENIDA DE CRISTO

Used by permission of Hope Publishing Co., Carol Stream, IL 60188 USA

CHILE

Dance-like ♩. = 66
Words: Santiago Stevenson
English: From Mark 13, Michael Perry
Music: Chilean melody
arranged Geoff Weaver
Capo 1(Bm)
TWO PARTS
Cm (Bm)
G7 (F♯)
1 La ve - ni - da de Cris - to se a - ce - rca. Pron - to
2 Si que - re - mos que Cris - to nos lle - ve a los
1 When the stars in their flight fall from the hea - vens, and the
2 Be on guard! Be pre-pared for Je - sus' com - ing; for we
vie - ne su i - gle - sia a bus - car. No dur -
cie - los con él a mo - rar. No se -
world has sur - ren - dered to night, and the
don't know the day or the hour, but we'll
G7 (F♯7)
Cm (Bm)
A♭7 (G7)
- ma - mos, es - te - mos a - ler - tos; ¡Vi - gi -
- a - mos ja - más ne - gli - gen - tes; ¡Tra - ba -
pil - lars of earth have been sha - ken, and the
hear of the wars of the na - tions, when the
Cm/G (Bm)
G (F♯)
- lad, vi - gi - lad, vi - gi - lad! Pron - to
- jad, tra - ba - jad, tra - ba - jad!
sun and the moon lose their light: Then we'll
kings of the earth lose their power.

There has been astonishing growth in the Protestant churches in Latin America in recent years. New Christians are encouraged to sing songs which grow from their own culture, and this lively dance song is a good example of such 'enculturation'. Add percussion instruments and guitars as you wish.

B♭ (A)
E♭ (D)
vie - ne Je - sús y nos lle - va a la her -
see the Lord come in his glo - ry, in the
B♭7 (A7)
E♭ (D)
G/B (F♯)
G
- mo - sa man-sión ce - les - tial. Pron-to vie-ne Je-sús a la
clouds he'll des-cend from his throne; he will send all his an - gels be -
Cm (Bm)
A♭ (G)
UNISON
Cm/G (Bm)
G7 (F♯7)
Cm (Bm)
tie-rra; nos i - re - mos con él a mo - rar.
- fore him, and with joy they will ga - ther his own.

3 *Arreglemos, estemos a cuentas*
con Jesús, el Cordero de Dios.
Del que ofende tengamos clemencia;
¡Perdonad, perdonad, perdonad!
Pronto viene . . .

4 *Perdonando, Jesús nos perdona,*
y nos lleva con él a reinar.
Ganaremos también la corona;
¡Vigilad, trabajad, perdonad!
Pronto viene . . .

3 We can trust in the presence of the Spirit,
he will teach us what we are to say;
and we need not be fearful or anxious,
for his grace will provide in that day.
Then we'll see the Lord . . .

4 When the leaves of the fig tree are emerging,
then we see that the summer is near,
even so, as these things start to happen
then you know that the Son will appear.
Then we'll see the Lord . . .

194 LET ALL THE ISLANDS RISE AND SING

PASEFIKA

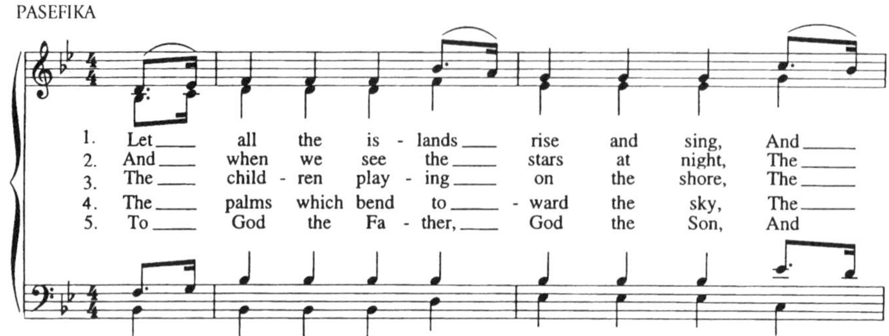
1. Let___ all the is - lands___ rise and sing, And___
2. And___ when we see the___ stars at night, The___
3. The___ child - ren play - ing___ on the shore, The___
4. The___ palms which bend to___ - ward the sky, The___
5. To___ God the Fa - ther,___ God the Son, And

to our God their__ prais - es bring; On___ strings and drum your
ma - ny worlds which__ cross the sky; The___ sun and moon which
sounds of laugh - ter___ which we hear; Their___ love in - creas - ing
clouds which hur - ry__ to and fro; The___ birds which fly both
God the Spi - rit,__ praise be done; My___ Christ the___ Lord

Fijian Popular Melody
Notated and Arranged by Veta Solomna
Author: L. Brittain

might pro - claim Sound the glo - ry of your name.
give us light, We ___ praise our God on high.
more and more, Re ___ - mind us God is here.
low and high, Give ___ joy to earth be - low.
up - on us pour the Spi - rit ev - er - more.
Pa - se - fi - ka, Pa - se - fi - ka,
Pa - se - fi - ka, Pa - se - fi - ka, With
throb - bing reef and ___ cor - al shore, For ___ fish and shell and
might - y whale, For your gifts our thanks we pour.

195 LOE DE ISA

Used by permission of Hope Publishing Co., Carol Stream, IL 60188 USA

Words: from the Pushto, Alison Blenkinsop
Music: unknown
arranged Geoff Weaver

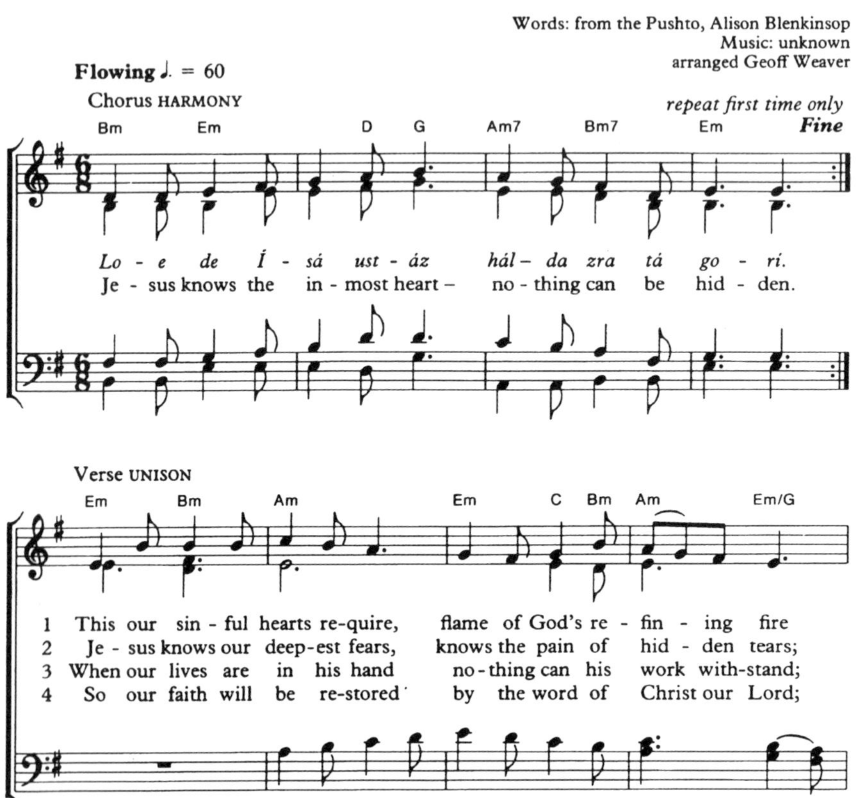
Flowing ♩. = 60
Chorus HARMONY
repeat first time only
Bm Em D G Am7 Bm7 Em Fine
Lo - e de Í - sá ust - áz hál – da zra tá go - rí.
Je - sus knows the in - most heart – no - thing can be hid - den.
Verse UNISON
Em Bm Am Em C Bm Am Em/G
1 This our sin - ful hearts re-quire, flame of God's re - fin - ing fire
2 Je - sus knows our deep-est fears, knows the pain of hid - den tears;
3 When our lives are in his hand no-thing can his work with-stand;
4 So our faith will be re-stored by the word of Christ our Lord;

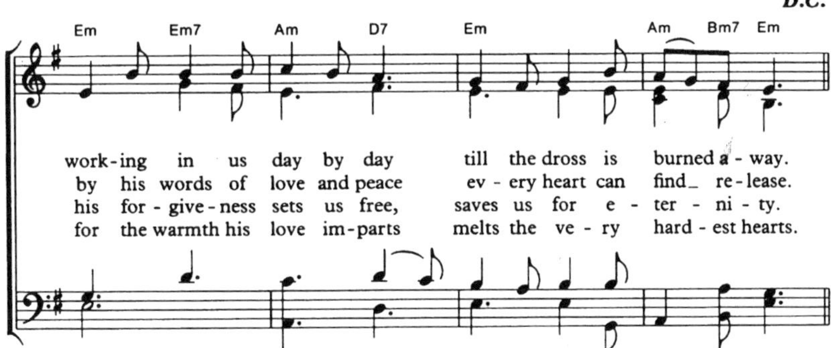
D.C.
Em
Em7
Am
D7
Em
Am
Bm7
Em
work-ing in us day by day till the dross is burned a - way.
by his words of love and peace ev - ery heart can find_ re-lease.
his for - give - ness sets us free, saves us for e - ter - ni - ty.
for the warmth his love im-parts melts the ve - ry hard - est hearts.

One of a number of songs from the Pushto-speaking Christians of Pakistan which have been collected by Alison Blenkinsop (formerly Fookes), who served as a missionary there. Both melody and text have a simplicity and directness which is very appealing.

196 LOOK AND LEARN

Words by John L. Bell & Graham Maule,

KOREA

Words: from Matthew 6: 23–34
John L. Bell
Music: Nah Young-Soo
arranged Geoff Weaver

Flowing ♩. = 56
G C6/G G D
1 Look and learn from the birds of the air, fly - ing high a-bove
2 Look and learn from the flowers of the field, bring - ing beau - ty and
3 What God wants_ should be___ our will; where God calls_ should
C/G D7/G G C/G G C G
wor - ry and fear; nei - ther sow - ing nor har - vest-ing seed,
col - our to life; nei - ther sew - ing nor tail - or - ing cloth,
be___ our goal. When we seek___ the King - dom first,
D C/G D7 G
yet they're gi - ven what - ev - er they need. If the God of
yet they're dressed in the fin - est at - tire. If the God of
all we've lost___ is ours___ a - gain. Let's be done with

On hearing this haunting pentatonic melody, many people are surprised to learn of its Korean origin. This should have an easy flow, not moving too slowly.

Em Bm Am D9 D7
earth and heaven cares for birds as much__ as this,
earth and heaven cares for flowers as much__ as this,
anx - ious thoughts, set a - side to - mor - row's cares,
G C/G G C G D C/G D7 G
won't he care much more for you, if you put_ your trust_ in him?
won't he care much more for you if you put_ your trust_ in him?
live each day_ that God pro-vides put-ting all__ our trust_ in him.

1 Look and learn from the birds of the air,
flying high above worry and fear;
neither sowing nor harvesting seed,
yet they're given whatever they need.
If the God of earth and heaven
cares for birds as much as this,
won't he care much more for you,
if you put your trust in him?

2 Look and learn from the flowers of the field,
bringing beauty and colour to life;
neither sewing nor tailoring cloth,
yet they're dressed in the finest attire.
If the God of earth and heaven
cares for flowers as much as this,
won't he care much more for you
if you put your trust in him?

3 What God wants should be our will;
where God calls should be our goal.
When we seek the Kingdom first,
all we've lost is ours again.
Let's be done with anxious thoughts,
set aside tomorrow's cares,
live each day that God provides
putting all our trust in him.

197 MAY THE PEACE OF GOD THE FATHER

ISRAEL

Words: unknown
in this version Word & Music
Music: Israeli melody
arranged David Peacock

Flowing ♩ = 74
Dm
F
G
A May the peace of God the Fa - ther
B and the grace of Christ, the
Am
B♭
Son,
A with the bless-ing of the Spi - rit –

F G Am F C
B God the ho - ly Three-in - One: A be up - on you
Dm Gm F C Dm
al-ways, and re-main B now and ev - er with you. A-men.

This haunting modal song of blessing is most effective when sung by two groups: the one responding to the other.

198 MAYENZIWE 'NTANDO YAKHO

SOUTH AFRICA

Words: from the Lord's Prayer
Music: transcribed by John L. Bell

Not too fast ♩ = 96

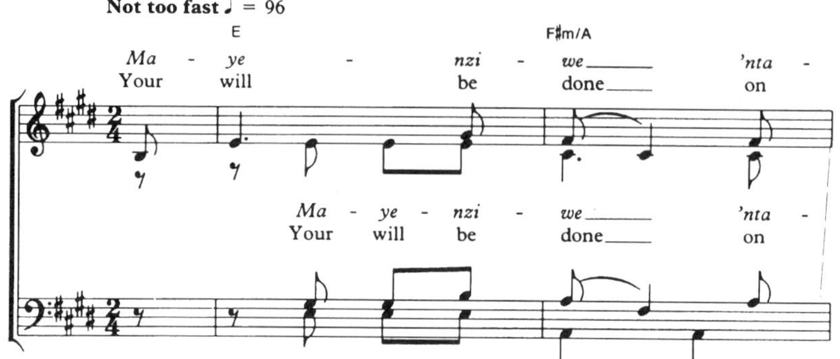
E
F♯m/A
Ma - ye - nzi - we 'nta -
Your will be done on
Ma - ye - nzi - we 'nta -
Your will be done on

E/B B E F♯/A
- ndo ya - kho. Ma - ye - nzi - we 'nta -
earth, O Lord. Your will be done on
- ndo ya - kho. Ma - ye - nzi - we 'nta -
earth, O Lord. Your will be done on

E/B B E F♯m B7 E
- ndo ya - kho. Ma - ye - nzi - we 'nta -
earth, O Lord. Your will be done on

A traditional song from South Africa, joyful and affirmative. This is best sung *a cappella*.

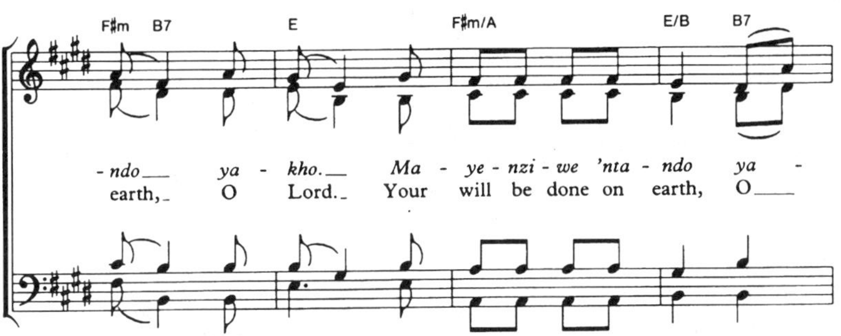
F♯m B7 E F♯m/A E/B B7
-ndo ya - kho. Ma - ye - nzi - we 'nta - ndo ya -
earth, O Lord. Your will be done on earth, O

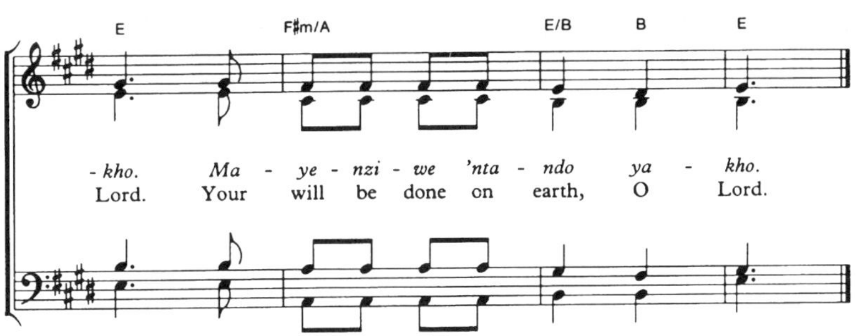
E F♯m/A E/B B E
- kho. Ma - ye - nzi - we 'nta - ndo ya - kho.
Lord. Your will be done on earth, O Lord.

Mayenziwe 'ntando yakho.
Mayenziwe 'ntando yakho.
Mayenziwe 'ntando yakho.
Mayenziwe 'ntando yakho.
Mayenziwe 'ntando yakho.

Your will be done on earth, O Lord.
Your will be done on earth, O Lord.
Your will be done on earth, O Lord.
Your will be done on earth, O Lord.
Your will be done on earth, O Lord.

199 MOTO UMEWAKA LEO

Used by permission of Hope Publishing Co., Carol Stream, IL 60188 USA

EAST AFRICA

Words and music: unknown
arranged Geoff Weaver

Lively ♩ = 108
G C G
Mo - to u - me - wa - ka le - o, Mo - to ni
God's fire is burn-ing in my soul, God's fire has
A D G C G
ka - zi ya Ye - su, Mo - to u - me - wa - ka le - o; Tu -
come to make me whole, God's fire is sweep-ing through the earth; praise

G/D
D7
G
- im - be hal - le - lu - jah mo - to u - me - wa - ka! Tu -
God, I've got God's fire and it's burn - ing in my soul! Praise
G/D
D7
G
- im - be hal - le - lu - jah mo - to u - me - wa - ka!
God – yes, hal - le - lu - jah it's burn - ing in my soul!

A song which most probably came out of the East African revival.
It needs to be sung with rhythm, fire and commitment.

200 NGAIH CHIAT TAHNAK KA TON LID AH

Used by permission of Hope Publishing Co., Carol Stream, IL 60188 USA

MYANMAR

Words: unknown
in this version Word & Music
Music: unknown
arranged David Peacock

Lilting ♩ = 108
D G D
Ngaih chiat tah - nak ka ton lid ah, a ka hnum tu
When I am sad and sor - row - ful, Je-sus is there;
A
hawi tha bik cu Je - suh a si
he's my best friend, my Sa - viour.
D G D
dwat mi hna nih thlan mual ran - liam lid can zon - gah
When all my friends have gone a - way, in that sad day,
G D/A A7 D G D
bawi Je - suh nih a ka um - pi.
Je - sus my Lord is with me. More

The recent history of Myanmar (Burma) has been one of great oppression and suffering. The editor recently met a young man who dared not return home to his family and this song was sung to him by another radical young Christian who feared for the future of his country. Many families have lost loved ones and the words of this song must be truly heartfelt.

A A7 D/A A G D
Sui le ngun nak in sung deuh mi maw_ hawi tha
pre - cious than sil-ver or gold – he's my best friend;
G/D D Bm
ngaih chiat can ah lea thin hnem tu
when I am sad and sor - row - ful
Em7 A D
maw_ hawi tha ka nun nak al cheen
he's my best friend; he's al-ways pre - sent
G D
le zan in a ka um - pi. Hawi tha bik
day and night in my life. My best
G D/A A7 D G D
cu Je - suh a si.
friend is Je - sus.

201 O LET THE POWER

Caribbean

Birchfield Aymer

trad. adapted B Aymer
arr. Patrick Prescod

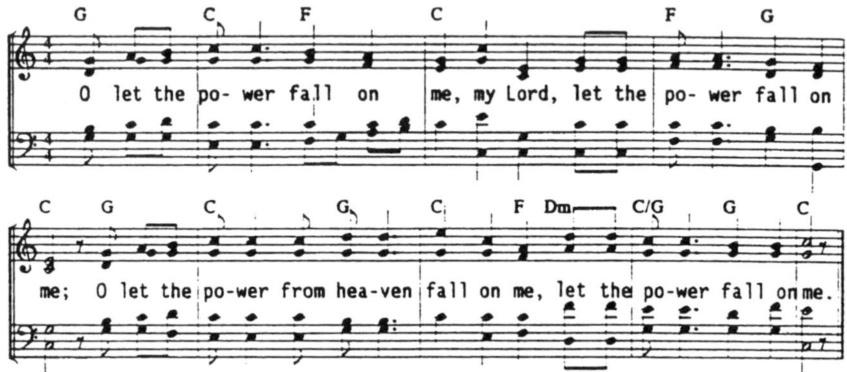
G C F C F G
O let the po- wer fall on me, my Lord, let the po- wer fall on
C G C G C F Dm C/G G C
me; O let the po-wer from hea-ven fall on me, let the po-wer fall on me.

1. O let the power fall on me, my Lord
Let the power fall on me;
O let the power from heaven fall on me,
Let the power fall on me.

2. For we want power to live as one, yes Lord,
We want power to live as one;
So as we pray and intercede for some,
May the Spirit make us one.

3. Send us the promised Comforter, O Christ,
Send us the promised Comforter;
And let our hearts be filled with love, O Christ,
When the Spirit come like Dove.

4. Give us the power here and now, O Christ,
Please for the power here and now;
Send us the power of grace and peace and love,
Send us the power of peace and love.

202 ON THE MOUNTAIN

Used by permission of Hope Publishing Co., Carol Stream, IL 60188 USA

NIGERIA

Words and music: collected Geoff Weaver
arranged Geoff Weaver

Confidently ♩ = 100

G
D/A
On the moun - tain, in the val - ley, on the

A7
D
D7
G
land and in the sea; on the moun - tain, in the

D/A
A7
D
val - ley, on the land and in the sea, hal - le-lu-jah! My

The Igbo Christians of Eastern Nigeria have many short songs of affirmation. This, with words partly drawn from the Psalms, reaffirms God's presence and goodness in all situations.

Poco meno mosso ♩ = 72
Em/G
D/A
God is my por - tion in the land of the liv - ing; my
A7
D
D7
Em/G
God is good for ev - er - more. My God is my por-tion in the
D/A
A7
D
land of the liv-ing; my God is good for ev - er - more.

On the mountain, in the valley,
on the land and in the sea;
on the mountain, in the valley,
on the land and in the sea, hallelujah!

My God is my portion
in the land of the living;
my God is good for evermore.
My God is my portion
in the land of the living;
my God is good for evermore.

203 PEOPLE OF FAITH

Taiwan

I–to Loh
para. James Minchin

Hengchhun melody
arr. I–to Loh

Peo- ple of faith, by God's com- - - mand
com- fort the ex- - - - iles, cap- - tives free;
na- tions con- front with pro- - - - phe- - - cy:
such words and deeds re- veal God's hand.

1. People of faith, by God's command
   Comfort the exiles, captives free,
   Nations confront with prophecy:
   Such words and deeds reveal God's hand.

2. God's light will clear the way ahead:
   Uproot and pull down what is wrong,
   Plant and rebuild, and make hope strong.
   Go forth with grace your daily bread.

204 PRABHOO LAYLAY

O Lord Jesus, enfold me in your arms

PAKISTAN

Words: Samuel Paul,
paraphrased Shirley Murray
Music: Samuel Paul
arranged Geoff Weaver

Flowing ♩ = 116
Chorus
Am
Dm
Pra-bhoo Lay-lay muj-hay Too Ba-hoñ Meñ ka-heen
O Lord Je-sus, en-fold me in your arms, let me
E7
Am
Fine
gir - na ja - aun gu - naa - hon meñ.
ne - ver be part - ed from your love;
Verse
Am
E7
1 Me - ra tan man aur dhan te - ray lee - ay, me - ra
2 Me - ray dil ko too ap - nay ruh say bhar me - ray
3 Pa - ape e - on ko main laau te - ray pass ab - di
1 All my be - ing and all that I poss - ess, all my
2 Let your Spi - rit be al - ways in my heart, and let
3 Let me bring to you oth - ers who are lost – in their
1.
Am
sa - ra jee - van te ray lee - ay.
dil ho se - raf te - ra ni ghar.
ku - shi pa - en jo hain ud aas.
life is com - mit - ted to you, Lord;
on - ly your Spi - rit live with - in;
sad - ness, may they dis - co - ver joy;

An unusual stylistic blend of syncopated rhythms with words of deep personal commitment. The verses may be sung as solos.

2.
Am
Am
- ay. Mu - jay lay chal tu ap nee raa - hoñ
ghar. Too he too ho me - ree ni - ga - ahon
aas. Vo bhee jaa - en te - ray ga - va - ahon
Lord; Come and turn all my foot-steps to your
- in. Let my vi - sion be on - ly what you
joy. In be - liev - ing, they'll wit - ness to your
Dm
E7
Am
May, ka-heen gir na ja-aun gu - na - ahon meñ. Mu - jay
may ka-heen gir na ja-aun gu - na - ahon meñ. Too he
may ka-heen gir na ja-aun gu - na - ahon meñ. Vo bhee
way, let me ne-ver be part-ed from your love; come and
are, let me ne-ver be part-ed from your love; let my
truth – let me ne-ver be part-ed from your love; in be -
A7
Dm
lay chal tu ap nee raa - hoñ May, ka heen
too ho me - ree ni - ga - ahon may ka - heen
jaa - en te - ray ga - va - ahon may ka - heen
turn all my foot-steps to your way, let me
vi - sion be on - ly what you are, let me
- liev - ing, they'll wit - ness to your truth – let me
Dm7/F
E
D.C. al Fine
gir na ja - aun gu - na - ahon meñ.
gir na ja - aun gu - na - ahon meñ.
gir na ja - aun gu - na - ahon meñ.
ne - ver be part - ed from your love.
ne - ver be part - ed from your love.
ne - ver be part - ed from your love.

205 RABB KI HOWE SANA HAMESHA

Used by permission of Hope Publishing Co., Carol Stream, IL 60188 USA

PAKISTAN

Words: from Psalm 150,
translated Alison Blenkinsop
Music: unknown
arranged Geoff Weaver

Fast and lively ♩ = 126

Capo 3(Bm) Dm (Bm)
F (D)
Am (F♯m)
Rabb-(a) ki ho - we_ sa-na ha-me - sha, rabb-(a) ki ho - we_

Dm (Bm)
B♭ (G)
sa - na. Sing the Lord's prai - ses for

F (D)
Am (F♯m)
F (D)
Fine
ev-er and ev - er;_ sing the Lord's prai - ses for ev-er.

An exuberant Hindi setting of Psalm 150. A performance will be enhanced by the use of rhythmic percussion and echo effects as suggested. Some pronunciation helps are:
Rabb has a little vowel after it – like 'rubber'
ki = key
howe = no way (slight 'v' sound to the 'w')
sana = sun-nah
hamesha = hu-may-sha

Am (F♯m)
Dm (Bm)
1 Let us praise the Lord with our voi - ces,
2 Let us praise the Lord in his tem - ple,
3 For he is the might - y cre - a - tor,
C (A)
F (D)
let us praise the Lord with our voi - ces,
let us praise the Lord in his tem - ple,
for he is the might - y cre - a - tor:
Gm (Em)
prais - ing his name for ev - er and ev - er,
thank - ing and prais - ing the Lord for ev - er,
tell of his glo - ry and power for ev - er,
B♭ (G)
F (D)
prais - ing his name for ev - er, ha - me - sha.
thank - ing and prais - ing the Lord, ha - me - sha.
tell of his glo - ry and power, ha - me - sha.

205 Contd.

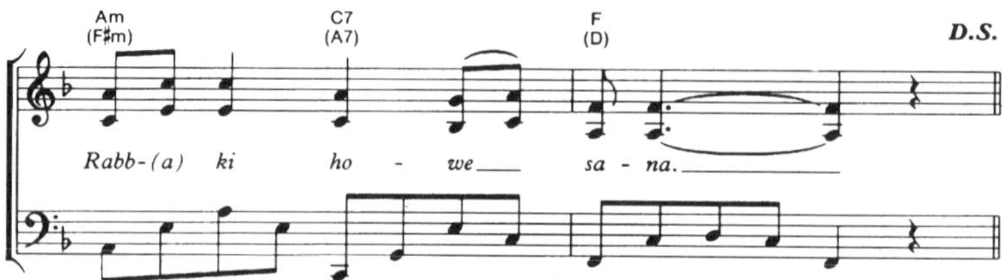
Am
(F♯m)
C7
(A7)
F
(D)
D.S.
Rabb-(a) ki ho - we sa - na.

Rabb ki howe sana hamesha,
rabb ki howe sana.
Sing the Lord's praises for ever and ever;
sing the Lord's praises for ever.

1 Let us praise the Lord with our voices,
let us praise the Lord with our voices,
praising his name for ever and ever,
praising his name for ever, *hamesha.*
Rabb ki howe sana.
Sing the Lord's praises . . .

2 Let us praise the Lord in his temple,
let us praise the Lord in his temple,
thanking and praising the Lord for ever,
thanking and praising the Lord, *hamesha.*
Rabb ki howe sana.
Sing the Lord's praises . . .

3 For he is the mighty creator,
for he is the mighty creator:
tell of his glory and power for ever,
tell of his glory and power, *hamesha.*
Rabb ki howe sana.
Sing the Lord's praises . . .

4 Loudly play the horns and the trumpets,
loudly play the horns and the trumpets;
play on the lute and the pipes together,
play on the lute and the pipes, *hamesha.*
Rabb ki howe sana.
Sing the Lord's praises . . .

5 Play with skill the violin and 'cello,
play with skill the violin and 'cello;
rattle the tambourine and drums together,
rattle the tambourine and drums, *hamesha.*
Rabb ki howe sana.
Sing the Lord's praises . . .

6 Play the flute so sweet and melodious,
play the flute so sweet and melodious;
clashing the cymbals and gongs together,
clashing the cymbals together, *hamesha.*
Rabb ki howe sana.
Sing the Lord's praises . . .

7 Everybody clap hands together,
everybody clap hands together;
sing the Lord's praises for ever and ever,
sing the Lord's praises for ever, *hamesha.*
Rabb ki howe sana.
Sing the Lord's praises . . .

206 SANTO

C G7 C F
San - to San - to San-to é o Se - nhor Deus do–u - ni -
Em Dm Am F G C
ver - so. Os ceus e a ter - ra es - tão chei - os da tua gló - ria! Ho -
G C C G7 Am
sa - na nas al - tu - ras! Ho - sa - na! Ben -
Dm Am F G C G
di - to o que vem em no - me do Se - nhor. Ho - sa - na nas al -
C G7 Am
tu - ras! Ho - sa - na.

Santo

Santo, Santo, Santo e o Senhor/Deus do Universo./Os ceus e a terra estao plenos da tua gloria!/Hosana nas alturas!/Hosana! Bendito o que vem em nome do Senhor/Hosana nas alturas!/Hosana!

Sanctus

Santo, Santo, Santo es el Senor/Dios poderoso./El cielo y la tierra/estan llenos de tu gloria./Hosana en las alturas./Hosana!/Bendito El que viene/en el nombre del Senor./Hosana en los cielos./Hosana!

Sanctus

Holy, Holy, Holy is the Lord/God of hosts./Heaven and earth/are full of your great glory./Hosanna in the highest,/hosanna!/Blessed is He/who comes in the name of the Lord./Hosanna in the highest!/Hosanna!

207 SANTO, SANTO

Used by permission of Hope Publishing Co., Carol Stream, IL 60188 USA

ARGENTINA

Words and music: unknown
arranged Geoff Weaver

Worshipfully ♩ = 84

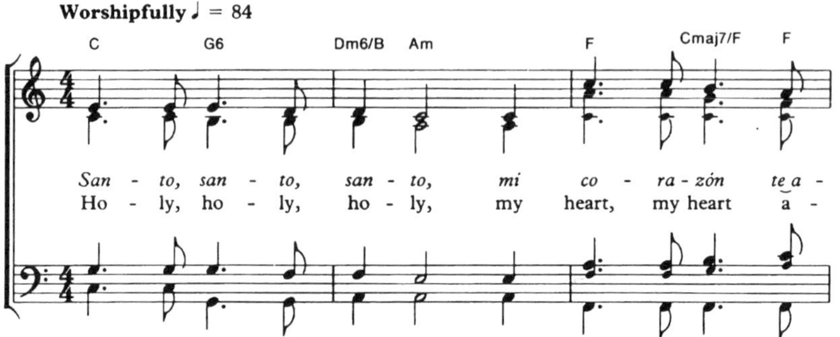
C G6 Dm6/B Am F Cmaj7/F F
San - to, san - to, san - to, mi co - ra - zón te a -
Ho - ly, ho - ly, ho - ly, my heart, my heart a -

F/C C F G
- do - ra! Mi co - ra - zón te
- dores you! My heart is glad to

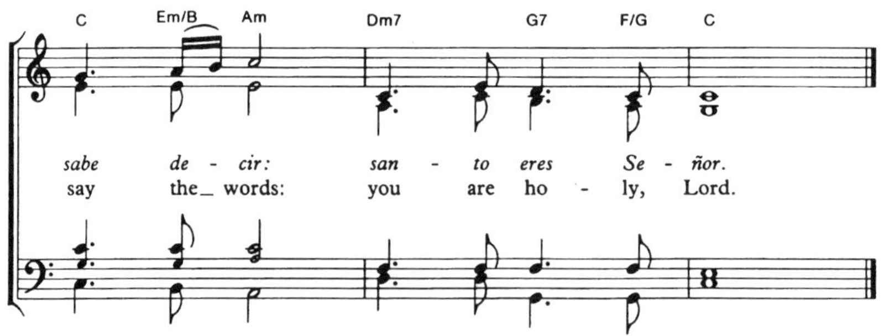
C Em/B Am Dm7 G7 F/G C
sabe de - cir: san - to eres Se - ñor.
say the_ words: you are ho - ly, Lord.

This heart-felt love song may be sung in unison, in two parts, or in rich harmony.

Santo, santo, santo,
mí corazón te adora!
Mí corazón te sabe decir:
santo eres Señor.

Holy, holy, holy,
my heart, my heart adores you!
My heart is glad to say the words:
you are holy, Lord.

INSTRUMENTAL OBLIGATO

Oboe

Flute

B♭ Clarinet

Simple part

208 SARANAM, SARANAM

Used by permission of Hope Publishing Co., Carol Stream, IL 60188 USA

PAKISTAN

Words: from Psalm 61 after D. T. Niles
Music: Punjabi melody arranged Geoff Weaver

With feeling ♩ = 88
Capo 1(D)
Sa - ra - nam, sa - ra - nam, sa - ra - nam,
Je - sus, Sav - iour, Lord, now to you I come, Sa - ra - nam, sa - ra-nam, sa - ra - nam; you my Rock, my re - fuge, my hea - venly home, Sa - ra - nam, sa - ra-nam, sa - ra - nam.
Fine

A hymn much loved by Christians from the Indian subcontinent, based on words by D. T. Niles and set to a Punjabi melody. 'Saranam' means 'refuge' or 'I take refuge'.

A♭
(G)
E♭
(D)
B♭7/D
(A7)
B♭
1 From the earth wher-ev-er I may be, out of des - pe - ra - tion and through
2 In your heart give me a hid - ing place, and be-neath your wings let me find
E♭
(D)
E♭7
A♭
(G)
a - go - ny, I cry in help - less - ness – O
shel - tering grace; O let me see the sun - shine
E♭
(D)
B♭7
(A7)
E♭
(D)
D.S.
ans - wer me, Sa - ra - nam, sa - ra - nam, sa - ra - nam.
of your face,

3 Then with joy to you my vows I'll pay,
and give thanks for all your mercy every day;
I'll humbly follow in your perfect way,
Saranam, saranam, saranam.
Jesus, Saviour . . .

4 Glory to the Father and the Son,
with the Holy Spirit ever Three-in-One;
we'll sing in heaven praises here begun,
Saranam, saranam, saranam.
Jesus, Saviour . . .

209 SENT BY THE LORD AM I

Used by permission of Hope Publishing Co., Carol Stream, IL 60188 USA

NICARAGUA

Words: from the oral tradition
translation Jorge Maldonodo
Music: traditional
arranged David Peacock

Confidently ♩ = 100
Capo 3(Dm)
Fm (Dm)
Sent by the Lord am I; my hands are rea-dy now to
B♭m/G (Gm)
C (A)
Fm (Dm)
make the earth the place in which the king-dom comes. Sent
HARMONY
by the Lord am I; my hands are rea - dy now to
B♭m/G (Gm)
C (A)
Fm (Dm)
make the earth the place in which the king-dom comes. The

A song from the folk tradition of Nicaragua. The use of the minor key somehow adds strength and resolve to the commitment to Christ's mission.

UNISON
Bbm7 (Gm7)
Eb (C)
Abmaj7 (F)
Dbmaj7 (Bb)
an - gels can - not change a world of hurt and pain in -
Bbm/G (Gm)
C (A)
F (D)
F/A
- to a world of love, of jus - tice and of peace. The
HARMONY
Bbm7 (Gm7)
Eb (C)
Abmaj7 (F)
Dbmaj7 (Bb)
task is mine to do, to set it real - ly free. Oh,
Bbm/G (Gm)
C (A)
F (D)
help me to o - bey; help me to do your will.

Sent by the Lord am I;
my hands are ready now
to make the earth the place
in which the kingdom comes.
Sent by the Lord am I;
my hands are ready now
to make the earth the place
in which the kingdom comes.

The angels cannot change
a world of hurt and pain
into a world of love,
of justice and of peace.
The task is mine to do,
to set it really free.
Oh, help me to obey;
help me to do your will.

210 SIYAHAMBA

Translation (Verse 1) & arrangement by Anders Nyberg.
Copyright © 1990 Wild Goose Publications, Iona Community,
840 Govan Road, Glasgow G51 3UU Scotland

SOUTH AFRICA

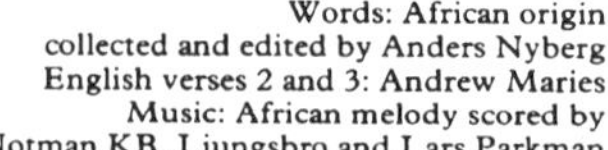
Words: African origin
collected and edited by Anders Nyberg
English verses 2 and 3: Andrew Maries
Music: African melody scored by
Notman KB, Ljungsbro and Lars Parkman

Joyfully ♩ = 120

G C

Si - ya - hamb' e - ku - kha - nye - ni 'kwen - khos, si - ya -

1. D G 2. D G

- hamb' e - ku - kha - nye - ni 'kwen - khos, si - ya - hamb' e - ku - kha - nye - ni 'kwen (kha - 'kwen - khos,

G7 C

- nye - ni 'kwen - khos). Si - ya - ham - ba ham - ba. (ham - ba; si - ya -

G C D G

- ham - ba, Oo ham - ba), si - ya Si - ya - hamb' e - ku - kha - nye - ni 'kwen - khos.

An exuberant song of hope from South Africa which has become popular in recent years. Experiment with variations in the harmony. It is hard to stand still while singing this song!

Joyfully ♩ = 120
G
C
We are march - ing in the light of God, we are
1.
D
G
2.
D
G
God
march-ing in the light of God,
we are march-ing in the light of, (the
G7
we are
C
march - ing
light of God).
We are march-ing, (march-ing, we are
G
C
D
G
Oh,
we are
march-ing, march-ing,) we are march-ing in the light of God!

OPTIONAL FURTHER VERSES

2 We are living in the love of God . . .

3 We are moving in the power of God . . .

211 SIZOHAMBA NAYE

SOUTH AFRICA

Words and music: unknown

Lively ♩ = 63

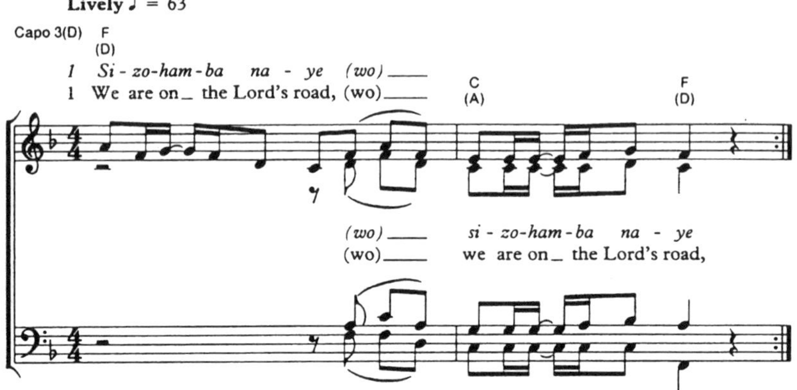
Capo 3(D) F
(D)
1 Si - zo-ham-ba na - ye (wo)
1 We are on the Lord's road, (wo)
C
(A)
F
(D)
(wo) si - zo-ham-ba na - ye
(wo) we are on the Lord's road,

B♭
(G)
Gm
(Em)
F
(D)
Dm
(Bm)
C7
(A7)
F
(D)
ngo-mhla wen - ja - bu - la
on our way to hea - ven -
si - zo - ham - ba na - ye
we are on the Lord's road,

B♭
(G)
Gm
(Em)
F
(D)
Dm
(Bm)
C7
(A7)
F
(D)
ngo-mhla wen - ja - bu - la
on our way to hea - ven -
si - zo - ham - ba na - ye.
we are on the Lord's road.

A lively song from South Africa. Try and feel the rhythms as exactly as possible.

1 *Sizohamba naye (wo) sizohamba naye*
Sizohamba naye . . .
ngomhla wenjabula
sizohamba naye
ngomhla wenjabula
sizohamba naye.

2 *Sizohalalisa (wo) sizohalalisa*
sizohalalisa . . .
ngomhla wenjabula
sizohalalisa naye
ngomhla wenjabula
sizohalalisa naye.

3 *Sizohlabelela (wo) sizohlabelela*
sizohlabelela . . .
ngomhla wenjabula
sizohlabelela naye
ngomhla wenjabula
sizohlabelela naye.

1 We are on the Lord's road,
we are on the Lord's road,
we are on the Lord's road,
we are on the Lord's road,
on our way to heaven –
we are on the Lord's road,
on our way to heaven –
we are on the Lord's road.

2 We shall sing the Lord's praise,
we shall sing the Lord's praise,
we shall sing the Lord's praise,
we shall sing the Lord's praise,
on our way to heaven –
we shall sing the Lord's praise,
on our way to heaven –
we shall sing the Lord's praise.

3 We shall live the Lord's word,
we shall live the Lord's word,
we shall live the Lord's word,
we shall live the Lord's word,
on our way to heaven –
we shall live the Lord's word,
on our way to heaven –
we shall live the Lord's word.

4 Hallelujah, amen,
hallelujah, amen,
hallelujah, amen,
hallelujah, amen,
on our way to heaven –
hallelujah, amen,
on our way to heaven –
hallelujah, amen.

212 TAMA NGAKAU

Used by permission of Hope Publishing Co., Carol Stream, IL 60188 USA

NEW ZEALAND

Words: from Romans 3:21–26
traditional Maori, paraphrased Michael Perry
Music: Maori traditional melody
arranged Geoff Weaver

With expression 𝅗𝅥 = 50

G D7 Em C G D7
1 Ta - ma nga - kau ma - ri - e, ta - ma
1 Lord of love, you come to bless all who

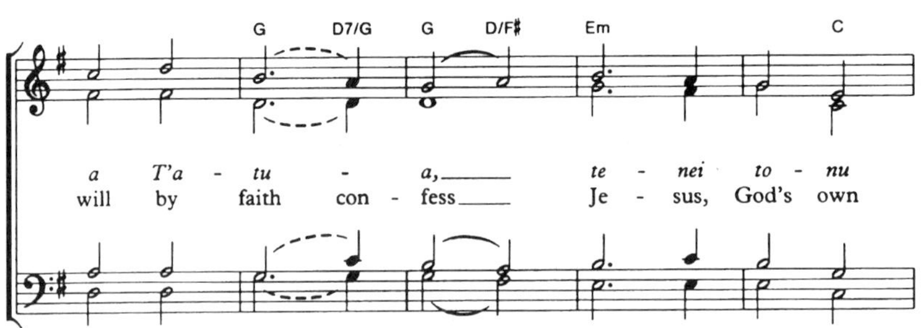

G D7/G G D/F♯ Em C
a T'a - tu - a, te - nei to - nu
will by faith con - fess Je - sus, God's own

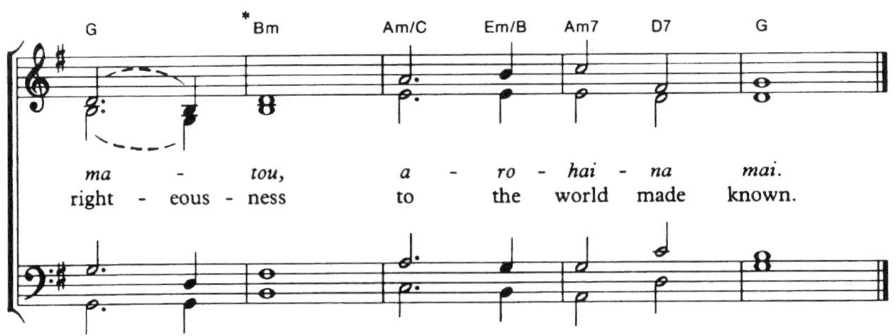

G *Bm Am/C Em/B Am7 D7 G
ma - tou, a - ro - hai - na mai.
right - eous - ness to the world made known.

A simple prayer, based on a traditional Maori melody, most effective when sung unaccompanied.

*ALTERNATIVE ENDING
G
D7
G/D
D7
G
- tou, a - ro - hai - na mai.
- ness to the world made known.

1 *Tama ngakau marie,*
tama a T'atua,
tenei tonu matou,
arohaina mai.

2 *Murua ra nga hara:*
wete kina mai,
enei here kino,
whakararu nei.

3 *Homai he aroha*
mou i mate nei
tenei ra, e Ihu
takina e koe.

1 Lord of love, you come to bless
all who will by faith confess
Jesus, God's own righteousness
to the world made known.

2 Bruised on Calvary's weary road,
bowed beneath the curse of God,
shedding the atoning blood
sacrifice is done.

3 By the arms you open wide,
by your wounded hands and side,
Jesus, we are justified,
saved by grace alone!

213 TATANACA, MAMANACA SARANTAÑANI

BOLIVIA

Words and music: Zoilo Yanapa
arranged Christopher Norton

Brightly ♩ = 72
Capo 3(Bm) Dm (Bm)
Gm7 (Em7)
C7 (A7)
F (D)
1 Ta - ta - na - ca, ma - ma - na - ca, Sa - ran - ta - ña - ni!
(2) Igle - sia na - ca - sa - ja ma - ya-ghasi-ña - ni,
1 Men and wo - men, let us walk, and let's walk to - ge-ther;
(2) Church be one strong bo - dy, walk-ing to - ge-ther;

Dm (Bm)
Gm7 (Em7)
C7 (A7)
F (D)
Ta - ta - na - ca, ma - ma - na - ca, Sa - ran - ta - ña - ni! Way - na -
ta - ke Igle - sia na - ca - sa - ja ma - ya-ghasi-ña - ni. Ma - ya -
men and wo - men, let us walk, and let's walk to - ge-ther. Bro-thers,
let the Church be one strong bo - dy, walk-ing to - ge-ther. Ev - ery

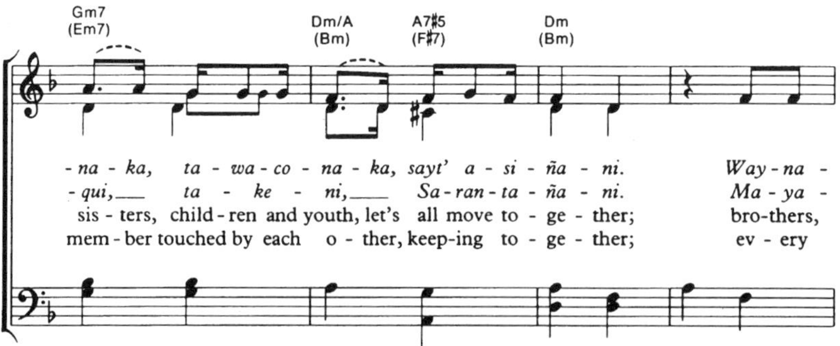
Gm7 (Em7)
Dm/A (Bm)
A7♯5 (F♯7)
Dm (Bm)
- na - ka, ta - wa - co - na - ka, sayt' a - si - ña - ni. Way - na -
- qui, ta - ke - ni, Sa - ran - ta - ña - ni. Ma - ya -
sis - ters, child - ren and youth, let's all move to - ge - ther; bro-thers,
mem - ber touched by each o - ther, keep-ing to - ge - ther; ev - ery

This dance-song comes from the Aymara people of Bolivia. With such vitality in their worship, it is not surprising that they are part of the fastest growing church in their country.

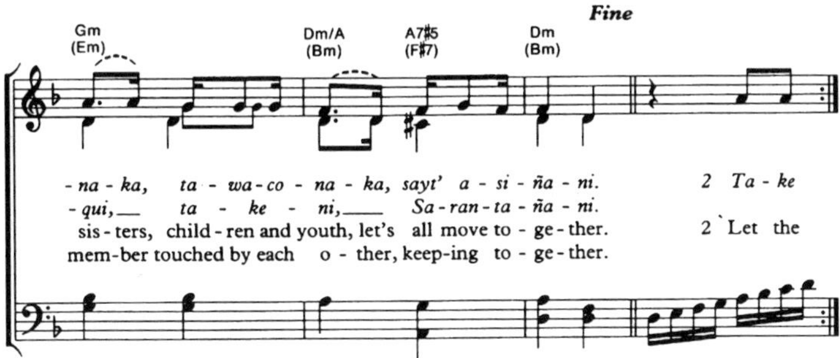
Fine
Gm
(Em)
Dm/A
(Bm)
A7♯5
(F♯7)
Dm
(Bm)
-na - ka, ta - wa-co - na - ka, sayt' a - si - ña - ni. 2 Ta - ke
-qui, ta - ke - ni, Sa-ran-ta - ña - ni.
sis-ters, child-ren and youth, let's all move to - ge-ther. 2 Let the
mem-ber touched by each o - ther, keep-ing to - ge-ther.

1 *Tatanaca, mamanaca, Sarantañani!*
Tatanaca, mamanaca, Sarantañani!
Waynanaka, tawaconaka, sayt' asiñani.
Waynanaka, tawaconaka, sayt' asiñani.

2 *Take Iglesia nacasaja mayaghasiñani,*
take Iglesia nacasaja mayaghasiñani.
Mayaqui, takeni, Sarantañani.
Mayaqui, takeni, Sarantañani.

1 Men and women, let us walk,
and let's walk together;
men and women, let us walk,
and let's walk together.
Brothers, sisters, children and youth,
let's all move together;
brothers, sisters, children and youth,
let's all move together.

2 Let the Church be one strong body,
walking together;
let the Church be one strong body,
walking together.
Every member touched by each other,
keeping together;
every member touched by each other,
keeping together.

214 THE RIGHT HAND OF GOD

CARIBBEAN

Words: after Patrick Prescord
Word & Music
Music: Noel Dexter
arranged Christopher Norton

Joyfully ♩ = 70

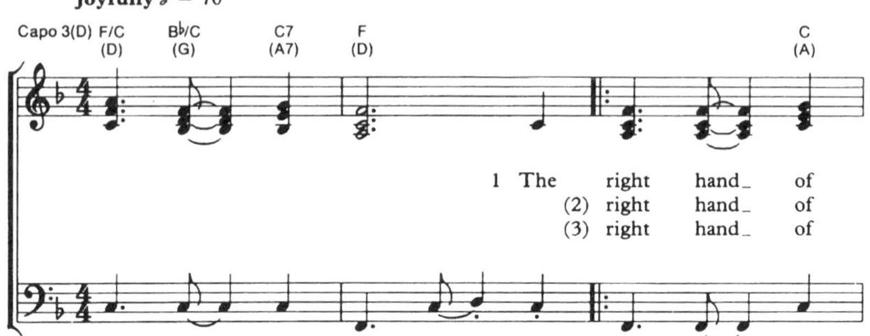

Capo 3(D) F/C (D) B♭/C (G) C7 (A7) F (D) C (A)
1 The right hand of
(2) right hand of
(3) right hand of

F (D) B♭ (G) C (A) F (D)
God is writ-ing in our land,
God is point-ing in our land,
God is strik-ing in our land,

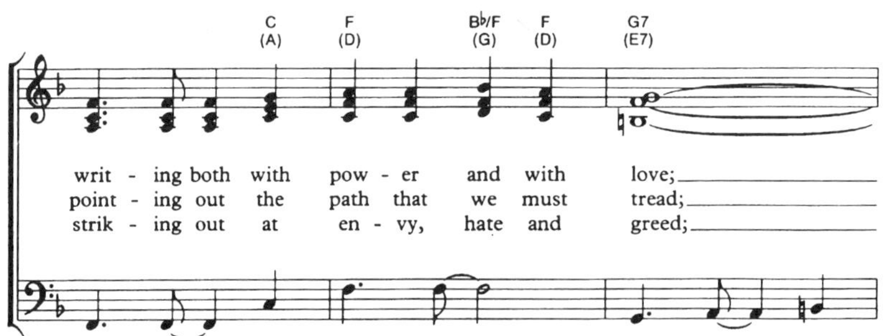

C (A) F (D) B♭/F (G) F (D) G7 (E7)
writ - ing both with pow - er and with love;
point - ing out the path that we must tread;
strik - ing out at en - vy, hate and greed;

A song of judgment, justice and mercy from the Caribbean.
It is very important to feel the rhythmic freedom here.

C (A) Am (F#m) Dm (Bm)
— our con-flicts and — our fears, our
— so cloud-ed is — the way, so
— our self-ish-ness — and lust, our
C/E (A) F (D) Gm7 (Em7) F/A (D) B♭ (G) F/A (D) Gm (Em)
tri-umphs and — our tears, are re-cord-ed by — the
ea-si-ly — we stray, but we're guid-ed by — the
pride, and deeds un-just are con-demned by — the

F/C (D) B♭/C (G) C7 (A7) F (D)
1. 2.
right hand of God. 2 The
right hand of God. 3 The
right hand of God. 4 The

4 The right hand of God is healing in our land,
healing broken bodies, minds and souls;
so when we bow in prayer,
the love of Christ is there
and we're healed by the right hand of God.

5 The right hand of God is planting in our land,
planting seeds of freedom, hope and love.
In this and every place
all we who live by grace
can be one with the right hand of God.

215 THUMA MINA

SOUTH AFRICA

Words and music:
transcribed from the singing of Lulu Dumazweni
arranged John L. Bell

As quickly as the mood requires
G
D
1 Thu - ma mi - na, thu - ma mi - na,
2 Ndi - ya vu - ma, ndi - ya vu - ma,
1 Send me, Je - sus; send me, Je - sus;
2 I am will - ing, I am will - ing;
Am
G
Em
D
G
thu - ma mi - na, Nko - si yam.
ndi - ya vu - ma, Nko - si yam.
send me, Je - sus; send me, Lord.
I am will - ing, will - ing, Lord.
LEADER
Thu - ma mi - na.
Send me Je - sus.

1 *Thuma mina, thuma mina,*
thuma mina, Nkosi yam.

2 *Ndiya vuma, ndiya vuma,*
ndiya vuma, Nkosi yam.

1 Send me, Jesus; send me, Jesus;
send me, Jesus; send me, Lord.

2 I am willing, I am willing;
I am willing, willing, Lord.

Words: South African and English Copyright control

216 TOUT EST FAIT POUR LA GLOIRE DE DIEU

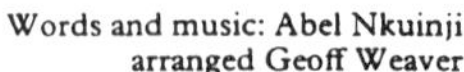
CAMEROON

Words and music: Abel Nkuinji
arranged Geoff Weaver

Rhythmic ♩ = 138

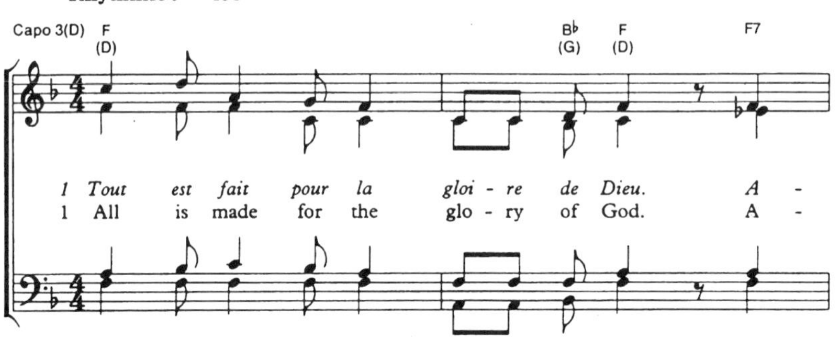
Capo 3(D)
F (D)
B♭ (G)
F (D)
F7
1 Tout est fait pour la gloi - re de Dieu. A -
1 All is made for the glo - ry of God. A -

B♭ (G)
B♭6
F (D)
- men, (A - men) a - men! Tout est fait pour la
- men, (A - men) a - men! All is made for the
SOLO Al - le - lu - ia
Al - le - lu - ia

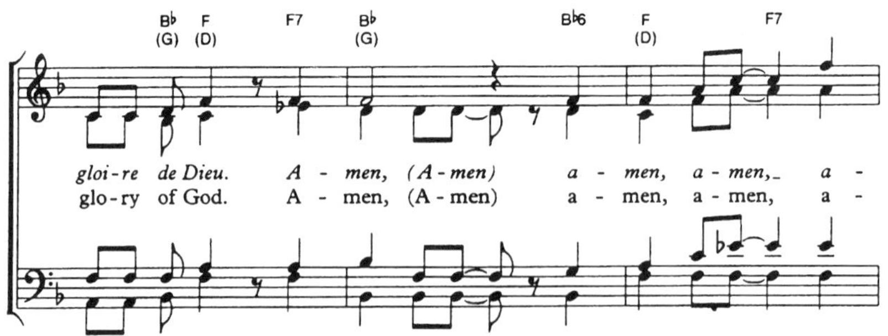
B♭ (G)
F (D)
F7
B♭ (G)
B♭6
F (D)
F7
gloi - re de Dieu. A - men, (A - men) a - men, a - men, a -
glo - ry of God. A - men, (A - men) a - men, a - men, a -

A lively rhythmic song from French-speaking West Africa. It can be extended indefinitely, as is the practice in Africa, by naming other subjects and creatures which exist for God's glory.

B♭
(G)
F
(D)
- men, (A - men) a - men! (A - men!) Tout est fait pour la
- men, (A - men) a - men! (A - men!) All is made for the

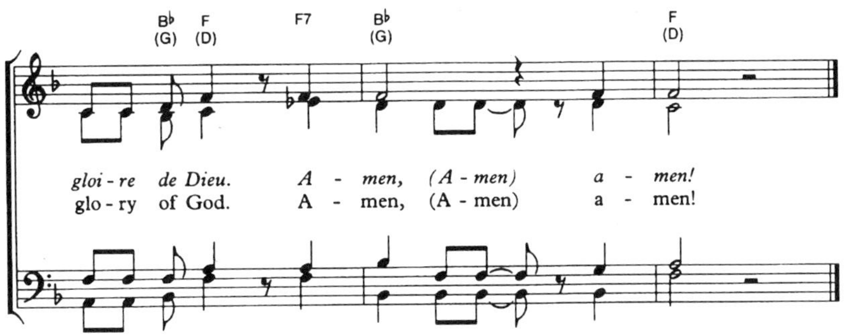
B♭ F F7 B♭ F
(G) (D) (G) (D)
gloi - re de Dieu. A - men, (A - men) a - men!
glo - ry of God. A - men, (A - men) a - men!

1 *Tout est fait pour la gloire de Dieu.*
Amen, amen!
Tout est fait pour la gloire de Dieu.
Amen, amen, amen, amen, amen!
Tout est fait pour la gloire de Dieu.
Amen, amen!

2 *La vie c'est pour la gloire de Dieu . . .*

3 *Le culte est pour la gloire de Dieu . . .*

1 All is made for the glory of God.
Amen, amen!
All is made for the glory of God.
Amen, amen, amen, amen, amen!
All is made for the glory of God.
Amen, amen!

2 Living is for the glory of God . . .

3 Worship is for the glory of God . . .

217 TUA PALAVRA

Dm
F6
Am6
Am
1.Tu - a pa - la - vra na vi - da
Gm9
A♭0
G7
C6
i fon - te que ja - mais se - ca
Dm
F6
Am7
Am
a - gua que a - ni - ma e res - tau - ra
B♭7
E7
Am
to - dos que a quei - ram be - ber.

1. Tua Palavra na vida
   é fonte que jamais seca,
   água que anima e restaura
   todos que a queiram beber.

2. Tua Palavra na vida
   é qual semente que brota,
   torna-se bom alimento,
   pão que não hã de faltar.

3. Tua Palavra na vida
   é luz que os passos clareia,
   para que ao fim no horizonte
   se veja o Reino de Deus.

Simei Monteiro (Brazil)

1. Your word in our lives, eternal,
   it is a clear founting flowing,
   water that gives strength and courage
   to all who draw near and drink.

2. Your word in our lives, eternal,
   seed of the Kingdom that's growing,
   it becomes bread for our tables,
   food for the feast without end.

3. Your word in our lives, eternal,
   is light that shines on the long road
   that leads us to the horizon
   and the bright Kingdom of God.

218 TUKUTENDEREZA YESU

Used by permission of Hope Publishing Co., Carol Stream, IL 60188 USA

EAST AFRICA

Words: from the Luganda, unknown
translated L. Rouse
Music: African, unknown
English: D. Boole
arranged David Peacock

Steadily ♩ = 90

G
Tu - ku - ten - de - re - za Ye - su, Ye - su

D D7/F♯ G
Omwa - na gw'en - di - ga; o - mu - sai - gwo gu - na -

D7 G
- zi - za‿n - kwe - ba - za, O - mu - lo - ko - zi.

The great song of the East African Revival, with all its resonances of 'walking in the light' and the transformation of so many lives. The Luganda version is based on an existing English hymn. The English text cannot be sung to the Luganda adaptation of the music.

ENGLISH VERSION

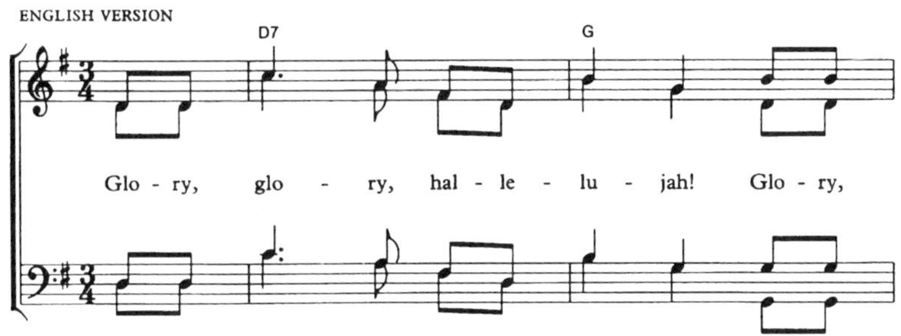
D7
G
Glo - ry, glo - ry, hal - le - lu - jah! Glo - ry,

A7
D
G
glo - ry to the Lamb! Oh, the cleans - ing blood has

Em7
A7
D7
G
reached me – glo - ry, glo - ry to the Lamb!

Tukutendereza Yesu,
Yesu Omwana gw'endiga;
omusaigwo gunaziza –
nkwebaza, Omulokozi.

Glory, glory, hallelujah!
Glory, glory to the Lamb!
Oh, the cleansing blood has reached me –
glory, glory to the Lamb!

219 VEM, JESUS NOSSA ESPERANCA

BRAZIL

Words: Jorge Rodriguez
Jaci C. Maraschin
Music: Marcilide de Oliveira Filko
arranged Christopher Norton
Rhythmically ♩ = 120
Capo 1(D)
E♭ (D) D♭ (C) E♭ (D) A♭7 (G7) B♭7 (A7)
1 Vem, Je - sus nos - sa es - pe - ran - ça nos - sas vi - das li - ber -
2 Vem te - cer um mun - do no - vo nos cam - in - hos de verd - a -
1 Come to be our hope, Lord Je - sus, come to set our peo - ple
2 Come to build your new cre - a - tion through the road of ser - vant -
E♭ (D) D♭ (C) E♭ (D)
- tar. Vem, nas - cer em nós, cri - an - ça vem o
- de; pa - ra que, a - fi - nal, o po - vo vi - va em
free; from op - pres - sion come, re - lease us, turn de -
- hood; give new life to ev - ery na - tion, chang - ing
A♭7 (G7) B♭7 (A7) E♭ (D) A♭ (G) B♭ (A)
teu po - der nos dar. Vem, li - ber - ta os pri - sio -
ple - na li - berd - ade. Vem, Je - sus, a - bre o fu -
- feat to vic - to - ry! Come, re - lease from ev - ery
e - vil in - to good. Come and o - pen our to -

Jaci Maraschin is one of Brazil's foremost Church composers. For him the dance finds its place in worship reflecting hope, while the flattened third portrays the pain of oppression. A light rhythmic accompaniment helps to bring out the dance-like character here.

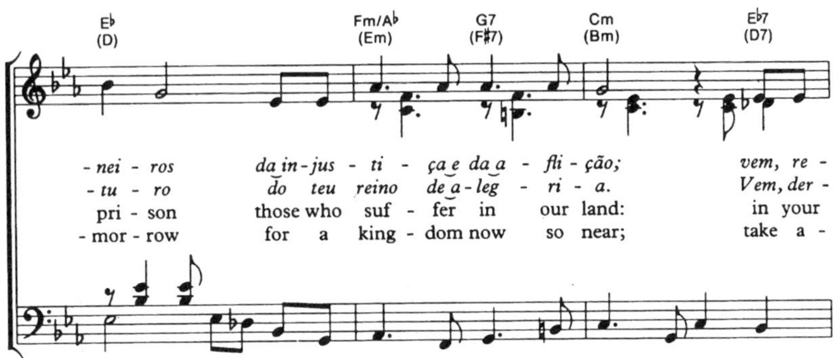
E♭ (D)
Fm/A♭ (Em)
G7 (F♯7)
Cm (Bm)
E♭7 (D7)
- nei - ros da in - jus - ti - ça e da a - fli - ção; vem, re -
- tu - ro do teu reino de a - leg - ri - a. Vem, der -
pri - son those who suf - fer in our land: in your
- mor - row for a king - dom now so near; take a -

A♭ (G)
B♭ (A)
E♭ (D)
C♭ (B♭)
A♭ (G)
B♭ (A)
E♭ (D)
- ú - ne os bra - si lei - ros em a - mor ___ e em com-preen-são.
- ruba o i-men - so mu - ro que se - para ___ a noite e o dia.
love we find the rea-son still to live ___ and un - der-stand.
- way all hu - man sor-row – give us hope ___ in place of fear.

1 Vem, Jesus nossa esperança
nossas vidas libertar.
Vem, nascer em nós, criança
vem o teu poder nos dar.
Vem, liberta os prisioneiros
da injustiça e da aflição;
vem, reúne os brasi leiros
em amor e em compreensão.

2 Vem tecer um mundo novo
nos caminhos de verdade;
para que, afinal, o povo
viva em plena liberdade.
Vem, Jesus, abre o futuro
do teu reino de alegria.
Vem, derruba o imenso muro
que separa a noite e o dia.

1 Come to be our hope, Lord Jesus,
come to set our people free;
from oppression come, release us,
turn defeat to victory!
Come, release from every prison
those who suffer in our land:
in your love we find the reason
still to live and understand.

2 Come to build your new creation
through the road of servanthood;
give new life to every nation,
changing evil into good.
Come and open our tomorrow
for a kingdom now so near;
take away all human sorrow –
give us hope in place of fear.

220 WERE YOU THERE

American folk hymn melody
arr. BERNARD S. MASSEY (1927–)

Unison

WERE you there when they crucified my Lord?
Were you there when they crucified my Lord?
Oh, sometimes it causes me to tremble, tremble, tremble;
Were you there when they crucified my Lord?

2 Were you there when they nailed him to the tree?

3 Were you there when they pierced him in the side?

4 Were you there when the sun refused to shine?

5 Were you there when they laid him in the tomb?

6 Were you there when God raised him from the dead?

American folk hymn

221 WHAT A GREAT MYSTERY

Francisco A. Feliciano

Based on a Bicol Folksong "Caturog na Nonoy"

(Gitara)
1. Far be-yond our mind's grasp and our tongue's de - clar - ing.
2. None of us is worth - y to re - ceive your es - sence.
1. Hin-di ko ma- i - sip, kay la - king hi - wa - ga.
2. Ang a - bang ling- kod mo'y di ka - ra pat da - pat.
You are here in mys - t'ry, quite - ly, tru - ly with-out fail:
In this meal to - geth er: yet, the gift is yours by choice.
Kay la - king pag - li ngap, pag pa - pa - ka - sa___ - kit
Sa-iyo'y ma - ki - sa - lo ma - ki-pag-ha - pu -___ nan

World

Lift - ted once on Cal - v'ry, sin and weak-ness bear - ing,
Death can nev - er snatch us from your ho - ly pres - ence,
Sa - la na-ming ta - o ng I - yong a - ku - in
Di na nga-na - na - is ng ma ra ming ba - gay
1.-3.
4.
O Lord, how won-der - ful you call us through the veil.
Your prom - ise is for life; we on - ly can re - joice.
Wa - lang hang - ga-nan Diyos, ang iyong pag - i - big.
Sa - pat na ma-da-mang I - kay ka - pi - ling.

3. Soon our hearts are lifted
to the realms above us,
Nourished and united
by the precious bread and wine.
Here what sweet contentment,
knowing that you love us!
We thank you for this feast,
this fellowship divine.

3. Nang aking malasap
alak at tinapay,
Aking kagalakan
ay walang mapagsidlan.
Di kinakailangang
akin pang wariin,
Kung bakit ang ligaya
ko'y walang patid.

4. Soon you bid us scatter,
share what we inherit.
From this home of blessing
where we taste your peace and grace.
May our lives be altars
glowing with your Spirit.
To light the lamps of those
who also seek your face.

4. Sana'y sa paglisan
sa iyong tahanan,
Aming mga puso
ay iyong lukuban.
Na maging dambana
ng iyong kabutihan,
Maging huwaran
ng pagmamahalan.

222 WHAT WONDROUS LOVE IS THIS

Used by permission of Hope Publishing Co., Carol Stream, IL 60188 USA

UNITED STATES OF AMERICA

Words and music: American folk hymn
arranged David Peacock

Simply 𝅗𝅥 = 80
Dm C F Am7(add2) Dm
1 What wond-rous love is this, O my soul, O my
(2) God and to the Lamb, I will sing, I will
(3) when from death I'm free, I'll sing on, I'll sing

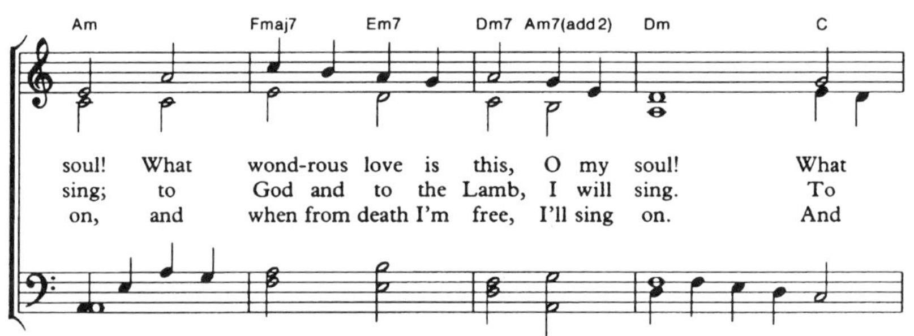
Am Fmaj7 Em7 Dm7 Am7(add2) Dm C
soul! What wond-rous love is this, O my soul! What
sing; to God and to the Lamb, I will sing. To
on, and when from death I'm free, I'll sing on. And

F B♭ Am Am7 G
wond-rous love is this that caused the Lord of bliss to
God and to the Lamb who is the great I AM, while
when from death I'm free, I'll sing and joy - ful be, and

A modal song of considerable character which should be sung simply and in unison.

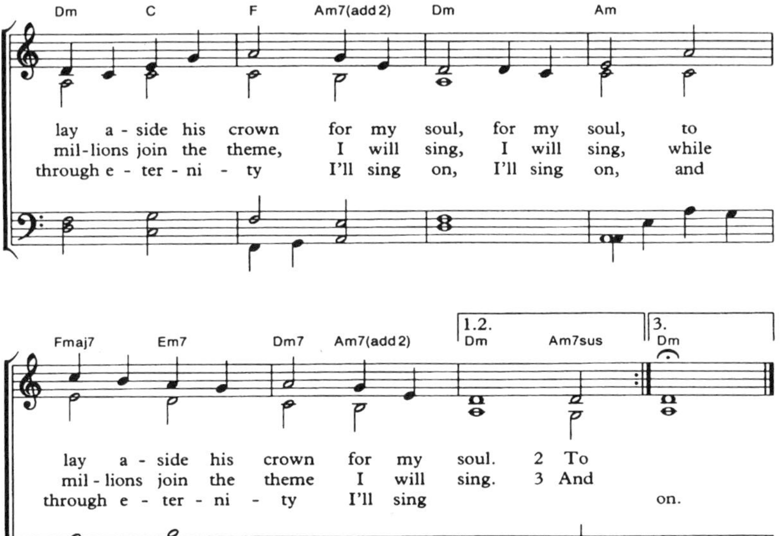
Dm C F Am7(add2) Dm Am
lay a - side his crown for my soul, for my soul, to
mil - lions join the theme, I will sing, I will sing, while
through e - ter - ni - ty I'll sing on, I'll sing on, and
Fmaj7 Em7 Dm7 Am7(add2) 1.2. Dm Am7sus 3. Dm
lay a - side his crown for my soul. 2 To
mil - lions join the theme I will sing. 3 And
through e - ter - ni - ty I'll sing on.

1 What wondrous love is this,
O my soul, O my soul!
What wondrous love is this, O my soul!
What wondrous love is this
that caused the Lord of bliss
to lay aside his crown
for my soul, for my soul,
to lay aside his crown for my soul.

2 To God and to the Lamb, I will sing, I will sing;
to God and to the Lamb, I will sing.
To God and to the Lamb
who is the great I AM,
while millions join the theme,
I will sing, I will sing,
while millions join the theme I will sing.

3 And when from death I'm free,
I'll sing on, I'll sing on,
and when from death I'm free, I'll sing on.
And when from death I'm free,
I'll sing and joyful be,
and through eternity
I'll sing on, I'll sing on,
and through eternity I'll sing on.

Chants and Responses

223 ADORAMUS TE, DOMINE

Mixed Voices
Music: Jacques Berthier (1923 -1994)
A
B
(hum)
A - do - ra - mus te Do- mi - ne.

224 AMEN

China

Chinese folk melody
arr. Jiang Pu–qi

(A)
(B)
A- - - men___, A- - - men___, A- - - - - - - - - - men.
A- - - men___, A- - - men___, A- - - - - - - - men.

Permission granted by the Asian Institute for Liturgy and Music, on behalf of the composer Mr. Jiang Puqi.

225 BLESS THE LORD

Ostinato Chorale

Music: Jacques Berthier (1923 -1994)

Mixed Voices
♩= 76
p
Bless the Lord my soul and bless his ho - ly name.
p

p
Bless the Lord my soul, who leads me in - to life.
p

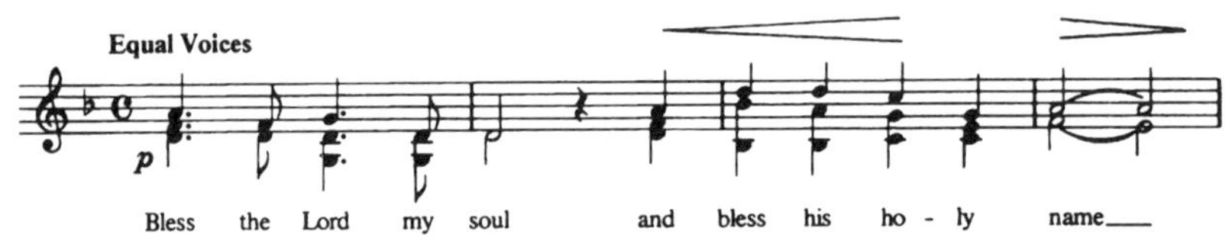
Equal Voices
p
Bless the Lord my soul and bless his ho - ly name

p
Bless the Lord my soul who leads me in - to life.

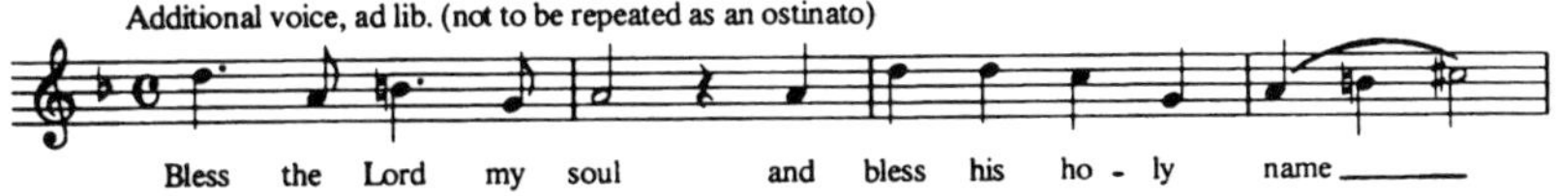
Additional voice, ad lib. (not to be repeated as an ostinato)
Bless the Lord my soul and bless his ho - ly name

Bless the Lord my soul who leads me in - to life.

Accompaniment

Keyboard or Guitar
Dm G Dm B♭ C F A

Dm G Dm B♭ C Dm

225 Contd.

Verses From Psalm 102 (103)

Cantor
1. It is he who for - gives all your guilt, who
heals ev - 'ry - one of your ills, who re - deems your life from the
grave, who crowns you with love and com - pas - sion.

2. The Lord is com - pas - sion and love, slow to
an - ger and rich in mer - cy. He does not treat us ac - cord - ing to our
sins nor re - pay us ac - cord - ing to our faults.

3. As a Fa - ther has com - pas - sion on his chil - dren, the Lord has
pi - ty on those who fear him; for he knows of what we are
made, he re - mem - bers that we are dust.

226 CELTIC ALLELUIA

ff AL LE - LU - IA, AL - LE - LU - IA,
ff Al - le - lu - ia, al - le - lu - ia,
Gt. ff
Ped. 8' + 16'
AL LE - LU - IA, AL - LE - LU - IA!
al le - lu - ia, al - le - lu - ia!

Words: Chris Walker
Music: Fintan O'Carroll

227 CHRISTE SALVATOR

Lord God, Son of the Father, have mercy on us

Ostinato Response

Music: Jacques Berthier (1923 -1994)

Mixed Voices
𝅗𝅥 = 50
p
mf
Chri-ste Sal - va - tor, Fi - li - us Pa - tris, do - na no - bis pa - cem.
(hum)
p
mf

Equal Voices
p
mf
Chri-ste Sal - va - tor, Fi - li - us Pa - tris, do - na no - bis pa - cem.

Accompaniment

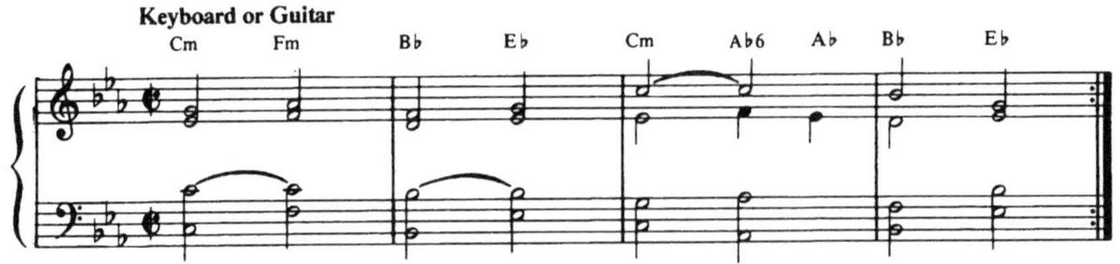
Keyboard or Guitar
Cm
Fm
B♭
E♭
Cm
A♭6
A♭
B♭
E♭

Chants

Verses Psalm 129 (130)

Cantor
(Miserere no - bis)
1. Out of the depths I cry to you, O Lord.
Lord, hear my voice! O let your ears be at - ten - tive to the
voice of my plead - ing.
2. If you, O Lord, should mark our
guilt, Lord, who would sur - vive? But with you is found for -
give - ness: for this we re - vere you.
3. My
soul is wait - ing for the Lord, I count on his word. My
soul is long - ing for the Lord, more than watch - man for day - break.
4. Be - cause with the Lord there is mer - cy and ful - ness of re -
dem - ption Is - ra - ël in - deed he will re - deem from all its in -
i - qui - ty.
5. Give praise to the Fa - ther al -
might - y, to his son Je - sus Christ, our Lord to the
spi - rit who dwells in our hearts, both now and for e - ver. A - men!

*Choose either part

227 Contd.

Other Verses Liturgical texts in various languages

English
(Miserere no bis)
1. You take a - way the sin of the world
2. By your pas - sion set us free, O Lord.
3
3. By your re - sur - rec - tion set us free, O Lord.
Spanish
(Miserere no - bis)
1. Tú que qui - tas el pe -
2
ca - do del mun - do 2. Por tu pa-sión, li - be - ra nos Se - ñor.
3
3. Por tu re - sur - rec - ción, li - be - ra nos Se - ñor.
German
(Miserere no bis)
1. Du nimmst 'hin - weg die Sün - de der Welt.
2. Durch dein Lei - den, Herr, be - frei - e uns.
*
3. Durch dei - ne Auf - er ste - hung be - frei - e uns.

*Choose either part

French
(Miserere no - bis)
2
Toi qui en - lè - ves le pè - ché du mon - de.
Par ta pas - sion, dé - li - vre nous, Sei - gneur.
Par ta ré - sur - rec - tion, dé - li - vre nous.
Italian
(Miserere no - bis)
Tu che to - gli i pec - ca - ti del
mon - - do. Con la
tu - a pas - sio - ne, li - be - ra - ci, Si - gno - re. Con la
tu - a ri - sur - re - zio - ne, li - be - ra - ci, Si - gno - re.
Amen (End)
(Miserere no - bis)
2
A - - - men!
2
A - - - - - men! A - - - - - men!

*Choose either part

228 COME ALL YOU PEOPLE

Tune & words: Alexander Gondo
Arrangement: JLB

(cantor)
energetically
U - ya - i mo - se, tin - a - ma - te Mwa - ri,
(women)
Come all you peo - ple, come and praise your Ma - ker,
U - ya - i mo - se, ti - na - ma - te Mwa - ri,
Come all you peo - ple, come and praise your Ma - ker,
(men)
Ahom
Ahom
U - ya - i mo - se, ti - na - ma - te Mwa - ri,
Come all you peo - ple, come and praise your Ma - ker,
U - ya - i mo - se, ti - na - ma - te Mwa - ri,
Come all you peo - ple, come and praise your Ma - ker,
Ahom
Ahom

U - ya - i mo - se, ti - na - ma - te Mwa - ri,
Come all you peo - ple, come and praise your Ma - ker,
U - ya - i mo - se, ti - na - ma - te Mwa - ri,
Come all you peo - ple, come and praise your Ma - ker,
Ahom
Ahom
[except last time]
U - ya - i mo - se zvi - no. ti - na - ma - te Mwa - ri,
Come now and wor - ship the Lord. Come and praise your Ma - ker,
U - ya - i mo - se zvi - no.
Come now and wor - ship the Lord.
Ahom
Ahom
Ahom

Uyai mose, tinamate Mwari (x3)
Uyai mose zvino.

Come all you people, come and praise your Maker (x3)
Come now and worship the Lord.

229 COME, O COME

From "Sound the Bamboo" published by the Christian Conference of Asia, 1990

Myanmar

Lajakle, Taura P'ya

University Christian Fellowship, Burma
para. I-to Loh and James Minchin

Burmese trad.

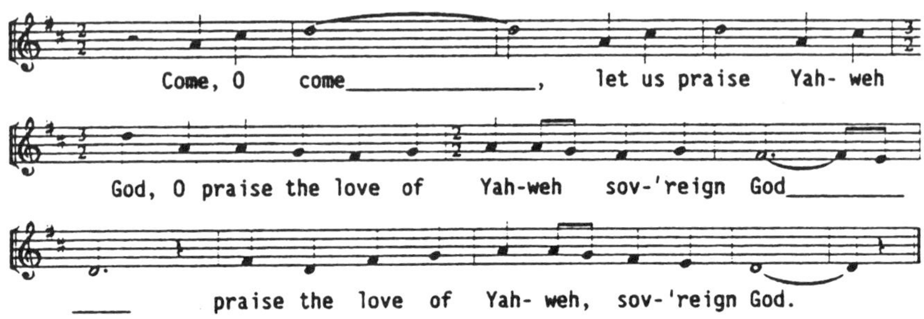

Come, O come, let us praise Yah- weh
God, O praise the love of Yah-weh sov-'reign God
praise the love of Yah- weh, sov-'reign God.

1. Come, O come, let us praise Yahweh God,
   O praise the love of Yahweh, sov'reign God,
   Praise the love of Yahweh, sov'reign God.

2. Come, O come, let us praise Christ, our King,
   O praise the grace of Christ, the Prince of Peace,
   Praise the grace of Christ, the Prince of Peace.

3. Come, O come, let us praise Spirit God,
   The fellowship of Holy Spirit God,
   Fellowship of Holy Spirit God.

Chants

1. Lajakle Tau-ra P'ya, Tau-ra P'ya i
   Metadaw ko chimon sohle,
   Metadaw ko chimon sohle.

2. Lajakle Kritaw P'ya, Kritaw P'ya i
   Jezudaw ko chimon sohle,
   Jezudaw ko chimon sohle.

3. Lajakle. Wingin P'ya, wingin P'ya i
   Meita hayah ko chimon sohle,
   Meita hayah ko chimon sohle.

230 GINOO MALOOY KA KANAMO

Used by permission of Hope Publishing Co., Carol Stream, IL 60188 USA

O Lord, have mercy

PHILIPPINES

KYRIE

Words: traditional
Music: as taught by Jeaneth Harris
arranged Geoff Weaver

With quiet intensity ♩ = 76

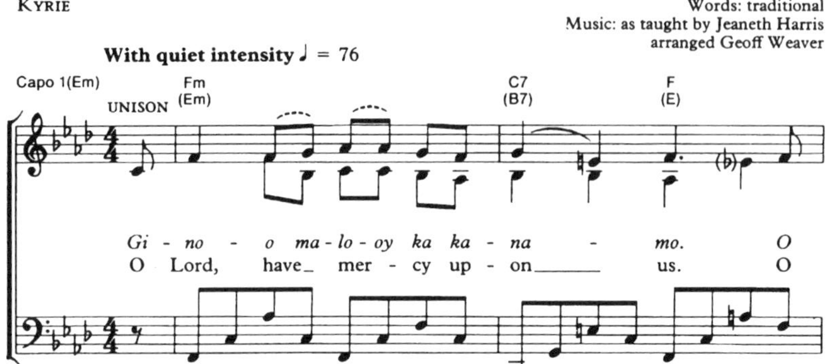

Capo 1(Em)
UNISON
Fm (Em)
C7 (B7)
F (E)
Gi - no - o ma - lo - oy ka ka - na - mo. O
O Lord, have_ mer - cy up - on_____ us. O

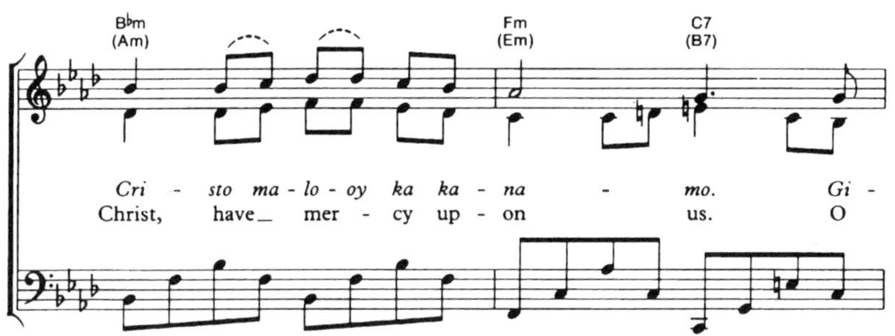

B♭m (Am)
Fm (Em)
C7 (B7)
Cri - sto ma - lo - oy ka ka - na - mo. Gi -
Christ, have_ mer - cy up - on us. O

D♭ (C)
A♭ (G)
Gm7/B♭ (F♯m)
C7 (B7)
Fm (Em)
- no - o ma - lo - oy ka ka - na - mo.
Lord, have_ mer - cy up - on_____ us.

A haunting, melancholy Kyrie (Lord, have mercy) from the Philippines, where so many people cry out in their sufferings and hardships.

HARMONY
Gi - no - o ma - lo - oy ka ka - na - mo. O
O Lord, have mer - cy up - on us. O
Cri - sto ma - lo - oy ka ka - na - mo. Gi -
Christ, have mer - cy up - on us. O
- no - o ma - lo - oy ka ka - na - mo.
Lord, have mer - cy up - on us.

Ginoo malooy ka kanamo.
O Cristo malooy ka kanamo.
Ginoo malooy ka kanamo.

O Lord, have mercy upon us.
O Christ, have mercy upon us.
O Lord, have mercy upon us.

231 GLORIA III

Glory to God in the highest. Alleluia!
Christ is born today, the Savior has appeared.

Principal Canon Music: Jacques Berthier (1923 -1994)

A = 80
B
Glo - ri - a, glo - ri - a, in ex - cel - sis De - o!
C
D
Glo - ri - a, glo - ri - a, al - le - lu - ia, al - le - lu - ia!
Secondary Canon - for Cantors or Choir (Unison, or in 2 Voice Canon at A and B).
1. Soprano, Tenor
A
Ho - di - e Chri - stus na - tus est, Sal - va - tor ap - pa - ru - it.
B
Al - le - lu - ia, al - le - lu - ia. (-ia). Glo - ri - a, glo - ri -
a, in ex - cel - sis De - o. Glo - ri - a, glo - ri - a, al - le - lu - - ia.
2. Alto, Bass (Variation in small notes)
A
Ho - di - e Chri - stus na - tus est, Sal - va - tor ap - pa - ru - it.
Ho - di - e Chri - stus na - tus est, Sal - va - tor ap - pa - ru - it.
B
(-it) Glo - ri - a, glo - ri - a, in ex - cel - sis De -
(-ia)
o. Glo - ri - a, glo - ri - a, al - le - lu - - ia.

Keyboard or Instruments

1
2
3

4

Guitar

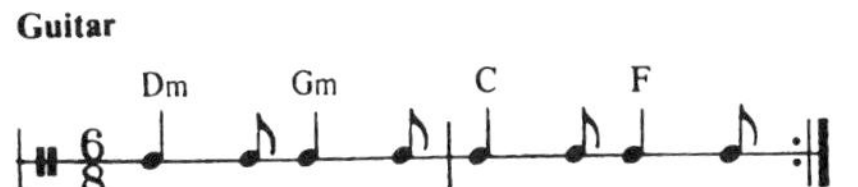
Dm
Gm
C
F

Rhythms may be added by small percussion instruments.

Choir

1
2
3
(hum)

4

232 GLORY TO GOD

Used by permission of Hope Publishing Co., Carol Steam, IL 60188 USA

PERU

Words and music: unknown

Lively but not too quickly ♩ = 132
LEADER
Glo-ry to God, glo-ry to God, glo - ry in the high - est!

ALL
Glo-ry to God, glo-ry to God, glo - ry in the high - est!

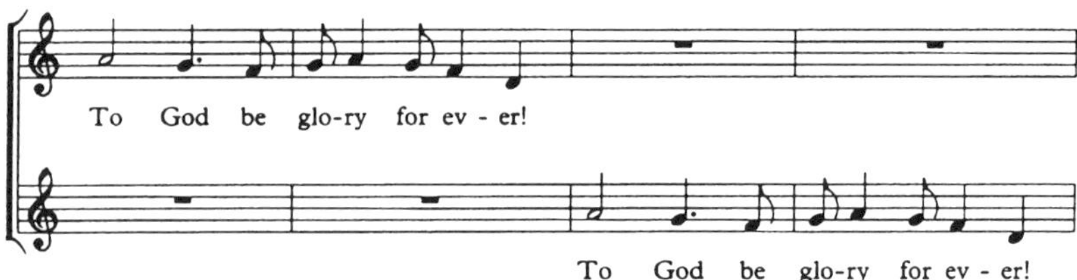

To God be glo-ry for ev - er!
To God be glo-ry for ev - er!

Al-le-lu-ia! A-men! Al-le-lu-ia! A-men!
GROUP 1
GROUP 2
Al-le-lu-ia! A-men! Al-le-lu-ia! A-men! Al-le-lu-ia! A-men!

This is ideal for celebrations and for any festive occasion. There are many ways of performing the Alleluias– feel free to experiment and to extend them. The song should be rhythmic but not too quick.

Al-le-lu-ia! A-men!
GROUP 3
Al-le-lu-ia! A-men! Al-le-lu-ia! A-men! Al-le-lu-ia! A-men! Al-le-lu-ia! A-men!

LEADER	Glory to God, glory to God, glory in the highest!
ALL	Glory to God, glory to God, glory in the highest!
LEADER	To God be glory for ever!
ALL	To God be glory for ever!
LEADER	Alleluia! Amen!
GROUP 1	Alleluia! Amen!
LEADER	Alleluia! Amen!
GROUPS 1, 2	Alleluia! Amen!
LEADER	Alleluia! Amen!
GROUPS 1, 2, 3	Alleluia! Amen!
ALL	Alleluia! Amen! Alleluia! Amen!

233 HALLELUJAH

ZIMBABWE

Words: traditional
Music: Abraham Maraire

Dynamically ♩. = 66
WOMEN
Hal - le - lu - jah, hal - le - lu - jah,
TENORS
Hal - le - lu - jah, hal - le - lu -,
BASSES
Hal - le - lu - jah, hal - le - lu - jah,

hal - le - lu - jah, hal - le - lu - jah!
hal - le - lu - jah, hal - le - lu - jah!
hal - le - lu - jah, hal - le - lu - jah!

An exuberant outburst, ideal as a congregational response before and after the Gospel reading. It moves quickly, effectively one beat to a bar.

234 HE BECAME POOR

He be-came poor that we may be rich
lov-ing the world and leav – ing his throne;
King of all Kings and Lord of all Lords,
Flesh of our flesh and bone of our bone.

235 HOSANNA

Canon
Music: Jacques Berthier (1923 -1994)
♩ = 116
A
B
C
D
Ho - san - na, ho - san - na, ho - san - na in ex - cel - sis. Ho -
Accompaniments
Keyboard
1
2
3
4
f
Guitar
E A B E
Choir
1
2
3
4
(hum)
Soprano or Instrument (at the end of the Canon)
1
In ex - cel - sis, in ex - cel - sis A - - men,
4
8
A - men, A - - men, A - men, A - - men, A - men, A - men,
12
A - men, A - men, A - men, A - men, A - men.

236 IMELA

Words and music:
Christ Church Gospel Band, Umani-Enugu
arranged Iona Community

Brightly ♩ = 88

Em
D
A
D
I - me - la, *i - me - la,* *i - me - la,* *O - ka - ka.*
We thank you, thank you Lord, we thank you, our great God.

Em
D
Bm
A7
D
I - me - la, *Chi - ne - ke.* *I - me - le* *On - y'o - ma.*
We thank you, gra-cious Lord, we thank you, our great God.

Imela, imela, imela, Okaka.
Imela, Chineke. Imele Ony'oma.

We thank you, thank you Lord,
we thank you, our great God.
We thank you, gracious Lord,
we thank you, our great God.

An Igbo song of thanksgiving, popular all over Nigeria. It requires freedom of expression, movement, handclaps, drumbeats and many repetitions to capture the authentic Nigerian flavour.

237 ISHWORO

Used by permission of Hope Publishing Co., Carol Stream, IL 60188 USA INDIA

KYRIE
Words: traditional
Music: unknown
arranged Geoff Weaver
Intensely ♩ = 84
SOLO
ALL
Ish - wo-ro, Ish - wo-ro da - ya ko - ro; Ish - wo-ro, Ish - wo-ro da - ya ko - ro.
Fa - ther in hea - ven, have mer-cy up - on us; Fa - ther in hea - ven, have mer-cy up - on us.
Ish - wo - ro da - ya ko - ro; Ish - wo - ro da - ya ko - ro.
Je - sus Christ, have mer-cy up - on us; Je - sus Christ, have mer-cy up - on us.
Ish - wo-ro, Ish - wo-ro da - ya ko - ro; Ish - wo-ro, Ish - wo-ro da - ya ko - ro.
Fa - ther in hea - ven, have mer-cy up - on us; Fa - ther in hea - ven, have mer-cy up - on us.
rit.
F♯m
A/C♯
F♯m/C♯
Bm
C♯m7

A solo-response Kyrie eleison (Lord, have mercy), characteristically Indian in its melodic shape. It should be sung with heartfelt yearning.

238 JESUS, REMEMBER ME

Ostinato Response

Music: Jacques Berthier (1923 -1994)

Mixed Voices
♩ = 69
Je - sus, re - mem - ber me when you come in - to your King - dom.
Je - sus, re - mem - ber me when you come in - to your King - dom.
Equal Voices
Je - sus, re - mem - ber me when you come in - to your King - dom.
Je - sus, re - mem - ber me when you come in - to your King - dom.

Accompaniment

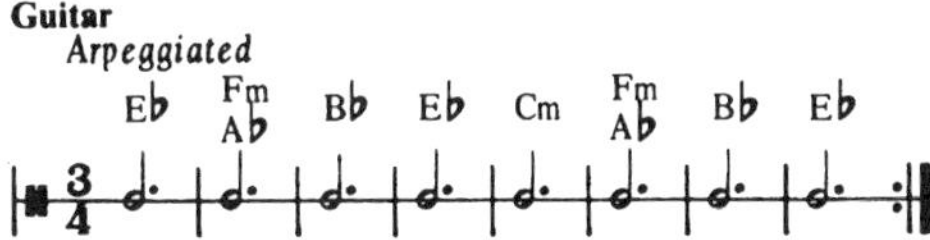

Guitar
Arpeggiated
E♭ Fm A♭ B♭ E♭ Cm Fm A♭ B♭ E♭

239 KINDLE A FLAME TO LIGHTEN THE DARK

Kind — le a flame to light — en the dark and

take all fear a — way. ——

240 KUMBAYA

Words & tune: Afro-Caribbean, traditional
Arrangement: JLB

firmly
(cantor) Kum - ba - ya my Lord, Kum - ba - ya
(all) Kum - ba - ya Kum - ba - ya my Lord, Kum - ba-
ya___ Kum - ba - ya my Lord, Kum - ba - ya___ O Lord,__ Kum - ba - ya.

1. Kumbaya, my Lord, Kumbaya (x3)
   O Lord Kumbaya.
2. Someone's crying, Lord, Kumbaya...
3. Someone's dying, Lord, Kumbaya...
4. Someone's shouting, Lord, Kumbaya...
5. Someone's praying, Lord, Kumbaya...
6. Kumbaya, my Lord... (as verse 1)

241 KYRIE ELEISON

Used by permission of HarperCollins Publishers Ltd.

RUSSIA

KYRIE

Words: traditional
Music: Russian Orthodox

Slowly ♩ = 60

Ky - ri - e e - lei - son. Ky - ri - e e - lei - son.
Lord, have mer - cy. Lord, have mer - cy.

Ky - ri - e e - lei - son.
Lord, have mer - cy.

Kyrie eleison.
Kyrie eleison.
Kyrie eleison.

Lord, have mercy.
Lord, have mercy.
Lord, have mercy.

Originally from the Russian Orthodox Church, this simple chant is ideal for encouraging a congregation to sing in harmony. It may be used repeatedly as a focus for meditation.

242 KYRIE ELEISON

Lord, have mercy

GHANA

Words: traditional
Music: Dinah Reindorf
arranged Geoff Weaver

Expressively ♩ = 76
Capo 3(Am) Cm (Am)
F7/C (D7)
Gaug/C (E)
Cm (Am)
Ky - ri - e e - le - i - son. Ky - ri - e e -
Lord, have mer - cy. Lord, have
F9 (D)
Gaug (E)
G7
Cm (Am)
Cm7 (Am7)
F7 (D7)
D7(add F) (B7)
- le - i - son. Ky - ri - e e - le - i - son.
mer - cy. Lord, have mer - cy.
Bdim (G♯dim)
Cm/G (Am)
Fm(♭9) (Dm)
Cm (Am)
Ky - ri - e e - lei - son.
Lord, have mer - cy on us.

It is not too fanciful to hear in this expressive Kyrie, with echoes of the blues in its final phrase, so much of the pain and suffering of Ghana's colonial past with its slave trade and enforced break-up of families. Dinah Reindorf, one of Ghana's leading musicians, composed this in response to a Passion Walk, walking in Christ's footsteps to the cross.

243 KYRIE ELEISON

Lord, have mercy.

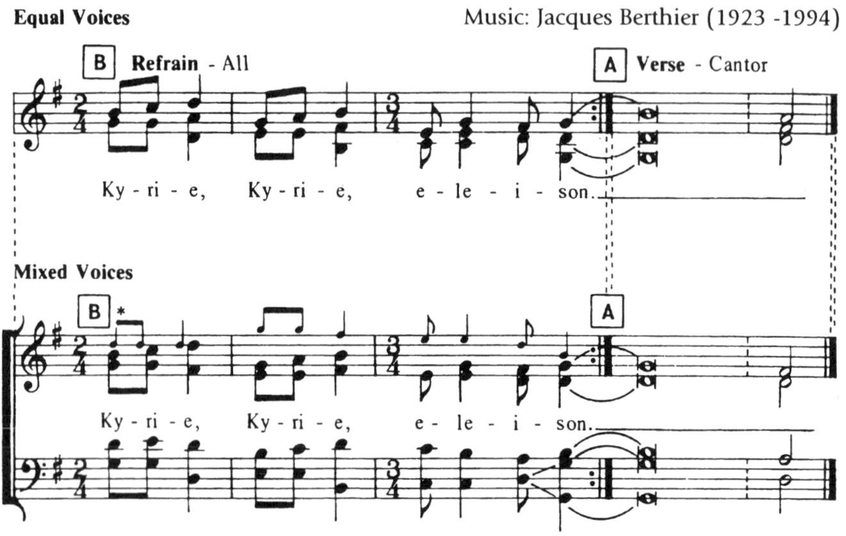
Equal Voices
Music: Jacques Berthier (1923 -1994)
B Refrain - All
A Verse - Cantor
Ky - ri - e, Ky - ri - e, e - le - i - son.
Mixed Voices
B *
A
Ky - ri - e, Ky - ri - e, e - le - i - son.
* Descant ad lib. 2nd time only

244 LAUDATE DOMINUM

Praise the Lord, all you peoples.

Ostinato Chorale

Mixed Voices

Music: Jacques Berthier (1923 -1994)

♩ = 116
Lau - da - te Do - mi - num, Lau - da - te Do - mi - num
om - nes gen - tes, Al - le - lu - ia. Al - le - lu - ia.
1.
2.
D.C.

Equal Voices

Lau - da - te Do - mi - num, Lau - da - te Do - mi - num om - nes

gen - tes, Al - le - lu - ia. Al - le - lu - ia.
1.
2.
D.C.

245 LAUDATE OMNES GENTES

All peoples, praise the Lord.

Ostinato Chorale

Music: Jacques Berthier (1923 -1994)

Mixed Voices

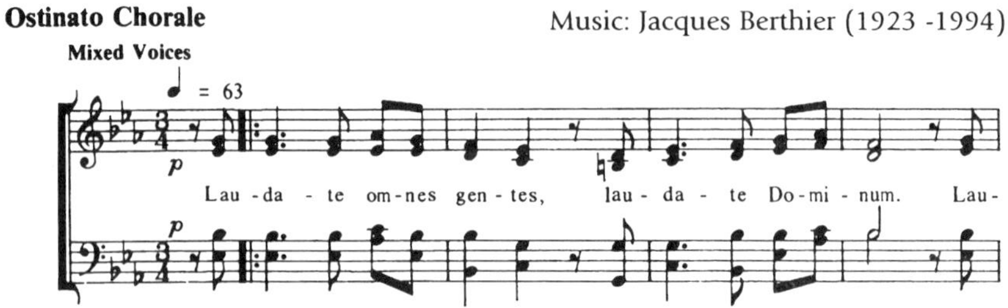
♩ = 63
p
Lau - da - te om - nes gen - tes, lau - da - te Do - mi - num. Lau -
p

(Fine)
da - te om - nes gen - tes, lau - da - te Do - mi - num! Lau -

Equal Voices

p
Lau - da - te om - nes gen - tes, lau - da - te Do - mi -
p

(Fine)
num. Lau - da - te om - nes gen - tes, lau - da - te Do - mi - num! Lau -

246 LORD, DRAW NEAR

(SOLO) Lord, draw near. (CHOIR) Lord, draw near. (ALL) DRAW

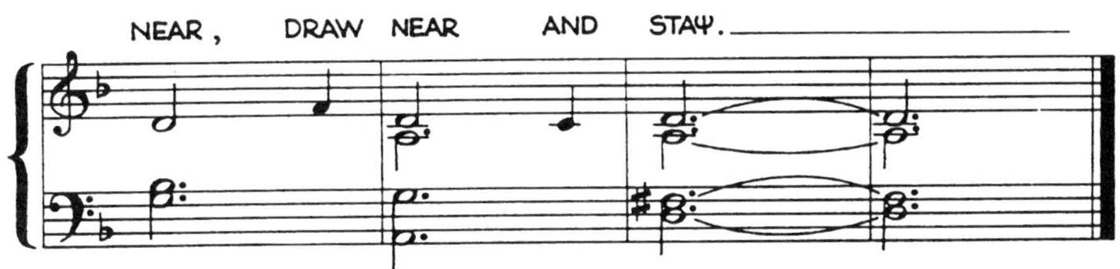
NEAR, DRAW NEAR AND STAY.

247 LORD, FORGIVE ME

Used by permission of Hope Publishing Co., Carol Stream, IL 60188 USA

CHINA

Words: Ellsworth Candlee
Music: Confucian Chant
arranged Geoff Weaver

♩ = 92
1 Lord, for - give___ me. Christ, have mer - cy!
2 Lord, for - give___ me. Christ, have mer - cy!
ORGAN PEDAL

I con - fess to you all my sin and shame.
Now to turn from sin, Lord, grant heaven - ly grace.

Save me, Lord, I cry. In your cross I trust,
Raised up and re-newed, may I fol - low you,

In the early 20th century, it was often said in China 'One Christian more means one Chinese less.' The use of an ancient Confucian chant in worship is one way in which Chinese Christians are able to root their faith in their Chinese culture and traditions.

Je - sus, Son of God, ho - ly, bless - èd one.
Je - sus, Son of God, ho - ly, bless - èd one.

1 Lord, forgive me. Christ, have mercy!
I confess to you all my sin and shame.
Save me, Lord, I cry.
In your cross I trust,
Jesus, Son of God, holy, blessèd one.

2 Lord, forgive me. Christ, have mercy!
Now to turn from sin, Lord,
grant heavenly grace.
Raised up and renewed,
may I follow you,
Jesus, Son of God, holy, blessèd one.

248 MISERERE NOBIS

Words: trad. liturgical

solemnly

Mi - se - re - re no - bis, mi - se - re - re

no - bis, Do - mi - ne.

Miserere nobis, Domine. (Have mercy on us, O Lord.)

249 MY PRAYERS RISE

UNITED STATES OF AMERICA

Words: from Psalm 141: 2
Arlo D. Duba
Music: Arlo D. Duba
arranged Geoff Weaver

Meditatively ♩ = 88

Capo 3(Bm)
Dm (Bm)
Gm (Em)
My prayers rise like___ in - cense, my

Dm (Bm)
Am7 (F#m7)
Dm (Bm)
hands like the eve - ning sac - ri - fice.

My prayers rise like incense,
my hands like the evening sacrifice.

This simple response was first sung as part of a service for justice, peace and the integrity of creation. It can be used effectively within a time of prayer.

250 NADA DE TURBE

Nothing can trouble

Nada te turbe

Na - da te tur - be, na - da te es - pan - te. Quien a Dios tie - ne
No - thing can trou - ble, no - thing can frigh - ten those who seek God shall

Am Dm⁷ G Em/C F Dm⁶

na - da le fal - ta. So - lo Dios bas - ta.
ne - ver go want - ing. God a - lone fills us.

E Am F Dm⁶ E Am

D.C.

251 O LORD HEAR MY PRAYER

From Psalm 101 (102)

Music: Jacques Berthier (1923 -1994)

Ostinato Chorale
Mixed Voices
♩= 72
O Lord hear my pray'r, O Lord hear my pray'r:
when I call an - swer me. O Lord hear my pray'r, O
Lord hear my pray'r Come and lis - ten to me. O
fine
Equal Voices
O Lord hear my pray'r, O Lord hear my pray'r:
when I call an - swer me. O Lord hear my pray'r, O
Lord hear my pray'r: come and lis - ten to me. O
fine
Accompaniment
Keyboard or Guitar
Em C6 D G C Am6 B Em C6 D G6 Am B Em
(Fine)

252 OUVE SENHOR

Used by permission of Hope Publishing Co., Carol Stream, IL 60188 USA

BRAZIL

Words: S. Monteiro
English: Word & Music
Music: unknown
arranged David Peacock

With expression ♩ = 84
Em
Am7
Ou - ve, Se - nhor, eu es - tou cla - man - do,
Mer - ci - ful Lord, in your lov - ing - kind - ness
D
B7
B7/E
Em
tem pie - da - de de mim e me res - pon - de.
hear our prayer, lis - ten to our in - ter - ces - sion.
Am7/E
Am7
Ou - ve, Se - nhor, eu es - tou cla - man - do,
Mer - ci - ful Lord, in your lov - ing - kind - ness
D
B7
B7/E
Em
tem pie - da - de de mim e me res - pon - de.
hear our prayer, lis - ten to our in - ter - ces - sion.

An impassioned plea, suitable for times of prayer, in a very Brazilian idiom.

253 SANNA

Used by permission of Hope Publishing Co., Carol Stream, IL 60188 USA

SOUTH AFRICA

Words: traditional
Music: unknown
arranged Geoff Weaver

Joyfully ♩ = 100
C G F C
San-na, san-na-ni-na, san-na, san-na, san-na.
(- na)
SOLO Ho - san - na, san -
G F C G7
San-na, san-na-ni-na, san-na, san-na, san-na.
SOLO Ho - san-na
San-na, san-na, san -
C C/G G7 C G7
- na san-na-ni-na, san-na, san-na, san-na.
SOLO Ho - san-na
San-na, san-na, san -
repeats
last time
C C/G G7 C D.C. C
- na san-na-ni-na, san-na, san-na, san-na.
- na.
SOLO Ho - san - na, san -

Sanna is a shortened form of *Hosanna*. It is very effective to start this song quietly, as if in a distant procession, and then to get louder and more exuberant as the imaginary procession draws nearer.

254 SENHOR TEM PIEDADE DE NÓS

O Lord, have mercy on us

BRAZIL

KYRIE

Music: Jaci C. Maraschin
arranged David Peacock

Gentle pulsating rhythm ♩ = 65

Capo 1(Am) B♭m (Am) Fm (Em)

Se - nhor, tem pie - da - de de
O Lord, have_ mer - cy on

B♭m (Am) Fm (Em) B♭m (Am)

nós. Se - nhor, tem pie - da - de de nós. Se -
us, O Lord, have mer - cy on us, O

Fm (Em) Cm (Bm) Fm (Em)

- nhor, tem pie - da - de de nós. Cris - to, tem pie - da - de de
Lord, have mer - cy on us. Christ, have mer - cy on

Underlying this wonderful Brazilian setting of the Kyrie, are the rhythms of the dance. The melodic line should be smooth, the accompaniment much less so.

nós.
us,
Cris-to, tem pie-da - de de nós.
Christ, have mer - cy on us,
Cm
(Bm)
B♭
(A)
Cm
(Bm)
B♭
(A)
Cris-to, tem pie-da - de de nós.
Christ, have mer - cy on us.
Se-nhor, tem pie-da - de de
O Lord, have mer - cy on
Fm
(Em)
Cm
(Bm)
B♭
(A)
Fm
(Em)
nós.
us,
Se-nhor, tem pie-da - de de nós.
O Lord, have mer - cy on us,
Se -
O
Cm7
(Bm7)
Fm
(Em)
- nhor, tem pie-da - de de nós.
Lord, have mer - cy on us.

255 STAY WITH ME

From Matthew 26

Ostinato Chorale Music: Jacques Berthier (1923 -1994)

Mixed Voices
♩= 72
p
Stay with me, re - main here with me, watch ___ and
pray ___ watch and pray ___
f
p
Equal Voices
Stay with me, re - main here with me, watch _ and pray, __ watch and pray.

Accompaniment
Keyboard or Guitar
Dm Gm Dm Gm Dm C F C Dm Asus A

Verses From Matthew 26, 36-42

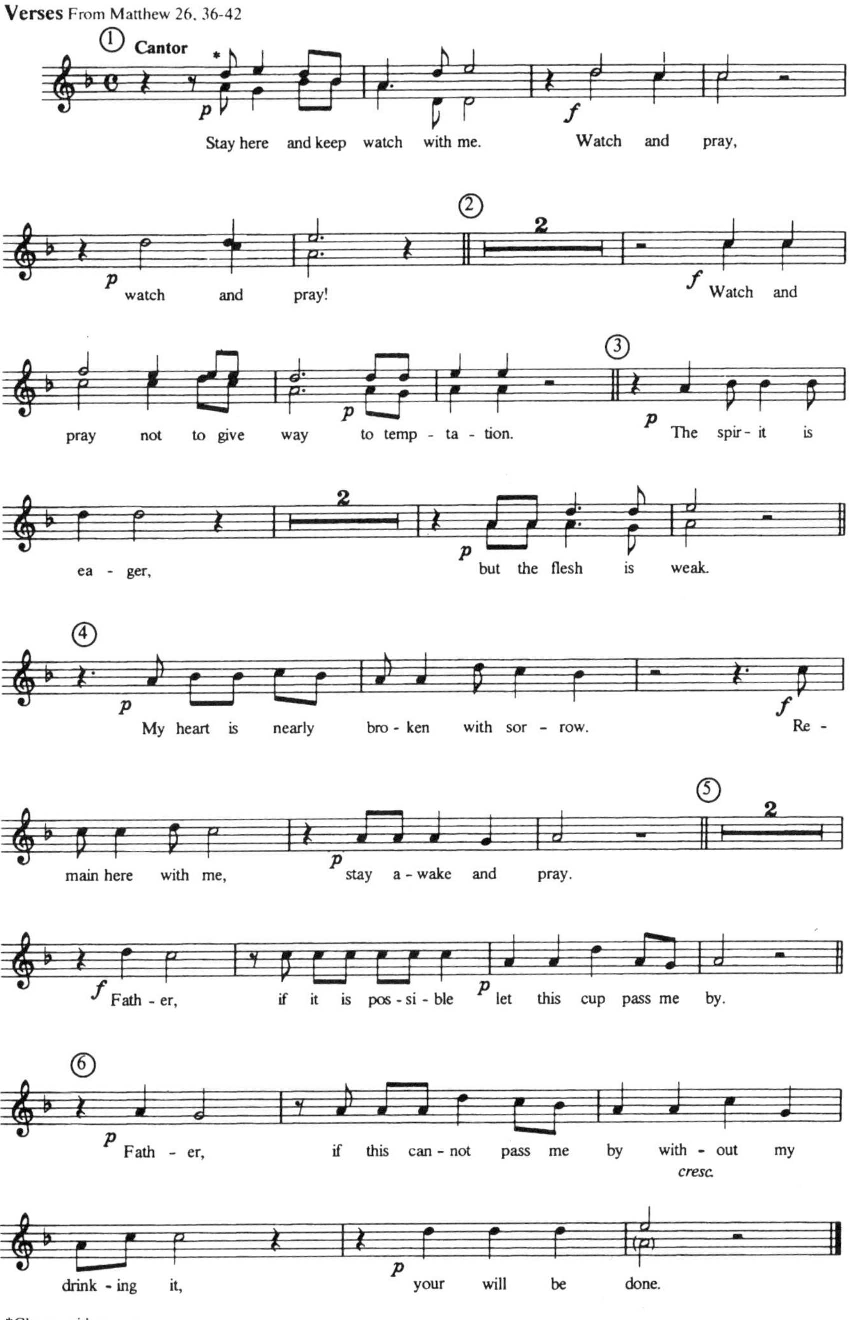

1 Cantor
Stay here and keep watch with me. Watch and pray,
watch and pray!
2
Watch and
pray not to give way to temp - ta - tion.
3
The spir - it is
ea - ger,
but the flesh is weak.
4
My heart is nearly bro - ken with sor - row. Re -
main here with me, stay a - wake and pray.
5
Fath - er, if it is pos - si - ble let this cup pass me by.
6
Fath - er, if this can - not pass me by with - out my
cresc.
drink - ing it, your will be done.

*Choose either part

256 STAY WITH US

After Luke 24 and Psalms 26 & 138

Music: Jacques Berthier (1923 -1994)

Ostinato Chorale
Mixed Voices
♩ = 72
p
Stay with us O Lord Je - sus Christ:
night will soon fall. Then stay with us O
mf
Lord Je - sus Christ: light in our dark - ness.
f
p subito
Equal Voices
Stay with us O Lord Jes-us Christ: night will soon fall. Do
stay with us O Lord Je - sus Christ: light in our dark - ness.
Accompaniment
Keyboard or Guitar
Gm
E♭
D
Dm7
E♭/D
C
F
B♭
Cm

257 SURREXIT CHRISTUS

Two Refrains Ostinato

Christ is risen. Sing to the Lord

Music: Jacques Berthier (1923 -1994)

Mixed Voices
A1
♩= 120
B
(hum)
Sur - re - xit Chris - tus al - le - lu - ia!
A2
C
(hum)
Can - ta - te Do - mi - no, al - le - lu - ia!
Choir Variation for B and C (can be sung at the same time as the standard version)
B
Sur - re - xit Christ - tus, al - le - lu - ia!
C
Can - ta - te Do - mi - no, al - le - lu - ia!
Equal Voices
A1
B
(hum)
Sur - re - xit Christ-tus, al - le - lu - ia!
A2
C
(hum)
Can - ta - te Do - mi - no, al - le - lu - ia!

Accompaniment
Keyboard or Guitar
D A Bm F♯m G F♯m7 Em A
D A Bm F♯m G D Em7 A D
Verses A1 and A2
Cantor
From Daniel, 3 (The praises of creation)
1. All you heav - ens, bless the Lord. Stars of the heav - ens
bless the Lord.
2. Sun and moon, bless the Lord.
And you, night and day, bless the Lord.
3. Frost and cold, bless the Lord.
Ice and snow, bless the Lord.
4. Fire and heat,
bless the Lord.
And you, light and dark - ness,
bless the Lord.
5. Spir - its and souls of the just, bless the Lord.
Saints and the hum - ble hear - ted, bless the Lord.

*Choose either part

From Psalm 117 (118)
2
1. Give thanks to the Lord, for he is good,

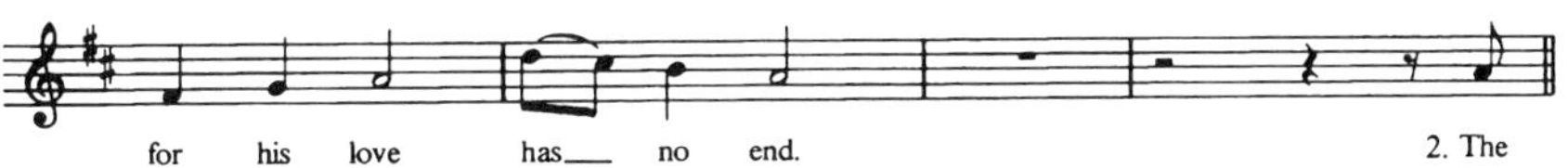
for his love has no end.
2. The

*
2
Lord is my strength, the Lord is my song;

2
he has been my Sa - vior.

2
3. I shall not die, I shall live,

2
I shall live and re - count his deeds.

*Choose either part

258 TAKE, O TAKE ME AS I AM

gently
Take, O take me as I am; sum - mon out what I shall be;
set your seal up - on my heart and live in me.

Take, O take me as I am;
summon out what I shall be;
set your seal upon my heart
and live in me.

259 TATA POKELELA

Used by permission of Hope Publishing Co., Carol Stream, IL 60188 USA

ZAMBIA

Everything is yours, Lord

Words: from 1 Chronicles 29, unknown
English: Word & Music
Music: unknown
arranged Geoff Weaver

Joyfully ♩ = 132

LEADER
D G D
Ta - ta po - ke - le - la If - ya - bu - pe fye - su,
Ev - ery-thing is yours, Lord; ev - ery-thing comes from you:

D/A A7 D
If - yo twa - mi pe - la le - lo.
all we have we of - fer to you.

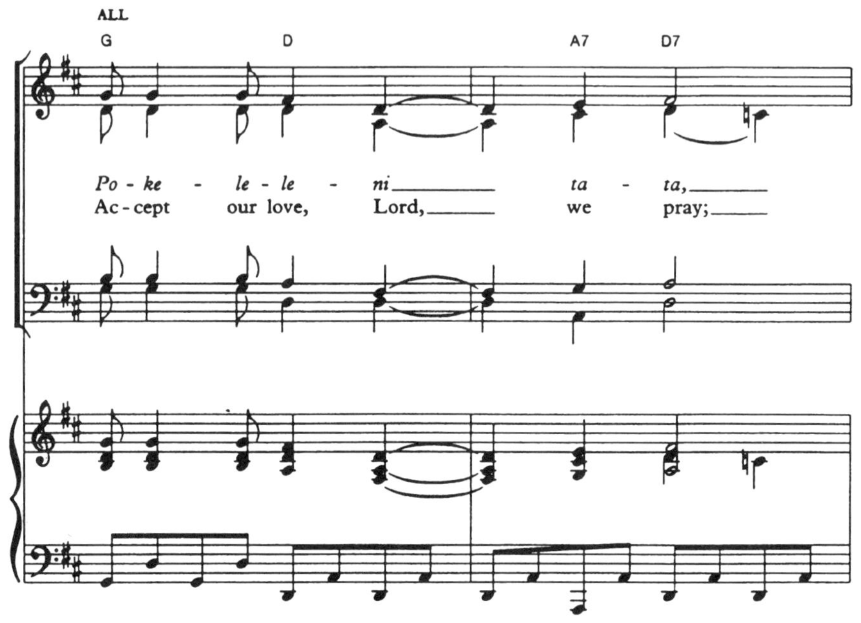
ALL
G
D
A7
D7
Po - ke - le - le - ni ta - ta,
Ac - cept our love, Lord, we pray;

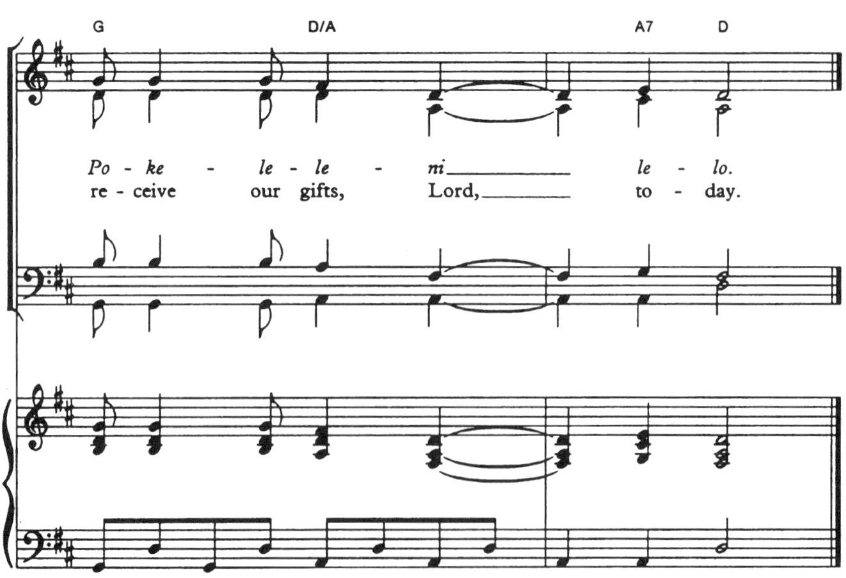
G
D/A
A7
D
Po - ke - le - le - ni le - lo.
re - ceive our gifts, Lord, to - day.

260 THE LORD IS MY LIGHT

Canon *From Psalm 26 (27)*

Music: Jacques Berthier (1923 -1994)

Theme I

Calmly ♩ = 66
A1
A2
B1
B2
fine
A1
The Lord is my light, my light and sal-vation: in him I trust, in him I trust. The

Theme II

A1
A2
B1
B2
fine
A1
The Lord is my light, my light and sal-vation: in him I trust, in him I trust. The

Each of the two themes can be sung *separately* either **in unison** or **as a round** (two voices only: coming in on A1 and B1)

The two themes can also be sung *together*, preferably with theme I for female voices and theme II for male voices.

Accompaniments

Keyboard or Guitar

1 Dm
G
2
3
4

Choir
1
2
3
4
(hum)

261 THROUGH OUR LIVES AND BY OUR PRAYERS

Through our lives and by our prayers, your King-dom come.

Words & music by John L. Bell & Graham Maule. Copyright © 1987 WGRG, Iona Community, 840 Govan Road, Glasgow G51 3UU Scotland

262 TUYO ES EL REINO

Used by permission of HarperCollins Publishers Ltd.

Yours is the kingdom

ARGENTINA

Words: from the Lord's Prayer
Music: Pablo D. Sosa
arranged Geoff Weaver

First time ♩. = 56
Second time ♩. = 66
Capo 3(Bm) Dm (Bm)
F (D)
Tu-yo es el rei - no, tu-yo el po - der, tuy - a la glo - ria y
Yours is the king - dom, yours is the power, yours is the glo - ry
A (F♯)
C (A)
siem-pre hide ser, siem-pre hide ser, siem-pre hide ser;
for ev - er-more, for ev - er-more, for ev - er-more;
B♭ (G)
Gm/B♭ (Em)
Am/C (F♯m)
Dm (Bm)
Gm (Em)
D (B)
tu-yo es el rei - no, el po - der y la glo-ria y siem-pre hide ser. A - men.
yours is the king-dom, the power and the glo - ry for ev - er-more. A - men.

The composer Pablo Sosa has written much music for worship with an authentically Latin American flavour. Here is the certainty of God's Kingdom allied to the vitality of the dance. It should be sung with vigour, a growing sense of excitement and a guitar and percussion accompaniment.

263 UBI CARITAS

Where charity and love are found, God himself is there.

Ostinato Response

Music: Jacques Berthier (1923 -1994)

Two or Three Equal Voices

A
Lento ♩ = 72
B
Two Voices
Third Voice ad lib.
U - bi ca - ri - tas___ et a - mor,___ U - bi ca - ri -
tas___ De - us i - bi - est.
3

Accompaniments

Keyboard or Instruments

A
B
p
p

Guitar

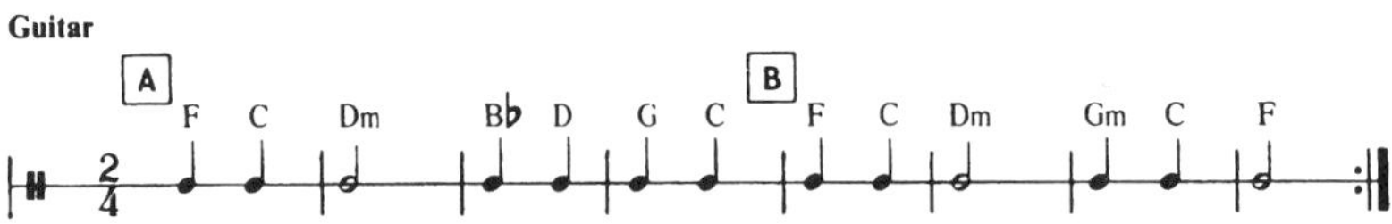
A
B
F C Dm Bb D G C F C Dm Gm C F

Bass (Cello, etc.)

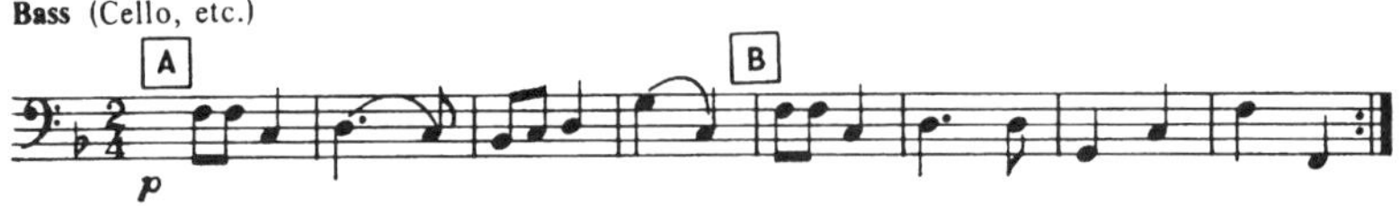
A
B
p

Choir
A
p
et a - mor
B
U - bi ca - ri - tas a - mor, U - bi ca - ri -
et a - mor,
tas, De - us i - bi est.
Verses B
Cantor
B
1. Your love, O Je - sus Christ, has gath - ered us to - geth - er.
B
2. May your love, O Je - sus Christ, be fore - most in our lives.
* B
3. Let us love one an - oth - er as God has loved us.
B
4. Let us be one in love to - geth - er in the one bread of Christ.
* B
5. The love of God in Je - sus Christ bears e - ter - nal joy.
* B
6. The love of God in Je - sus Christ will nev - er have an end.
* Choose either part.

264 VENI SANCTE SPIRITUS

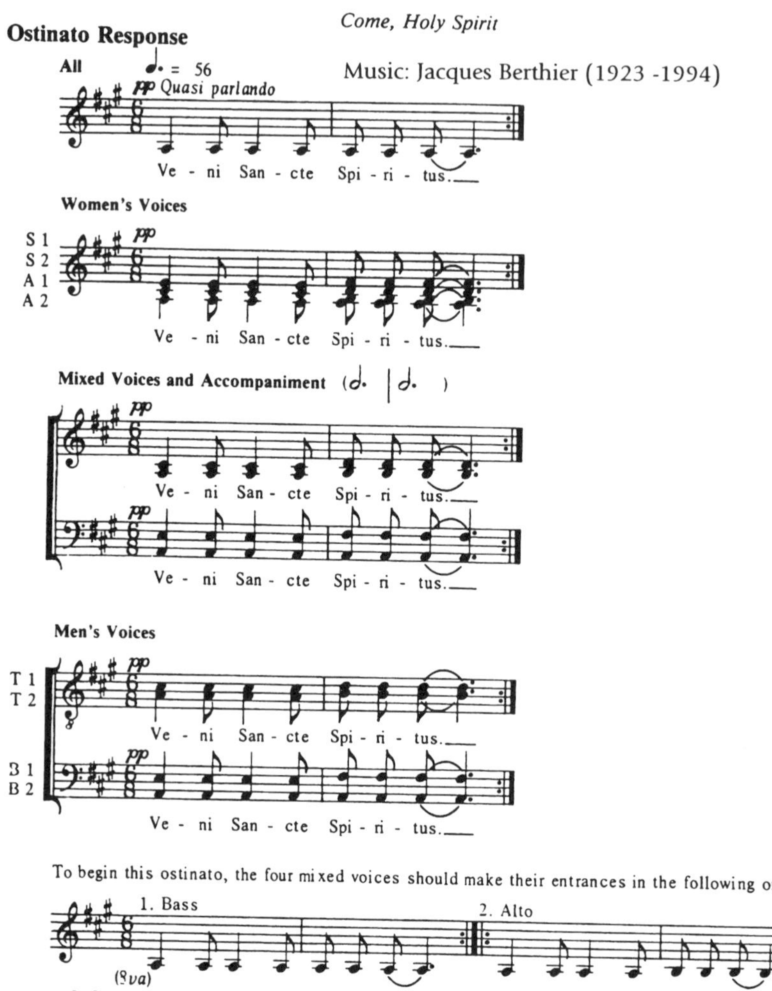

Ostinato Response
Come, Holy Spirit
Music: Jacques Berthier (1923 -1994)
All
♩. = 56
pp Quasi parlando
Ve - ni San - cte Spi - ri - tus.
Women's Voices
S 1
S 2
A 1
A 2
pp
Ve - ni San - cte Spi - ri - tus.
Mixed Voices and Accompaniment
pp
Ve - ni San - cte Spi - ri - tus.
pp
Ve - ni San - cte Spi - ri - tus.
Men's Voices
T 1
T 2
pp
Ve - ni San - cte Spi - ri - tus.
B 1
B 2
pp
Ve - ni San - cte Spi - ri - tus.
To begin this ostinato, the four mixed voices should make their entrances in the following order:
1. Bass
(8va)
2. Alto
3. Soprano
4. Tenor
(8va)

Accompaniment

Guitar

Verses

As the ostinato continues, vocal and instrumental verses are sung or played as desired with some space always left between the verses (after the cantor's "Veni Sancte Spiritus").

Cantor
1
1. Come, Ho - ly Spir - it, from heav - en shine forth with your glo - rious light.
Ve - ni San - cte Spi - ri - tus. 2. Come, Fa - ther of the poor, come, gen - er - ous
Spir - it, come, light of our hearts. Ve - ni San - cte Spi - ri - tus.

2
1. Come from the four winds, O Spir - it, come breath of God; dis -
perse the shad - ows ov - er us, re - new and strength - en your peo - ple.
Ve - ni San - cte Spi - ri - tus. 2. Fa - ther of the poor come to our pov - er - ty.
Show - er up - on us the sev - en gifts of your grace. Be the light of our lives oh
come. Ve - ni San - cte Spi - ri - tus. 3. You are our on - ly com - fort - er,
Peace of the soul. In the heat you shade us; in our la - bor you re -
fresh us, and in trou - ble you are our strength. Ve - ni San - cte

264 Contd.

Spi - ri - tus.__ 4. Kin - dle in our hearts the flame of your love that in the dark - ness_
__ of the world it may glow and reach to all__ for ev - er.__ Ve - ni . .

* Choose either part.

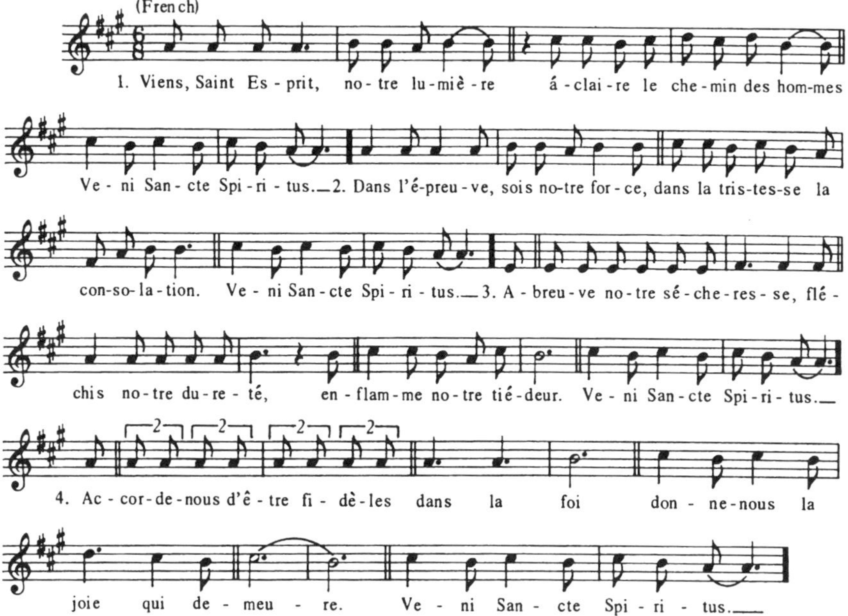
(French)
1. Viens, Saint Es - prit, no - tre lu - miè - re á - clai - re le che - min des hom-mes
Ve - ni San - cte Spi - ri - tus.__ 2. Dans l'é-preu - ve, sois no-tre for - ce, dans la tris-tes-se la
con-so- la - tion. Ve - ni San - cte Spi - ri - tus.__ 3. A - breu - ve no - tre sé - che - res - se, flé -
chis no - tre du - re - té, en - flam - me no - tre tié - deur. Ve - ni San - cte Spi - ri - tus.__
4. Ac - cor - de-nous d'ê - tre fi - dè - les dans la foi don - ne-nous la
joie qui de - meu - re. Ve - ni San - cte Spi - ri - tus.__

(German)
1. Komm, Hei - li - ger Geist, lass den Glanz dei - ner Herr - lich-keit vom

Him-mel er - strah - - len. Ve - ni San - cte Spi - ri - tus.___ 2. Komm, Va - ter der
Ar - men, Komm, Ur-sprung al - ler Ga - ben, Komm, Licht der Her - zen. Ve - ni . .

(Spanish)
(Veni) Ven! Ven! Es - pí - ri - tu San - - to. (Ve-ni San-cte S. . .) Ven!
Ven! Pa - - - dre, Pa - - - dre___ de los po - bres. (Ve-ni San-cte) Ven! Ven!
luz de los co - ra - zo - nes Ve - ni San - cte Spi - ri - tus!___

(Italian)
1. Vie - ni San - to Spi - ri - to___ riem - pi i cuo - ri dei tuoi_fe - de - li
e ac - cen - di in es - si il fuo - co del tu - o___ a - mo - re. Ve - ni San - cte
Spi - ri - tus.___ 2. Con - so - la - to - re per - fet - - to; os - pi - te mi - te dell'
a - ni - ma; dol - cis - si - mo sol - lie - vo. Ve - ni San - cte Spi - ri - tus.___

265 WA WA WA EMIMIMO

Words used by permission of HarperCollins Publishers Ltd.

Come, O Holy Spirit, come

NIGERIA

Words and music: unknown
arranged Geoff Weaver

♩ = 88 or ♩ = 120

Capo 3(D) F
(D)

Wa wa wa E-mi-mi - mo.
Come, O Ho-ly Spi-rit, come.

Wa wa wa A-lag-ba -
Come, Al-might-y Spi-rit,

E-mi - o - lo - ye
Ho-ly Spi-rit, come.

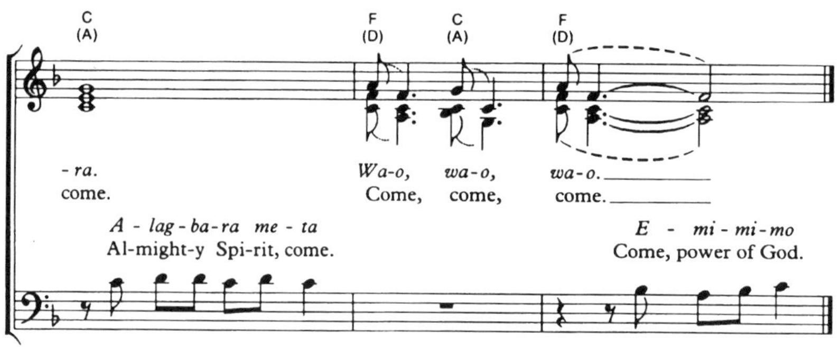
C
(A)
F
(D)
C
(A)
F
(D)
- ra.
come.
Wa-o,
Come,
wa-o,
come,
wa-o.
come.
A - lag-ba-ra me - ta
Al-might-y Spi-rit, come.
E - mi-mi-mo
Come, power of God.

Wa wa wa Emimimo.
Wa wa wa Alagbara.
Wao, wao, wao.

Come, O Holy Spirit, come.
Come, Almighty Spirit, come.
Come, come, come.

First 3 times: sing at slow tempo ♩ = 88: 1. top line only (with tenor response); 2. add lower alto; 3. add guitar (first beat of every bar only); 4th time onwards sing faster at ♩ = 120. Add the middle part then percussion and more rhythmic guitar.

This Yoruba invocation of the Holy Spirit is very effective when sung slowly and quietly, gradually introducing voices and instruments on each repetition as indicated. A change of tempo with drums and clapping provides an exciting conclusion, always greeted with enthusiasm by Africans.

266 WAIT FOR THE LORD

After James 5 and Psalm 26 (27)

Music: Jacques Berthier (1923 -1994)

Ostinato Response
Mixed Voices
Lento 𝅗𝅥 = 48
p
Wait for the Lord, whose day is near.
p
mf
Wait for the Lord: keep watch, take heart!
mf
Equal Voices
p
Wait for the Lord, whose day is near.
mf
Wait for the Lord: keep watch, take heart!
Accompaniment
Keyboard or Guitar
Em
C
Am
B
Em
D
G
Am
B
Em

Verses (in this case, the response is not repeated as an ostinato, but the response and verses are sung one after the other)

Choir (humming) or Keyboard
... heart
(hum)
Cantor
1. Pre - pare the way for the Lord Make a straight path for Him. (Is. 40)
2. The glo - ry of the Lord shall be re - vealed. (Is. 40)
3. All the earth will see the Lord. (Is. 40)
4. Re - joice in the Lord al - ways He is at hand. (Phil. 4)
5. Seek first the king-dom of God, seek and you shall find. (Mat. 6-7)
6. Joy and glad-ness for all who seek the Lord. (Ps. 69)
7. I wait-ed for the Lord he heard my cry. (Ps. 39)
8. Our eyes are fixed on the Lord our God. (Ps. 122)
9. O Lord show us your way. Guide us in your truth. (Ps. 118)
10. Pre - pare the way for the Lord.

267 WE BELIEVE

Glaubt und sprecht
Philippinen
1 We be - lieve: Ma-ra - na - tha, Light of the Day.
2 Glaubt und sprecht: Un-ser Herr kommt, e - wi-ges Licht!
We be - lieve: Ma - ra - na - tha,
Glaubt und sprecht: Un - ser Herr kommt,
1 We be - lieve:
2 Glaubt und sprecht:
1 We be - - lieve,
2 Ja, es gilt,
Light of the Day.
e - wi - ges Licht!
Ma - ra - na - tha, Light of the Day.
Un - ser Herr kommt, e - wi - ges Licht!
we be - lieve.
ja, es gilt.

1 = englisch, 2 = deutsch

Melodie: Francisco F. Feliciano. Text zu Offenbarung 22,5 und 20. 2: Dieter Trautwein © beim Autor. © 2: Strube, München

268 YOUR KINGDOM COME

RUSSIA

Words and music: N. Zabolotski
arranged John L. Bell

Steadily ♩ = 112
Your king-dom come, O Lord. Your king-dom come, O Lord. Your

king-dom come, O Lord._ Your king-dom come, O Lord.

Your kingdom come, O Lord.
Your kingdom come, O Lord.
Your kingdom come, O Lord.
Your kingdom come, O Lord.

Written for a W.C.C. Conference in Melbourne in 1980, the composer Nicolai Zabolotski asked that the song should start softly, almost in a questioning way, and should grow in strength and confidence until the final phrase which asserts the hope that God's Kingdom is coming.

Worship Songs

269 A NEW COMMANDMENT

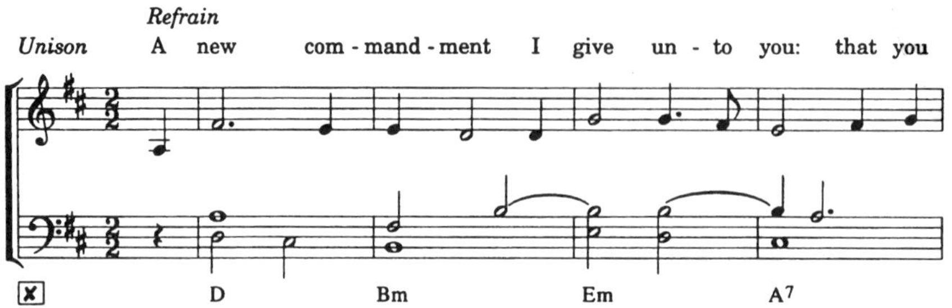
Refrain
Unison
A new com - mand - ment I give un - to you: that you
D
Bm
Em
A7

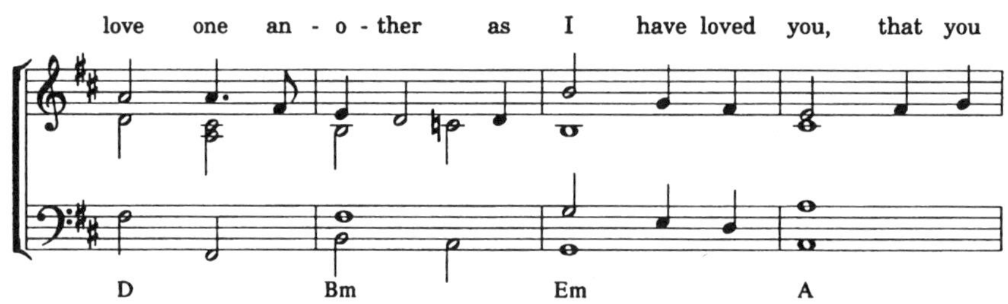
love one an - o - ther as I have loved you, that you
D
Bm
Em
A

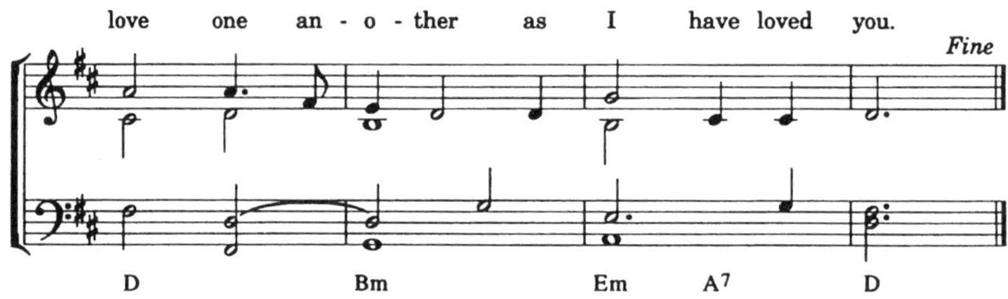
love one an - o - ther as I have loved you.
Fine
D
Bm
Em
A7
D

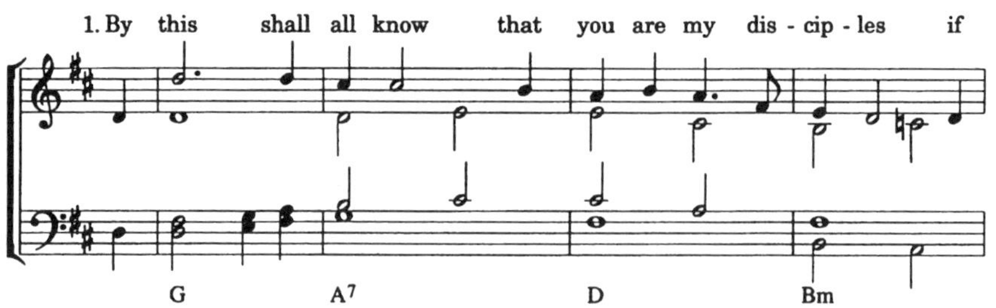
1. By this shall all know that you are my dis - cip - les if
G
A7
D
Bm

you have love one for an - o - ther. By
G A A7 D D7
this shall all know that you are my dis - cip - les if
G A7 D Bm
you have love one for an - o - ther.
D.C.
G A A7 D

2. You are my friends if you do what I command you.
Without my help you can do nothing.
You are my friends if you do what I command you.
Without my help you can do nothing.

3. I am the true vine, my Father is the gard'ner.
Abide in me: I will be with you.
I am the true vine, my Father is the gard'ner.
Abide in me: I will be with you.

4. True love is patient, not arrogant or boastful;
love bears all things, love is eternal.
True love is patient, not arrogant or boastful;
love bears all things, love is eternal.

Text: v. 1 unknown, based on John 13:34-35
vs. 2-4 Aniceto Nazareth, based on John 15 and 1 Corinthians 13
Music: unknown arr. Richard Lloyd (*b.* 1933)

270 ABBA, FATHER, LET ME BE

Unison
Ab - ba, Fa - ther, let me be yours and
Capo 2
G C D7 G C

yours a - lone. May my will for -
D G C

e - ver be more and more your own.
D7 G C D7 G

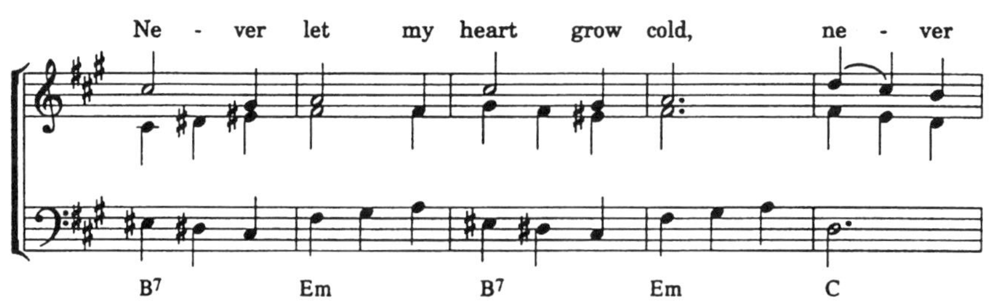
Ne - ver let my heart grow cold, ne - ver
B7 Em B7 Em C

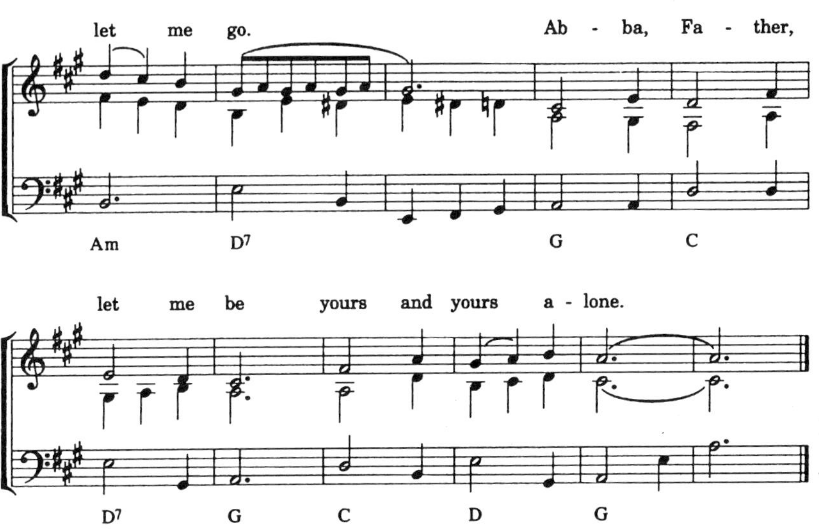
let me go. Ab - ba, Fa - ther,
Am D7 G C
let me be yours and yours a - lone.
D7 G C D G

Text: Dave Bilbrough
Music: Dave Bilbrough arr. Christopher Tambling (*b.* 1964)

271 ALL HEAVEN DECLARES

Unison 1. All heav'n de - clares the glo - ry of the
A Amaj7 D Esus 4 E
ri - sen Lord. Who can com - pare
D/A A Amaj7 D
with the beau - ty of the Lord? For e - ver he will be
Esus4 E D/A A D
the Lamb up - on the throne. I glad - ly bow the
E A E/G♯ F♯m7

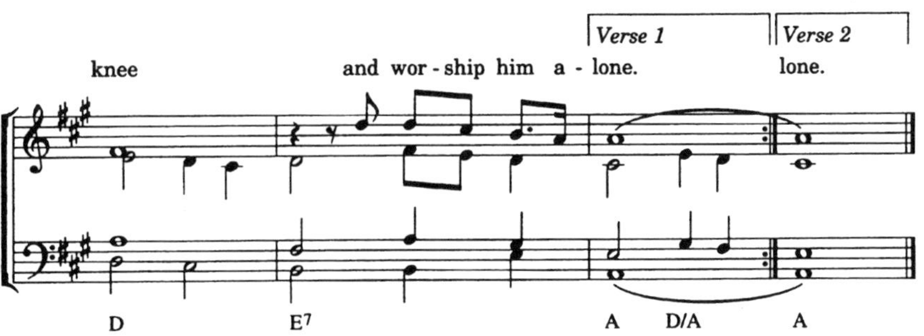
Verse 1
Verse 2
knee
and wor - ship him a - lone.
lone.
D
E7
A
D/A
A

2. I will proclaim
   the glory of the risen Lord,
   who once was slain
   to reconcile us to God.
   For ever you will be
   the Lamb upon the throne;
   I gladly bow the knee,
   and worship you alone.

Text: Noel and Tricia Richards
Music: Noel and Tricia Richards arr. Malcolm Archer (*b.* 1952)

272 ALLELUIA NO. 1

ALLELUIA NO.1 99 and Refrain

Refrain
Unison Al - le - lu - ia, al - le - lu - ia, give thanks to the ri - sen Lord, al - le -
Capo 3
D Bm Em A7

lu - ia, al - le - lu - ia, give praise to his name.
Fine
D Bm A7 D

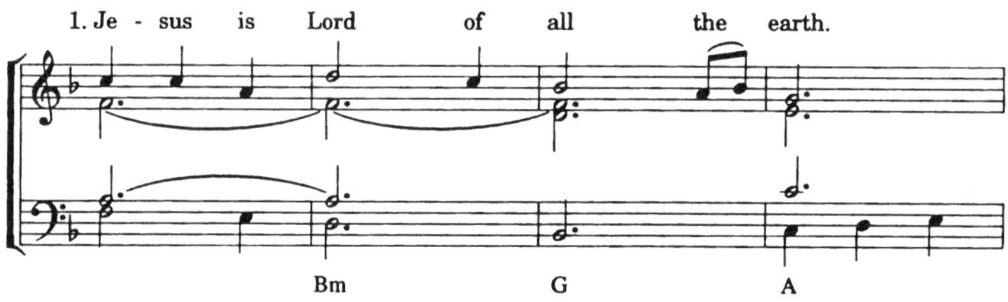
1. Je - sus is Lord of all the earth.
Bm G A

He is the King of cre - a - tion.
D.C.
D Bm G A7

2. Spread the good news o'er all the earth.
Jesus has died and is risen.

3. We have been crucified with Christ.
Now we shall live for ever.

4. God has proclaimed the just reward:
'Life for us all, alleluia!'

5. Come, let us praise the living God,
joyfully sing to our Saviour.

273 AS THE DEER PANTS FOR THE WATER

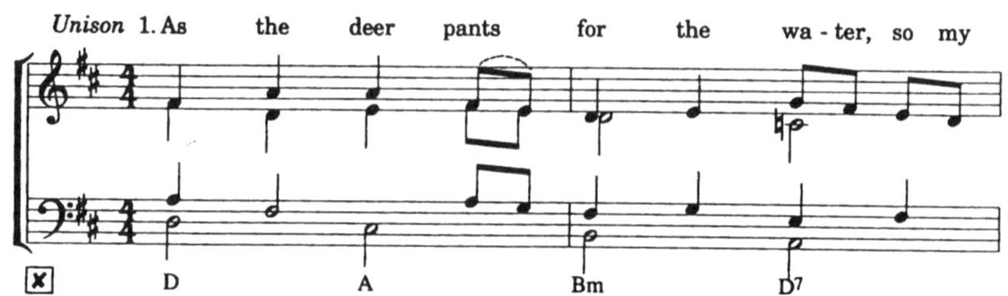

Unison 1. As the deer pants for the wa - ter, so my
D A Bm D7

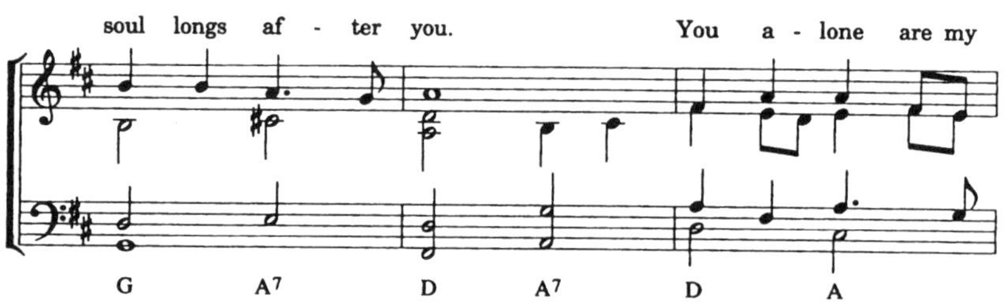

soul longs af - ter you. You a - lone are my
G A7 D A7 D A

heart's de - sire and I long to wor - ship you.
Bm D7 G A D

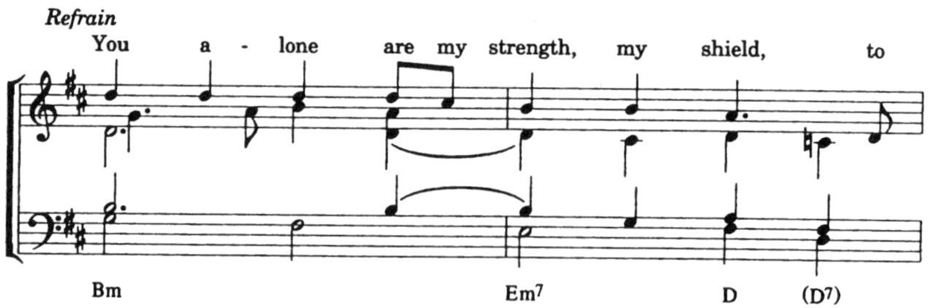

Refrain
You a - lone are my strength, my shield, to
Bm Em7 D (D7)

2. I want you more than gold or silver,
   only you can satisfy.
   You alone are the real joy-giver
   and the apple of my eye.

3. You're my friend and you are my brother,
   even though you are a king.
   I love you more than any other,
   so much more than anything.

Text: Martin Nystrom, based on Psalm 42:1-2
Music: Martin Nystrom arr. Richard Lloyd (*b.* 1933)

274 BE STILL AND KNOW THAT I AM GOD

BE STILL AND KNOW 888
Unison 1. Be still and know that I am
D
A7
God. Be still and know that I am
D
G
E7

God. Be still and know that I am God.
A7 D A7 D

2. I am the Lord that healeth thee.
I am the Lord that healeth thee.
I am the Lord that healeth thee.

3. In thee, O Lord, I put my trust.
In thee, O Lord, I put my trust.
In thee, O Lord, I put my trust.

Text: unknown, based on Psalm 46
Music: unknown arr. Adrian Vernon Fish (*b.* 1956)

275 BE STILL FOR THE PRESENCE OF THE LORD

Unison 1. Be still, for the pre-sence of the Lord, the Ho-ly One, is here;

D F♯m Bm Em A7

come, bow be-fore him now, with rev-er-ence and fear.

D F♯m Bm Em A7

In him no sin is found, we stand on ho-ly ground.

G D G D

Be still, for the pre-sence of the Lord, the Ho-ly One, is here.

G A F♯m Bm Em A7 D

2. Be still, for the glory of the Lord is shining all around;
he burns with holy fire, with splendour he is crowned.
How awesome is the sight, our radiant King of Light!
Be still, for the glory of the Lord is shining all around.

3. Be still, for the power of the Lord is moving in this place,
he comes to cleanse and heal, to minister his grace.
No work too hard for him, in faith receive from him;
be still, for the power of the Lord is moving in this place.

Text: David J. Evans (*b.* 1957)
Music: David J. Evans (*b.* 1957) arr. Norman Warren (*b.* 1934)

276 BREAK THOU THE BREAD OF LIFE

Capo 3(C)
LATHBURY
Peacefully

William F. Sherwin (1826-88)

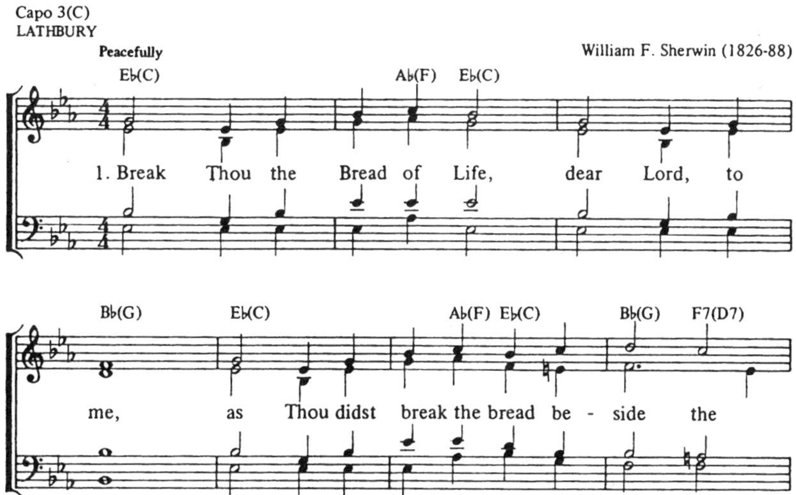

E♭(C)
A♭(F) E♭(C)
1. Break Thou the Bread of Life, dear Lord, to
B♭(G)
E♭(C)
A♭(F) E♭(C)
B♭(G) F7(D7)
me, as Thou didst break the bread be - side the

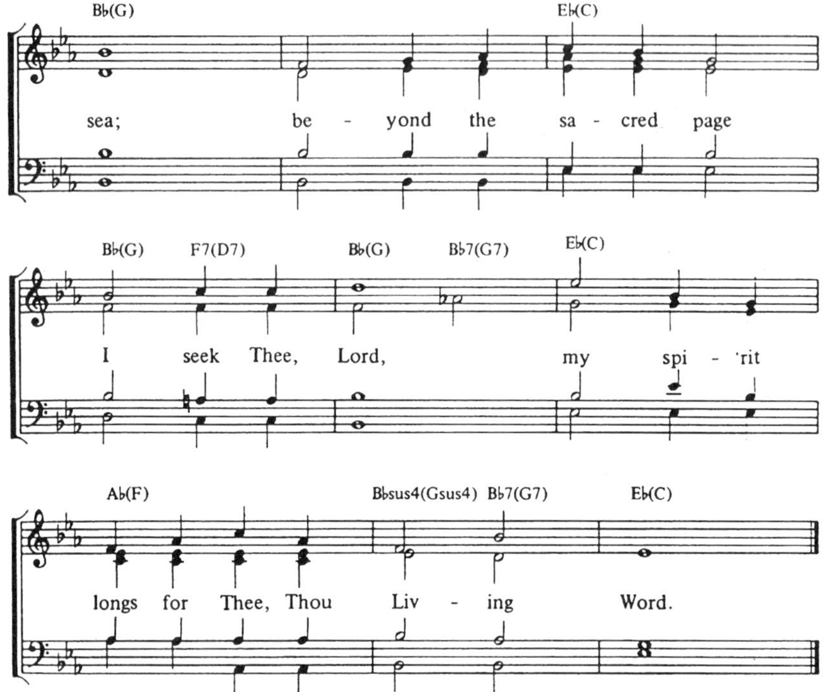

Bb(G)
Eb(C)
sea; be - yond the sa - cred page
Bb(G) F7(D7) Bb(G) Bb7(G7) Eb(C)
I seek Thee, Lord, my spi - 'rit
Ab(F) Bbsus4(Gsus4) Bb7(G7) Eb(C)
longs for Thee, Thou Liv - ing Word.

2. Thou art the Bread of Life,
O Lord, to me,
Thy holy Word the truth
That saveth me;
Give me to eat and live
With Thee above,
Teach me to love Thy truth,
For Thou art love.

3. O send Thy Spirit, Lord,
Now unto me,
That He may touch my eyes
And make me see;
Show me the truth concealed
Within Thy Word,
And in Thy Book revealed,
I see Thee, Lord.

4. Bless Thou the Bread of Life
To me, to me,
As Thou didst bless the loaves
By Galilee;
Then shall all bondage cease,
All fetters fall,
And I shall find my peace,
My all in all.

Mary A. Lathbury (1841-1913)
vv. 2 & 3 Alexander Groves (1843-1909)
Mt 6:11; Mk 14:22; Jn 6:11, 35

277 FATHER WE ADORE YOU

This may be sung in unison as a round, with entries at A, B *and* C

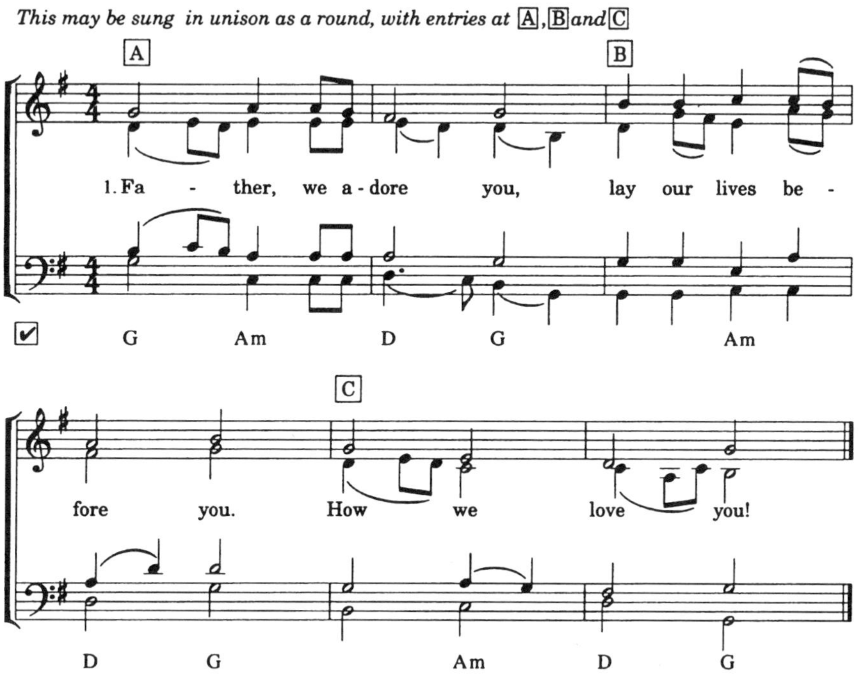
A
B
1. Fa - ther, we a - dore you, lay our lives be -
G Am D G Am
C
fore you. How we love you!
D G Am D G

2. Jesus, we adore you,
lay our lives before you.
How we love you!

3. Spirit, we adore you,
lay our lives before you.
How we love you!

Text: Terrye Coelho (*b.* 1952)
Music: Terrye Coelho (*b.* 1952) arr. Colin Hand (*b.* 1929)

278 GLORIFY YOUR NAME

1. Fa - ther, we love you, we praise you, we a - dore you.
C Dm G C
Glo - ri - fy your name in all the earth. (in all the earth.)
Dm G G7
Glo - ri - fy your name, glo - ri - fy your name,
C Dm E7 Am
glo - ri - fy your name in all the earth. (in all the earth.)
Dm G7 C

2. Jesus, we love you,
   we praise you, we adore you.
   Glorify your name in all the earth.
   Glorify your name, glorify your name,
   glorify your name in all the earth.

3. Spirit, we love you,
   we praise you, we adore you.
   Glorify your name in all the earth.
   Glorify your name, glorify your name,
   glorify your name in all the earth.

279 HALLELUJAH MY FATHER

Unison
Hal - le - lu - jah, my Fa - ther, for
D A7
giv - ing us your Son; send - ing him in -
G D
to the world to be giv - en up for all,
A7 G D
know - ing we would bruise him and smite him from the
G D G D

earth! Hal - le - lu - jah, my Fa - ther, in his
A7
D
A7

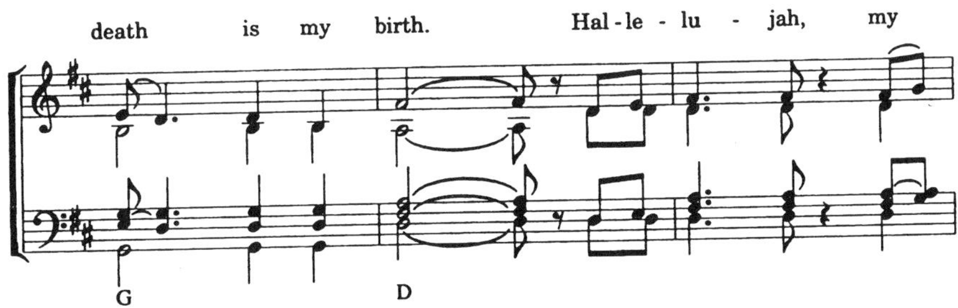
death is my birth. Hal - le - lu - jah, my
G
D

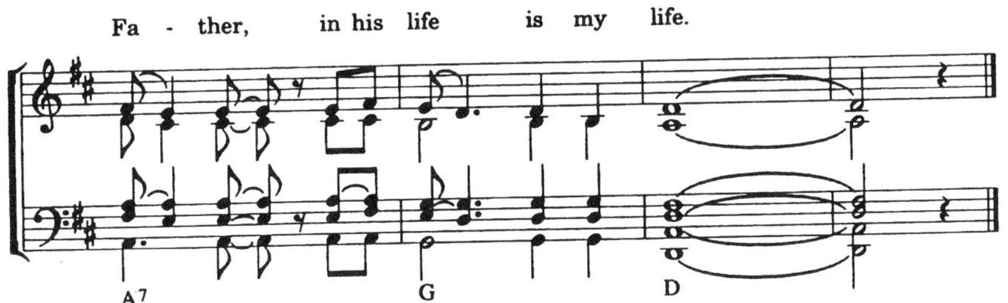
Fa - ther, in his life is my life.
A7
G
D

Text and music: Tim Cullen, alt.

280 HE IS LORD

Unison
1. He is Lord, he is Lord.
He is ri - sen from the dead and he is Lord.
Ev - 'ry knee shall bow, ev - 'ry tongue con -
fess that Je - sus Christ is Lord.
D G D D7 G
Em Am D7
G Em C
Am G D7 G

2. He is King, he is King.
   He is risen from the dead and he is King.
   Ev'ry knee shall bow, ev'ry tongue confess
   that Jesus Christ is King.

3. He is love, he is love.
   He is risen from the dead and he is love.
   Ev'ry knee shall bow, ev'ry tongue confess
   that Jesus Christ is love.

Text: unknown
Music: unknown arr. Adrian Vernon Fish (*b*. 1956)

281 HOLY, HOLY, HOLY IS THE LORD

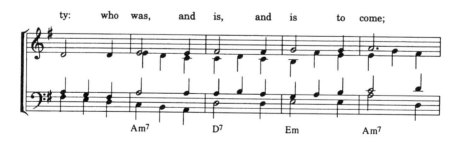

Unison 1. Ho - ly, ho - ly, ho - ly is the Lord, ho - ly is the
G Em Bm Am
Lord God al - migh - ty. Ho - ly, ho - ly,
D D7 G Em
ho - ly is the Lord, ho - ly is the Lord God al - migh -
Bm Am7 D
ty: who was, and is, and is to come;
Am7 D7 Em Am7

ho - ly, ho - ly, ho - ly is the Lord.
G G7 Em Am D7 G

2. Jesus, Jesus, Jesus is the Lord,
Jesus is the Lord God almighty:
Jesus, Jesus, Jesus is the Lord,
Jesus is the Lord God almighty:
who was, and is, and is to come;
Jesus, Jesus, Jesus is the Lord.

3. Worthy, worthy, worthy is the Lord,
worthy is the Lord God almighty:
worthy, worthy, worthy is the Lord,
worthy is the Lord God almighty:
who was, and is, and is to come;
worthy, worthy, worthy is the Lord.

4. Glory, glory, glory to the Lord,
glory to the Lord God almighty:
glory, glory, glory to the Lord,
glory to the Lord God almighty:
who was, and is, and is to come;
glory, glory, glory to the Lord.

Text: unknown
Music: unknown arr. Colin Hand (*b.* 1929)

282 HOSANNA, HOSANNA

Unison 1. Ho - san - na, ho - san - na, ho -
2. Glo - ry, glo - ry,
G D
san - na in the high - est! Ho - san - na, ho -
glo - ry to the King of kings! Glo - ry,
Em C D G
san - na, ho - san - na in the high -
glo - ry, glo - ry to the King of
D Em C
est! Lord, we lift up your name
kings! Lord, we lift up your name
D C D G

with hearts full of praise;
with hearts full of praise;
be ex- alt-ed, O
be ex- alt-ed, O
C
D
G
C
D
Lord, our God! Ho - san - na in the high - est!
Lord, our God! Glo - ry to the King of kings!
G
D/F♯
Em
C
D
G

Text: Carl Tuttle, based on Matthew 21:9
Music: Carl Tuttle arr. Malcolm Archer (*b.* 1952)

283 I AM THE BREAD OF LIFE

Unison
1. I am the bread of life. You who come to me shall not
2. The bread that I will give is my flesh for the life of the
3. Un - less you eat of the flesh of the Son of
A
C♯m
D

hun - ger; and who be - lieve in me shall not thirst.
world, and if you eat of this bread,
Man, and drink of his blood, and
E7
A
C♯m
D

No - one can come to me un - less the Fa - ther beck - ons.
you shall live for e - ver, you shall live for e - ver.
drink of his blood, you shall not have life with - in you.
A D Bm E
Refrain
And I will raise you up, and I will raise you
E7 A E A A7 D
over to verses 4 & 5
up, and I will raise you up on the last day.
E7 A D A E7 A

4. I am the re - sur - rec - tion, I am the
5. Yes, Lord, I be - lieve that you are the
A
C♯m
D
life. If you be - lieve in me,
Christ, the Son of God,
E7
A
C♯m
D
e - ven though you die, you shall live for e - ver.
who has come in - to the world.
A
D
Bm
E

Refrain
And I will raise you up, and I will raise you
E7 A E A A7 D

up, and I will raise you up on the last day.
E7 A D A E7 A

Text: Suzanne Toolan (*b.* 1927)
Music: Suzanne Toolan (*b.* 1927) arr. Colin Hand (*b.* 1929)

284 I LOVE YOU LORD

Unison I love you, Lord, and I lift my voice
Capo 3 D A7

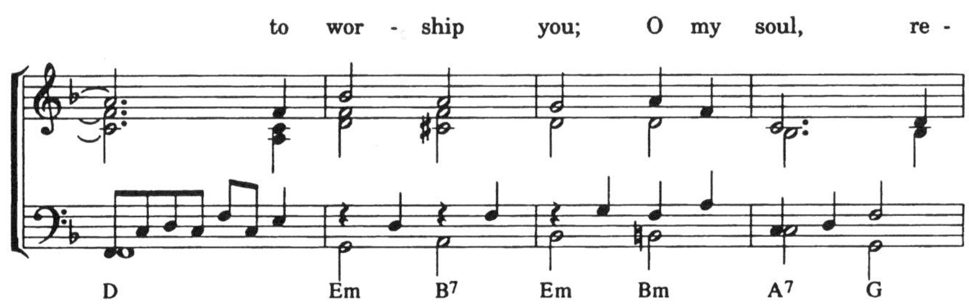
to wor - ship you; O my soul, re -
D Em B7 Em Bm A7 G

joice. Take joy, my King, in what you hear,
A7 D A7

may it be a sweet, sweet sound in your ear.
D D7 Em Bm Em A7 D A7 D

Text: Laurie Klein
Music: Laurie Klein arr. Noel Rawsthorne (*b.* 1929)

285 JESUS STAND AMONG US AT THE MEETING OF OUR LIVES

Unison 1. Je - sus, stand a - mong us at the meet - ing of our
D Em7 A7
lives, be our sweet a - gree - ment at the
D Em7 D Bm7 Em7 G
meet - ing of our eyes. Refrain O Je - sus, we
A7 D Em7 G A7
love you, so we gath - er here,
D Bm7 G A7 D D7

join our hearts in u - ni-ty and take a-way
G Em F♯m7 E7
1st time our fear.
Em A7
2nd time our fear.
Em A7 D Em D

2. So to you we're gath'ring out of each and ev'ry land,
Christ the love between us at the joining of our hands.

Optional verse for Communion

3. Jesus stand among us at the breaking of the bread;
join us as one body as we worship you, our Head.

Text: Graham Kendrick (*b.* 1950)
Music: Graham Kendrick (*b.* 1950) arr. Noel Rawsthorne (*b.* 1929)

286 JESUS YOU ARE CHANGING ME

Marilyn Baker

Jer 18: 6; 2 Cor 3: 18

Capo 3 (C)

Prayerfully
Eb(C) Bb(G) Eb(C)
Je - sus, You are chang - ing me,
Bb7/F(G7) Ab/Eb(F) Eb(C) Ab/C(F) Eb(C)
by Your Spi - rit You're mak - ing me like
F7(D7) Bb7(G7) Eb(C) Bb(G)
You. Je - sus, You're trans-
Eb(C) G7(E7) Cm(Am)
- form - ing me, that Your love - li-ness may be
F(D) Bb7(G7)
seen in all I do.

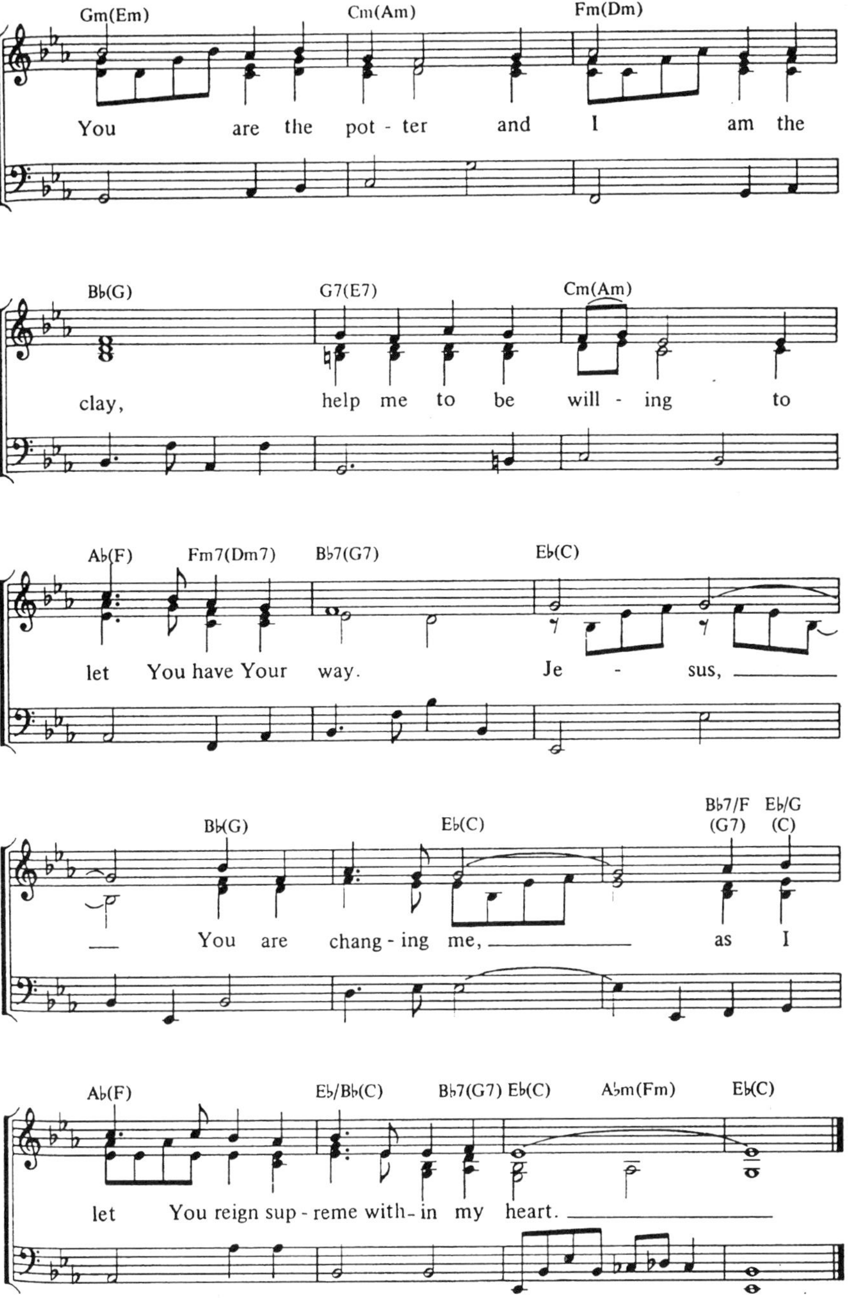
Gm(Em)
Cm(Am)
Fm(Dm)
You are the pot - ter and I am the
Bb(G)
G7(E7)
Cm(Am)
clay, help me to be will - ing to
Ab(F)
Fm7(Dm7)
Bb7(G7)
Eb(C)
let You have Your way. Je - sus,
Bb(G)
Eb(C)
Bb7/F (G7)
Eb/G (C)
You are chang - ing me, as I
Ab(F)
Eb/Bb(C)
Bb7(G7)
Eb(C)
Abm(Fm)
Eb(C)
let You reign sup - reme with - in my heart.

287 MAKE ME A CHANNEL OF YOUR PEACE

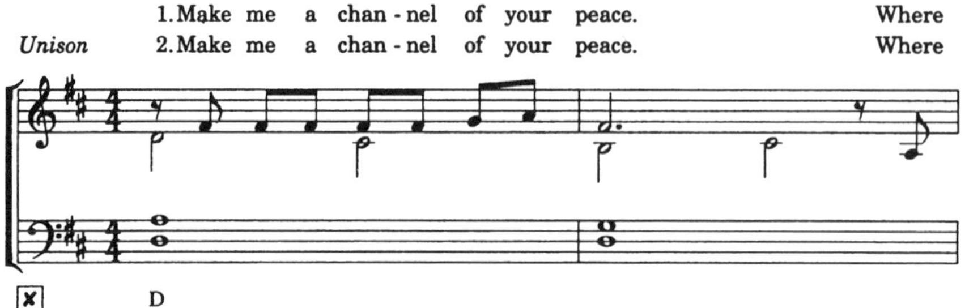
1. Make me a chan - nel of your peace. Where
Unison 2. Make me a chan - nel of your peace. Where
D

there is ha - tred, let me bring your love. Where
there's des - pair in life, let me bring hope. Where
A7

there is in - ju - ry, your par - don, Lord, and
there is dark - ness, on - ly light, and

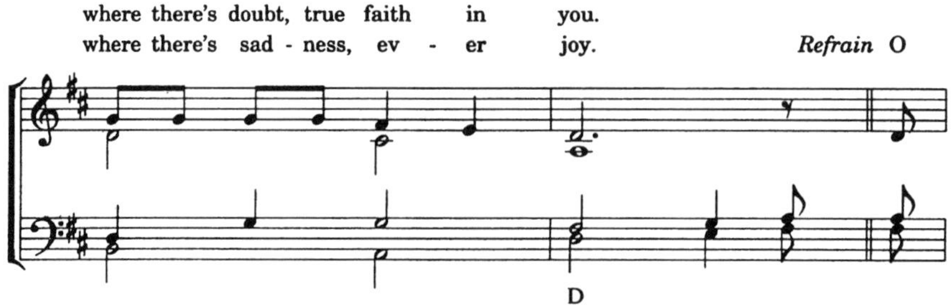
where there's doubt, true faith in you.
where there's sad - ness, ev - er joy. Refrain O
D

Mas - ter, grant that I may ne - ver seek so
G
D

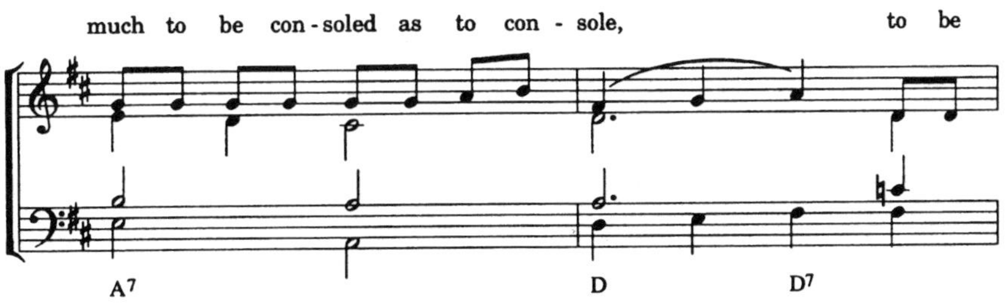
much to be con - soled as to con - sole, to be
A7
D
D7

un - der - stood, as to un - der - stand, to be
G
D

loved, as to love with all my soul.
D.C. to verse 2
over to verse 3
E7
A
A7

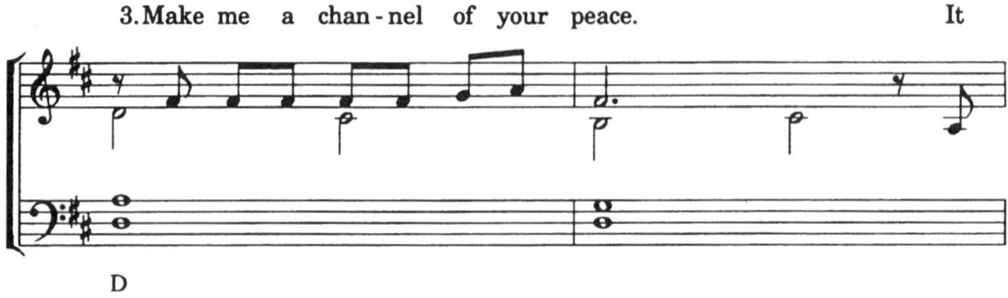
3. Make me a chan - nel of your peace. It
D

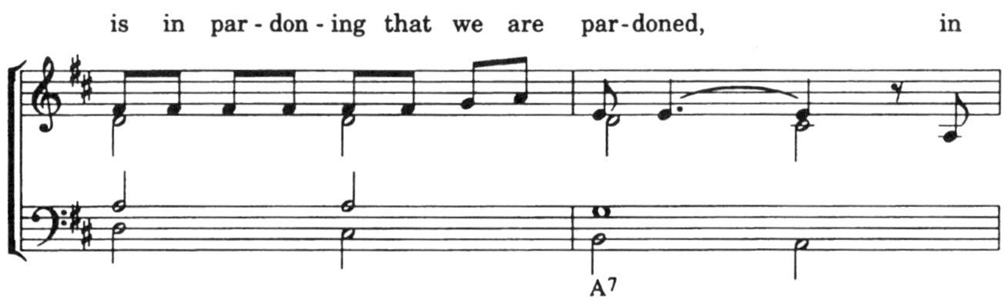
is in par - don - ing that we are par - doned, in
A7

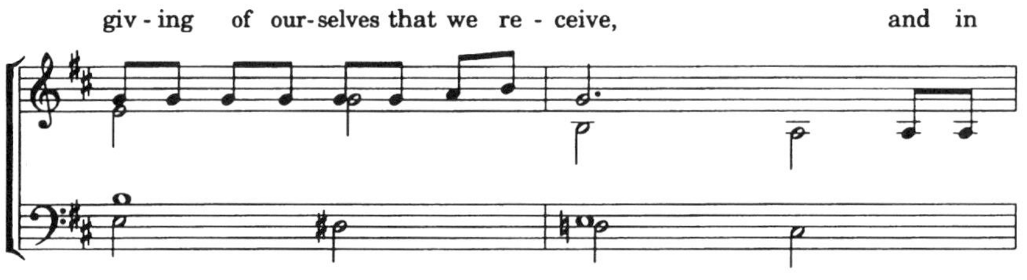
giv - ing of our - selves that we re - ceive, and in

dy - ing that we're born to e - ter - nal life.
D

Text: Sebastian Temple (*b.* 1928) based on the Prayer of St Francis
Music: Sebastian Temple (*b.* 1928) arr. Norman Warren (*b.* 1934)

288 O HOLY SPIRIT BREATHE ON ME

F
Gm
C7
Am
O Ho- ly Spi - rit __ breathe on me, ____ O Ho- ly Spi - rit __
Ped.
G7
Dm7
breathe on me, ____ and cleanse a- way my sin, ____ fill me with love with - in: ___
Gm7
F Gm Am Gm F
Last Verse
_ O Ho- ly Spi - rit __ breathe on me.

2. O Holy Spirit fill my life,
O Holy Spirit fill my life,
Take all my pride from me,
Give me humility:
O Holy Spirit breathe on me!

3. O Holy Spirit make me new,
O Holy Spirit make me new,
Make Jesus real to me,
Give me his purity:
O Holy Spirit breathe on me!

4. O Holy Spirit wind of God,
O Holy Spirit wind of God,
Give me your power today,
To live for you always:
O Holy Spirit breathe on me!

289 PRAISE YOU LORD

Capo 3 (C)
With majesty
Nettie Rose
Is 61:1
E♭(C) Cm(Am) A♭(F) B♭(G)
1. Praise You, Lord, for the won - der of Your heal - ing.
E♭(C) G(E) Cm(Am) F7(D7) B♭(G) B♭7(G7)
Praise You, Lord, for Your love so free - ly given,
E♭(C) E♭7(C7) A♭(F) A♭m(Fm)
out - pour-ing a - noin-ting, flow-ing in to heal our wounds.
E♭(C) G(E) Cm(Am) B♭7(G7) E♭(C)
Praise You, Lord, for Your love for me.

2. Praise You, Lord, for Your gift of liberation.
Praise You, Lord, You have set the captives free;
The chains that bind are broken by the sharpness of Your sword,
Praise You, Lord, You gave Your life for me.

3. Praise You, Lord, You have born the depths of sorrow.
Praise You, Lord, for Your anguish on the tree;
The nails that tore Your body and the pain that tore Your soul.
Praise You, Lord, Your tears, they fell for me.

4. Praise You, Lord, You have turned our thorns to roses.
Glory, Lord, as they bloom upon Your brow.
The path of pain is hallowed, for Your love has made it sweet,
Praise You, Lord, and may I love You now.

290 SEEK YE FIRST

SEEK YE FIRST Irregular and Refrain

This may be sung as a round, the second entry beginning at the double bar.

Unison 1. Seek ye first the king - dom of God, and his right - eous -
D F♯m G D G D

ness, and all these things shall be add - ed un - to you;
A4 A D F♯m G D

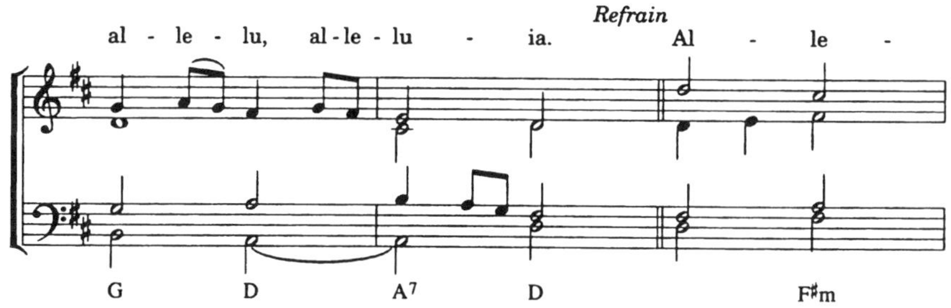

al - le - lu, al - le - lu - ia.
Refrain
Al - le -
G D A7 D F♯m

lu - ia, al - le - lu - ia, al - le -
G D G D A4 A D F♯m

lu - ia, al - le - lu, al-le-lu - ia.
G D G D A7 D

2. You shall not live by bread alone,
   but by ev'ry word
   that proceeds from the mouth of God;
   allelu, alleluia.

3. Ask and it shall be given unto you,
   seek and ye shall find;
   knock, and it shall be opened unto you;
   allelu, alleluia.

Text: v.1: Karen Lafferty (*b.* 1948) vs. 2 & 3: unknown; based on Matthew 4: 4; 6: 33; 7: 7
Music: Karen Lafferty (*b.* 1948) arr. Adrian Vernon Fish (*b.* 1956)

291 SING HALLELUJAH TO THE LORD

Capo 3 (Am)

Linda Stassen

With feeling
Cm(Am) Gm(Em) Cm(Am) Gm(Em) Cm(Am) E♭(C)
(Women) Sing Hal-le - lu-jah to the Lord,
(Men) 1. Sing Hal-le -lu-jah to the Lord, sing Hal-le -lu-jah to the
G(E) Cm(Am) Gm(Em) A♭(F) E♭(C)
sing Hal-le-lu - jah, Hal le - lu - jah,
Lord, sing Hal-le - lu - jah, sing Hal-le - lu - jah,
(Together)
Cm(Am) Gm(Em)
1st time
Cm(Am)
Last time
C(A)
sing Hal-le -lu-jah to the Lord. Lord.

2. Jesus is risen from the dead . . . *etc.*

3. Jesus is Lord of heaven and earth . . . *etc.*

4. Jesus is living in His church . . . *etc.*

5. Jesus is coming for His own . . . *etc.*

292 SPIRIT OF THE LIVING GOD

Spi - rit of the liv - ing God, fall a-fresh on me.
Capo 3 D Em B7 Em D A D
Spi - rit of the liv - ing God, fall a-fresh on me.
G D G A A7 D
Melt me, mould me, fill me, use me.
G D E A A7
Spi - rit of the liv - ing God, fall a-fresh on me.
D Em B7 Em D A D

Text and music: Daniel Iverson (1890 - 1972)

293 SUCH LOVE

Unison 1. Such love, pure as the whit - est snow;
3
A D Bm D7 Gmaj7
such love weeps for the shame I know;
3
Em A/C♯ Bm A D
such love, pay-ing the debt I owe;
3
Bm F♯7 Bm G D
O Je - sus, such love.
Bm G D Bm A7 D G D

2. Such love, stilling my restlessness;
   such love, filling my emptiness;
   such love, showing me holiness;
   O Jesus, such love.

3. Such love springs from eternity;
   such love, streaming through his
   such love, fountain of life to me;
   O Jesus, such love.

Text: Graham Kendrick (*b.* 1950)
Music: Graham Kendrick (*b.* 1950) arr. Colin Hand (*b.* 1929)

294 THE LIGHT OF CHRIST

Flowing
Refrain
C
Part 1. The light of Christ
Parta 2. The light of Christ
F Dm G C
come in - to the world, light of
has come in - to the world, the
F G C
1.-3.
Christ has come in - to the world.
light of Christ has come.

Verses
F
C
F
G
1. All must now be born a - gain to see the king - dom of
2. God gave up his on - ly Son out of love for the
3. The light of God has come to us so that we might have sal -
C
F
G
C
God; the wa - ter and the Spi - rit bring new
world, so that all who be - lieve in him will
va - tion; from the dark - ness of our sins we walk in - to
Dm
G
D.C.
4. C
life in God's love.
live for ev - er. world.
glo - ry with Christ Je - sus.

295 THERE IS A REDEEMER

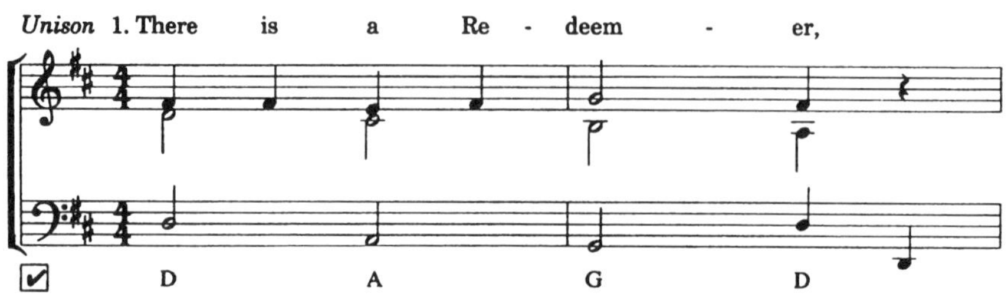
Unison 1. There is a Re - deem - er,
D A G D

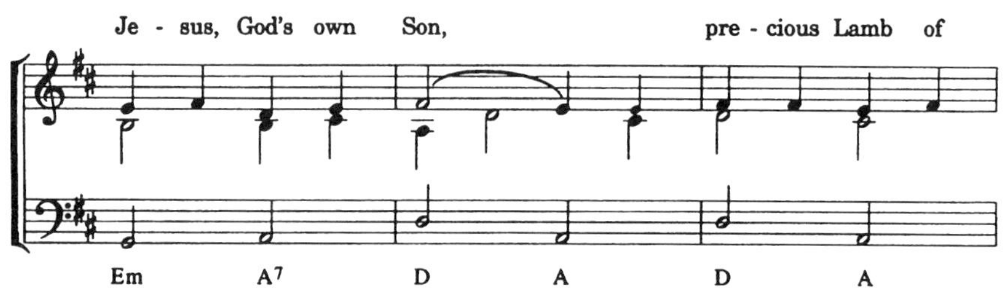
Je - sus, God's own Son, pre - cious Lamb of
Em A7 D A D A

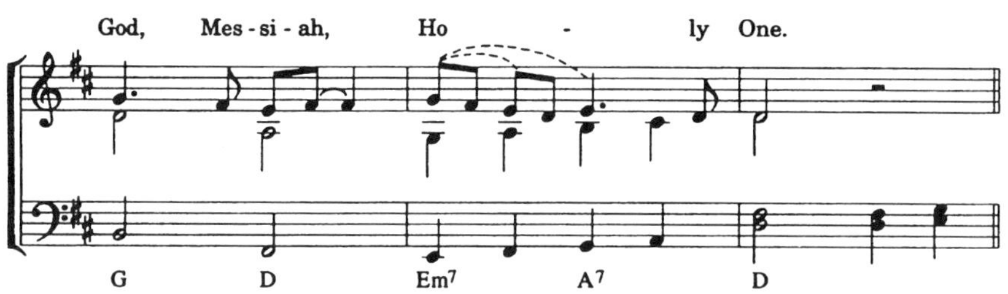
God, Mes - si - ah, Ho - ly One.
G D Em7 A7 D

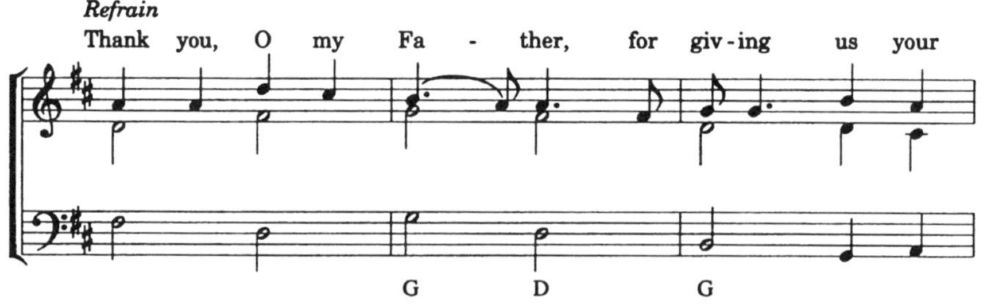
Refrain
Thank you, O my Fa - ther, for giv - ing us your
G D G

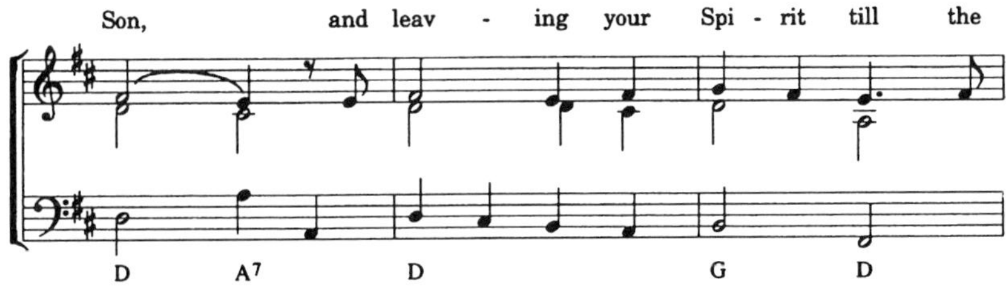
Son, and leav - ing your Spi - rit till the
D A7 D G D

verses 1&2
last time
work on earth is done. done.
D.C.
Em7 A7 D A7 D

2. Jesus, my Redeemer,
   name above all names,
   precious Lamb of God, Messiah,
   O for sinners slain.

3. When I stand in glory,
   I will see his face,
   and there I'll serve my King for ever,
   in that holy place.

Text: Melody Green, based on Scripture
Music: Melody Green arr. Christopher Tambling (*b.* 1964)

296 YOU ARE THE VINE

Capo 2(C)

Danny Daniels
Jn 13:34-35; 15:1-11

Smoothly
D(C)
Em7(Dm7)
D(C)
You are the Vine, we are the

1st time
G(F)
D(C)
G(F)
branch - es, keep us a - bid - ing in

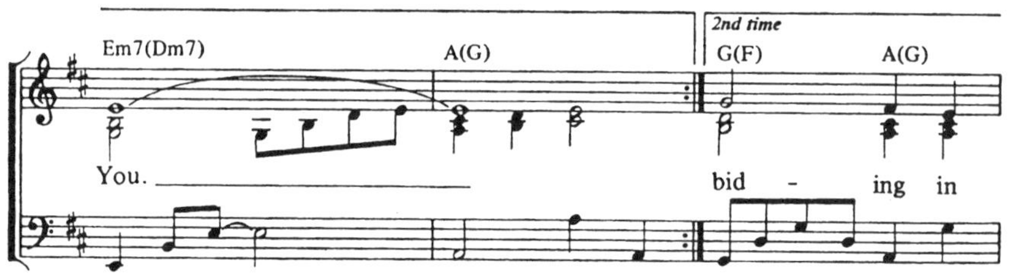
2nd time
Em7(Dm7)
A(G)
G(F)
A(G)
You.
bid - ing in

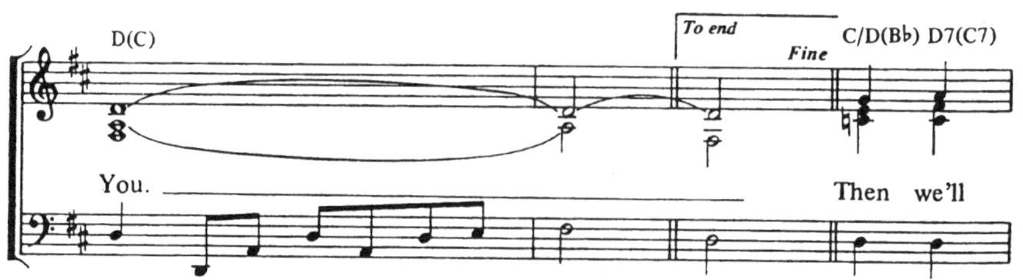
To end
Fine
D(C)
C/D(B♭) D7(C7)
You.
Then we'll

G(F)
Em(Dm)
F♯m(Em)
go
in Your love,
Bm(Am)
Em(Dm)
A(G)
then we'll go
in Your
D(C)
C/D(B♭) D7(C7)
G(F)
name,
that the world
Em(Dm)
F♯m(Em)
Bm(Am)
will sure - ly know
that You have
Em7(Dm7)
Em/A(Dm/G)
A(G)
D.C. al Fine
pow - er to heal and to save.

HYMNAL SOURCE INFORMATION

ABINGDON PRESS
201 8th Avenue, South; Nashville, Tennessee 37202, USA
(The United Methodist Hymnal)

ATELIERS ET PRESSES DE TAIZE
71250 Taize Community, France
(Music from Taize - Vols. One & Two - Vocal Editions)

CHRISTIAN CONFERENCE OF ASIAN
96, 2nd District, Pak Tin Village, Mei Tin Road, Shatin, N. T., Hong Kong
(E. A. C. C. Hymnal)

HYMNS ANCIENT & MODERN LIMITED
St. Mary's Works, St. Mary's Plain, Norwich, Norfolk NR3 3BH, UK
(Hymns Ancient & Modern New Standard, The New English Hymnal)

KEVIN MAYHEW LTD.
Rattlesden, Bury St. Edmunds, Suffolk IP30 0SZ, UK
(Hymns Old and New)

MARSHALL PICKERING
HarperCollins Publishers, 77-85 Fulham Palace Road, London W6 8JB, UK
(World Praise, Let's Praise!)

OXFORD UNIVERSITY PRESS
70 Baker Street, London W1M 1DJ, UK
(*Rejoice & Sing, 1991*; The following songs were reproduced by permission of Oxford University Press: 2, 3, 7, 8, 9, 10, 11, 14, 17, 18, 20, 21, 22, 26, 27, 29, 31, 33, 34, 35, 36, 37, 38, 40, 41, 43, 45, 47, 48, 51, 57, 58, 62, 63, 64, 65, 69, 70, 75, 79, 80, 81, 83, 84, 86, 87, 88, 89, 90, 91, 93, 99, 100, 101, 102, 103, 105, 112, 116, 118, 119, 120, 122, 126, 129, 130, 131, 134, 137, 142, 143, 144, 145, 147, 148, 149, 150, 153, 159, 160, 161, 162, 163, 166, 220)

STRUBE VERLANG GMBH - Munchen and BASILEIA-VERLAG - Basel
(Thuma Mina)

THE COUNCIL FOR WORLD MISSION
11 Carteret Street, London SW1H 9DL, UK
(Drawn to the Wonder)

WILD GOOSE RESOURCE GROUP
Iona Community, 840 Govan Road, Glasgow G51 3UU, Scotland
(Come All You People, Heaven Shall Not Wait, Love from Below)

INDEX OF FIRST LINES AND TITLES